rocks in this area, the cross is strangely white and pristine. Rumors exist of a tunnel from somewhere on the mountain leading directly to the Mission Inn, used by Miller's associates during Prohibition. Teenagers and others prone to wild tales still search for the elusive subterranean passage, with no luck so far, but the legends refuse to die out.

Near the crest of the north end of the peak are the remnants of a graceful, though defaced, painting of a horse, fading to obscurity on a flat rock. Since it looks like something out of the Lascaux caves, some tourists have insisted that it was made by some ancient "Indian," but there's no record of it before the mid-twentieth century.

Among the most enduring legends of Mount Rubidoux are the stories of furtive "attack midgets." Locals reportedly tell of small stones raining down on them during solitary walks. Also described are small piles of rocks left on the trails, usually in groups of three, and even occasional sightings of the diminutive demons. On the flip side of the spirit tales are the large, shadowy figures that have been reported walking near the peaks late at night. Resembling the "watchers" of the central coast ranges or the equally mysterious robed forms said to wander the slopes of Mount Shasta, the silent, hooded spirits seem to be replaying some ancient ceremony along Mount Rubidoux's windswept peaks.

FRANK A. MILLER
MOUNT
RUBIDOUX
MEMORIAL PARK
A GIFT TO THE CITIZENS OF RIVERSIDE
BY FRANK A. MILLER, INC. NOV. 28, 1955
FIRST EASTER SUNRISE SERVICE
APRIL 11, 1909

The Secret Language of Boontling

If you have ever found yourself deeking at your applehead's ose and thinking that you might ply her with a heelch of frattey and perhaps a few horns of steinbers in the hopes of some boarch burlapping after the big tidrik, you are not only checking out your girlfriend's backside and thinking you can fill her with large quantities of wine and perhaps a few glasses of beer in the hopes of some romance after the big party, you are also harpin' (or rather speaking) Boontling.

Boontling is the once secret language created around 1880 in the small and isolated farming community of Boonville in Anderson Valley. The parlance is said to contain over one thousand unique words and phrases.

Some say the lingo was used to speak in code in front of outsiders. As longtime Boonville resident Bobby Glover once quipped to Johnny Carson on *The Tonight Show,* "My mother used to say never trust anybody until you've known them at least twenty years . . . and even then be damned careful!"

Others say the manufactured jargon, which contains a good amount of sexual inference, was made up so the menfolk could speak plainly in front of the children, and still others say it's possible it was the other way around: kids trying to have their own special language that the adults wouldn't understand.

Linguists agree that Boontling's roots are drawn from a mixture of English, Scottish, Irish, Spanish, and Pomo Indian words. Today it's a dying language, but there are still visible traces of the vernacular in town. The pay phone is called a Bucky Walters (after buck—a code name for a nickel—and Walter—the first man in Boonville to own a phone), and a cup of coffee is still written on some restaurant menus as a horn of Zeese (after a man nicknamed Z.C., who made particularly bitter coffee).

Visit Boonville. Brightlighters (cityfolk) are welcome.

Chronicle / Eric Luse

*Boonville resident
Bobby Glover*

La Llorona—The Phantom Banshee

In the tree-lined arroyo of Trabuco Creek at O'Neill Regional Park in Orange County dwells one of the most feared phantoms in all of Mexican legend and lore, La Llorona. And while she is known to haunt many locations throughout southern California as well as the rest of the American Southwest, the area of Trabuco Creek is one of her most notorious stomping grounds.

La Llorona ("the crier") gets her name from her ghostly, bansheelike wail. Legend has it that she was an evil woman who cheated on her husband and drowned her three children because they kept her from her lover. God then condemned her to walk the earth for all eternity, searching for her drowned children.

It's said that she steals the souls of living children, and she's often invoked by Mexican mothers to frighten naughty niños. Tradition also has it that if you see La Llorona, you or someone close to you will die within a week. The origin of the legend is unknown, although some believe it dates back to Aztec times.

Many modern Mexican Americans believe in La Llorona and swear that she still bedevils the living. They say she continues to walk southern California's hill country at night, her long, jet-black hair and black dress blowing in the wind, an evil counterpart to California's many Women in White ghosts. But where her face should be, they whisper, there is the head of a horse.

Trabuco Creek is rumored to be the spot where the wicked woman drowned her children. And on moonlit nights, they say, you can see her black-clad form bending over the creek bed, her pale arms elbow-deep in the waters, searching for her lost babies.

Screaming Tree—Lakeside

The Screaming Trees were a Seattle band with a strong cult following. The band broke up in 1999, but the original screaming tree, we hear, is still going strong in the town of Lakeside.

Legend instructs the seeker to drive to the end of a dirt road in Lakeside, an eastern suburb of San Diego. Look for a feedlot and/or slaughterhouse, and pull up next to a lone tree in a clearing, 1.7 miles after the end of the paved road. Honk three times and the ghost of a murdered girl will scream at the top of her disembodied lungs, replaying the last moments of her life at the foot of this gnarled trunk.

In fact, this does look like the perfect place for a killing; homes are few and far between, and rusting cars share yard space with trash and makeshift lean-tos at most of the roadside dwellings. More well-to-do residents up on the ridgeline are surrounded by orchards and fences to keep the riffraff out. A dry creek bed slaloms through the rock-strewn valley, providing water for horses and cattle in the springtime, and flash floods after a good rain.

An area resident cornered outside the local Circle K gave conflicting directions and warnings about crazies with shotguns and bad attitudes. "All the trees are haunted around here!" she said, laughing. "You must be looking for the meth lab." She claimed to have a great view of the mountainside from her place across the valley and hinted at all sorts of nefarious activity seen from her backyard. Then she walked on down the road.

Local legend, or a *Scooby Doo*–like cover-up of a redneck speed factory? The answers lie with the intrepid explorer or the San Diego Sheriff's Department.

The Screaming Tree might be located near the end of Willow Road off Highway 67.

Deadly Nuclear Waste Under Rec Center?

In the late 1970s, U.C.L.A. professor Dan Hirsch heard from some of his students that the future site of the Barrington Recreation Center in the tony L.A. suburb of Brentwood was sitting atop a dark secret. There was talk that Veterans Administration doctors and staff had been quietly dumping nuclear waste from the hospital into a landfill for almost twenty years.

Hirsch formed a coalition of his students to look into the charges and soon found that the rumors were true. They uncovered a paper trail indicating that the V.A. had indeed used the area as a dump for waste from the radiation therapy program, "secret" human experiments, and perhaps even from a small reactor. "The main concern here is that the radiation could have gotten into the soil, which in turn would have been absorbed into the vegetation. Remember, this stuff sticks around for years, hundreds of years," Hirsch is quoted as saying in the book *L. A. Exposed,* by Paul Young.

What Hirsch and his students didn't count on was a bizarre confrontation with a Brentwood lobby group, who absolutely insisted that soccer and baseball fields be built on the radioactive real estate. These people, wealthy parents of local kids, didn't believe the stories about the V.A. dumping, perhaps thinking that some developer had planted them to scare away the competition.

The Nuclear Regulatory Commission (NRC) was called in to investigate. After a perfunctory sweep of the area with a Geiger counter, the NRC pronounced the area safe. Not satisfied, Hirsch was able to secure an LAPD helicopter to fly him over the property with an infrared camera, which might reveal radioactive "hot spots." However, on the appointed day, he arrived to find that someone had gone over the area with a bulldozer, wiping out any vegetation that would show up hot on the infrared pictures. Hirsch was later told that the timing of the plowing was merely a coincidence, that the fire department had planned to plow the area for fire control for some time.

If the waste is buried more than a few feet underground, the radiation should be well contained and the NRC can be trusted in this case, even though it didn't take the simple and obvious step of obtaining soil samples. If you are the cautious type, though, it might be a good idea to limit visits to the Barrington Recreation Center to a half hour or less.

In late September 1999, someone filed a Freedom of Information Act request with the NRC to see the secret findings on the Barrington property. However, to read them, you have to go to Rockville, Maryland, where the NRC headquarters and public reading room are located. Request "Landfill site at 330 S. Barrington Ave., Brentwood, CA, permit/license & inspection reports, FOIA/PA99-374." Good luck.

Los Angeles's Hyperion Treatment Plant, as it is officially known, is the second largest complex of its kind in the United States (Chicago's is number one). The plant typically processes about 350 million gallons of soupy grey wastewater per day from a nexus of 6,500 miles of sewer line, most of it from homes and apartments. The treated water is not fit to drink, but meets EPA standards, and is piped five miles offshore and released 190 feet below the ocean's surface.

Over the years, some pretty scary stuff has been caught in the main intake gates. Raw sewage flows through "bar screens" to prevent larger objects from clogging up the works down the line. A sort of mechanical rake drops fifteen feet into the murky depths to comb objects from the steel bars and then dumps a congealed mass of partially decomposed toilet paper, empty pharmaceutical blister packs, and other unidentifiable gunk into a hopper, which sits just above eye level for easy inspection. It's a lovely place to visit.

And the really weird thing is that people want to see this stuff. Hyperion offers tours, and people line up regularly to take them. We asked unflappable tour guide Nancy Carr what else has turned up, apart from the obvious. "We've had bowling balls, two-by-fours, hypodermic needles, and a few body parts," she says cheerfully. BODY PARTS?

"When that happens, by law, we have to call the police so that they can investigate," says Carr. She adds that she usually doesn't ask for the juicy details.

Although there is an obvious public fascination with what turns up in the sewers, the day-to-day operations of the Hyperion facility are almost as interesting. The sterile solid waste, politely referred to as biosolids, left over from various bacteriological purification processes, is used to fertilize a 4,600-acre farm in Kern County (ironically called Green Acres) that was purchased by the city in 2000. "L.A. bought the farm. I love saying that," jokes Carr. The land is used to grow barley, alfalfa, corn, and other crops, but calm down—the product is fed only to livestock. Ultimately, this means that your beef, chicken, and pork are actually recycled, which is pretty darned efficient.

So what is the legend of Hyperion? Well, all kinds of things are rumored to have shown up in the city's sewer treatment plant, from live reptiles to fetuses to mobsters' decapitated heads. But our mission here is to set the record straight. We have the real list of wacky things flushed down the toilets of southern California. In his 2002 book *L.A. Exposed*, Paul Young reports that "staff members admit that they've found . . . bags of money, a finger, a mattress, various sex toys, a full set of kitchen cabinets, a complete motorcycle, a five-foot grease ball, and a *fully intact, adult male horse*."

For tours of the Hyperion Plant, contact public relations at (310) 648-5363.

A Pizzeria That Really Delivers!

What do buns in the oven have to do with an upscale Italian bistro tucked between equally chichi boutiques on this quiet residential street? Read on.

When chef-owner Ed LaDou opened Caioti Pizza Cafe (pronounced *ki-o-te*) in North Hollywood in 1986, he had no idea that his place would become a hot spot for overdue mothers. LaDou learned his craft at world-class eateries like Spago, where he almost single-handedly invented the now ubiquitous California Pizza, using ingredients like roasted eggplant and barbequed chicken. However, it was one of his salads that was destined to put Caioti on the map.

The restaurant moved to Studio City in the late 1990s. Sometime in 1993, a pregnant woman who was well past her due date stopped by and ordered the romaine and watercress salad with balsamic dressing. The next day she went into labor. She told an overdue friend what had happened. The friend came to the restaurant, ordered the same salad, and the same thing happened. A local legend, and quite a few babies, were born.

"We get pregnant women in here every day. Sometimes twenty or more," says one of the waitresses. "We don't even have to ask what they want. We just bring it out."

Although at first he was a bit miffed that it was his humble salad that was attracting customers, LaDou eventually embraced his dubious celebrity. Doctors are reluctant to prescribe the salad as a remedy for reluctant babies, but some apparently do suggest that their worried patients make the pilgrimage to Caioti. The legendary salad may do nothing more than calm a few nerves and allow nature to take its course, but why knock it? For those looking for a scientific explanation, there is some medical evidence that balsamic vinegar may cause uterine contractions.

Do Ed a favor when you go and at least order a pizza. They are really very good.

Turnbull Canyon Legends

Satanists, kidnappers, ghosts, and supposedly, a gravity hill — this canyon, popular with hikers, mountain bikers, and road racers hides many dark secrets. The chaparral-covered mountain with its twisted road lies between the suburban sprawl of Whittier on one side and the capitalist paradise called the City of Industry on the other. While signs along the trails warn strolling couples and fitness nuts about mountain lions and rattlesnakes, the more sinister features of this area are known only to some unfortunate locals as well as finer connoisseurs of the weird.

History tells us that like many unhallowed places in North America, the area now known as Turnbull Canyon was considered off-limits by the local Indians. They named it Hutukngna, which supposedly means "the dark place."

In 1845, the Spanish governor of Alta California deeded most of the land in what is now Whittier to two settlers, John Rowland and William Workman, who emigrated from Taos, New Mexico. Their huge 49,000-acre spread included the present site of Turnbull Canyon. Workman was not well liked by the local Indians, who initially staged constant raids on

An insane asylum apparently was once located somewhere in the now weed-choked floor of Turnbull Canyon. It flourished in the 1930s, but burned down in the early 1940s. Sometime around 1962, a group of teenagers were partying in the ruins, and legend has it that one of the more daring boys was killed by the remains of a long-dormant electroshock device, which pumped several thousand volts through his drug-addled brain.

Witnesses have also experienced ghosts of children (presumably victims of the kidnapping cult) and other figures swinging by the neck from the limbs of scraggly trees, although most of the scarier information on the canyon comes from a Web site of dubious provenance.

However, a real tragedy did occur on the road in October 2002 when a seventeen-year-old girl was killed and later dragged behind a car for five miles. A few years later a local motorcycle officer was killed by a drunk, possibly road-racing, driver on the east end of Turnbull Canyon Road. The constant twists and turns are an irresistible lure to fans of a new sport called Drifting, in which the driver attempts to negotiate turns by skidding through them. The cop was killed on a night detail that was dispatched to nab Drifters.

The location of the gravity hill spot is so debated that it is well nigh impossible to find, but we wouldn't advise stopping anyway, since you're liable to be rear-ended by a thrill-crazed racer and become yet another tragic ghost that haunts Turnbull Canyon.

his property. To protect his family, he built a tunnel and living space under his home. Later, when the Indians actually worked for him, they reported seeing ghosts and "witches" in the subterranean passage, which ended at the family burial ground. Workman was also involved in a plot to usurp the governor who had originally given him his land, and he carried this bad juju to the end of his life. He lost most of his property and money in a failed banking enterprise with his son-in-law and shot himself in 1876.

During the Depression years, rumors started that Turnbull Canyon was the site of strange rituals involving a child- and baby-selling cult. Some claim that the area is still used for satanic worship or something equally evil. An anonymous source recently reported that an old metal sign far up the canyon was spray-painted with the words "Die Jesus."

I've Heard It All

I live near Turnbull Canyon and yes I've heard about all this. It is one scary place to be in if you're by yourself and you aren't familiar with it. I remember seeing people walking around with hoods on, but I'm not sure. For sure though, I know that there are many devil worshipers/cults in that area. Also, they found some rapist/killer hiding there.–*Counterlock, drifting.com*

Peg-leg Smith's Lost Gold

They promise to tell lies, whole lies, and nothing but lies. On the first Saturday of April (as near enough to the first of April as weekday workers can get) the town of Borrego Springs hosts its annual Peg-Leg Smith Liars' Contest to honor a man who told one of the most legendary and enduring stretchers of all in these parts.

Thomas J. Smith was born in 1801 in the Kentucky hills. As a young man, he made a name for himself as an explorer, fur trapper, prospector, and Indian slave trader. As a sideline, he also practiced horse thievery. Smith left the lower half of his right leg in Wyoming after an Indian skirmish and acquired the nickname by which history now knows him—Peg-Leg Smith. The horse-stealing business was going really well, but by 1840 the authorities had broken up his gang, and Peg-Leg returned to prospecting. We know this much for sure.

It's hard to tell what parts of the next bit of the story are true, or what are part of Peg-Leg's most ultimately successful business, lying about the details to rook his newest mark.

During an expedition to the Borrego Badlands in 1836, Smith and a group of trappers from St. Louis had not seen water for four days. The group found themselves crossing the Salton Sink, trudging westward into a distant range of mountains where they hoped to find a creek or spring. As events and nerves turned desperate, one of the party was dispatched on a scouting sortie up a nearby canyon. As he reached the top of a small range of buttes, he found himself surrounded by a field of black, metallic rocks. He nonchalantly picked up a sample and saw a gleam of yellow in the fading light of sunset. He thought the stuff was copper but pocketed a few chunks for the assayer in

BE A PEG-LEG
LIAR
.I KNOW IT'S AROUND HERE SOME-WHERE
B O R R E G O
December 31st

the next town just the same. The following day, in a last-ditch effort, the men found a cool spring at the base of a tall peak and slaked their thirst. The mountain was named Smith, in honor of their leader and guide.

When the band arrived in civilization, the blackish rocks were tested and discovered to contain chunks of pure gold. Why Smith or his party didn't immediately return to the remote buttes is a mystery, but suspiciously, after gold fever hit the state in 1849, he organized an expedition to relocate his amazing find. The group set off from San Francisco, headed toward the southern desert. In a classic episode of karmic justice, sometime during the trip, Indian guides made off with most of the supplies in the dead of night. Smith was forced to abandon the search and disappeared somewhere near San Bernardino.

He turned up again many years later in San Francisco, hobbling along the streets, dressed in a beaver-skin hat and willing to tell anyone who would listen how to find his fabulous strike out in the Borrego Desert. Some of the more gullible parted with cash, and later, it took just a couple of shots of whiskey to pry hand-drawn maps and bogus mining claims out of the aging and alcoholic prospector. Smith died in a Bay Area hospital in 1866.

Tales of suspiciously wealthy Indians kept the Lost Peg-Leg Gold story alive in the lore of the Southwest. In the 1920s, Hollywood set designer Harry Oliver started the Peg-Leg Smith Club. Each New Year's Eve, Oliver and his group gathered in a spot near Borrego Springs where Smith was said to have started his expeditions and held what they called "burning parties." Local artist John Hilton would throw his past year's "mistakes" into the flames.

Oliver stepped up the fun in 1949, when the first liars' contest was held at the site. The group erected a monument that still stands today. The sign at the side of the road instructs: LET HIM WHO SEEKS PEGLEG'S GOLD ADD TEN ROCKS TO THIS. The pile grows steadily every year and, in recent years, has reached nearly ten feet.

After an interruption of several years, the liars' contest was renewed by a former newspaperman, Bill Jennings. Contestants need only sign up to participate and must tell a tall tale involving Peg-Leg Smith and/or gold. The winner gets the title Greatest Prevaricator for one year and a trophy (baseball, bowling, or otherwise) harvested from the local thrift store. Recent tales have featured Smith using a penguin as a compass, and a rhino with gold toenails as his traveling companion. Meanwhile, perhaps Peg-Leg Smith's lost gold still sits on a lone butte somewhere up nearby Coyote Canyon.

If you stop, don't forget to open the old mailbox and sign the guestbook.

PEG-LEG SMITH'S GOLD
Where it was found and where it is lost.

You might think that mysterious artifacts and crumbling temples are found only in remote parts of the world, in impenetrable jungles or hostile deserts. But unexplained structures and cryptic remnants of lost civilizations can sometimes be found in your own backyard.

Many archaeologists and historians believe a large portion of California's history has vanished in the folds of time. Native American petroglyphs have been found in caves, crevices, and rock shelters throughout the state, but these, some experts assert, give only a small hint of the civilizations and people who wandered our state back in the dawn of time. In addition to the brief postcards from the past left behind by indigenous cultures, there is evidence that visitors from places as far away as China may have come to the western coast of the continent when it was still a wilderness. These visitors made their journeys long before Christopher Columbus "discovered" America, and they left behind mysterious reminders of their presence.

How did the creators of these puzzling artifacts and the builders of these stone structures get to this land? Where did they come from and why did they leave? Nobody can say for sure, but these ancient sojourners have given us sites to ponder and cryptic messages to decipher.

Examining these lost pages from the book of history opens up an entirely new realm of possibilities just as fascinating as the heritage we thought we knew. Whether or not you choose to believe that ancient civilizations once inhabited the land we now know as California, one thing is certain: This state we call home has been a very weird place for a very very long time!

Ancient Mysteries and Unnatural Wonders

Maze Stone Reveals Unknown Designs

A big, striking petroglyph of unknown origin graces a small mountain area called Maze Stone County Park in Hemet, Riverside County. Inscribed on a large boulder, the three-foot-square figure is a maze formed by four interlocking swastikas. The design is almost unknown among Indian petroglyphs, and archaeologists attribute it to the so-called Maze Culture, which left only one similar design, miles to the south in San Diego County. Other people have other explanations. Maze Stone has been labeled everything from a 15,000-year-old remnant of the Cascadians, thought to be the ancestors of the Maya, to a religious symbol left by Chinese Buddhist monks at about A.D. 500. The latter theory is popular among historians seeking to prove that the Chinese beat Columbus to North America by at least a thousand years. To see the puzzling petroglyph, take state highway 74, then go north 3.2 miles on California Avenue to Maze Stone Park.

MAZE STONE

THIS PICTOGRAPH REPRESENTING A MAZE, IS AN OUTSTANDING EXAMPLE OF THE WORK OF PREHISTORIC PEOPLES. IT, WITH 5.75 ACRES OF LAND, WAS DONATED TO RIVERSIDE COUNTY AS A COUNTY PARK ON APRIL 15, 1956, BY MR. AND MRS. ROGER E. MILLER.

REGISTERED LANDMARK NO. 557

PLAQUE PLACED BY CALIFORNIA STATE PARK COMMISSION IN COOPERATION WITH RIVERSIDE COUNTY BOARD OF SUPERVISORS AND HEMET WOMAN'S CLUB, FEBRUARY 9, 1957.

Welcome to Ancient California—Gateway to Fu Shang

Bob Meistrell ran a scuba equipment shop in Palos Verdes. One day in 1975, he and his friend Wayne Baldwin were indulging their passion for diving and looking for lobsters and abalones to put on the barbeque back home. Although the fruits of the sea eluded them, their foray off the rocky reefs of the peninsula turned up something that would puzzle and disturb mainstream archaeology for years.

Spotting an unusual round object thirty-five feet down on the sea bottom, Meistrell and Baldwin hauled the thing, which turned out to be a 305-pound rock, to the surface and carted it back to the shop. The rock was almost perfectly round, with a circular hole bored in the center. In the next few weeks, they searched the area and eventually discovered about thirty-five more stones of similar appearance.

The artifacts soon came to the attention of James Moriarty III, a professor of history and archaeology at the University of San Diego. After five years of research, Moriarty and his associate Larry Pierson concluded that the stones were anchors from an ancient shipwreck, possibly dating back some two thousand years. The largest object eventually brought to the surface weighed almost half a ton, leading the researchers to surmise that the ship it had come from was in excess of one hundred feet from stem to stern and may have carried a crew of fifty or more. The timbers of the ancient wreck had long since been battered to splinters on the treacherous coast of the Palos Verdes peninsula. Through correspondence with scientists in Southeast Asia, Moriarty and Pierson deduced that the sandstone from which the anchors and

ballast were fashioned was a type native to southern China. Although historians have begun to take the idea of Chinese explorers more seriously in the last few years, at the time it was academic heresy to suggest that a non-European race had reached the shores of western North America almost 1,500 years before the Spanish made their first forays here in the sixteenth century. Mainstream archaeology massed to protect the status quo by first suggesting that the artifacts were merely leftover anchors from immigrant Chinese fishermen of the nineteenth and early twentieth centuries. But this explanation for the origin of the stones was refuted, since contemporary photographic evidence proved that the Chinese in California chose to employ readily available and much more practical metal anchors.

But that was not all that was found on the seabed near the Palos Verdes promontory: Two columnlike stones carved with grooves and holes, as well as a stone sphere weighing almost a ton with a groove cut around its circumference, were also recovered. No one could venture a guess as to what these objects were for and whence they came. Henriette Mertz, in her book *Pale Ink,* delved into the ancient Chinese legend of the land of Fu Shang. Although other scholars have found fault with her analysis, Mertz translated the old Chinese units of measure into miles and found that the tales of Fu Shang placed its location precisely at the California coast. Reading the stories told by

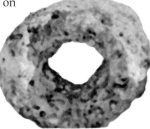

the explorers, she also thought she recognized descriptions of Mount Shasta and the Grand Canyon.

The anchors found by the Palos Verdes divers weren't the first erratic Chinese artifacts to show up in America. A U.S. Geological Survey dredging operation had pulled up a similar object seventy-five miles off California's coast. And earlier in the century, ancient Chinese inscriptions and relics had turned up in odd places around the West. Archaic Chinese rock writing had been found in a Nevada canyon, and a peculiar little idol covered with old Chinese characters was unearthed in Granby, Colorado: two more pieces in a vast, centuries-old Chinese puzzle.

For now, the academic battle still rages about the Palos Verdes artifacts. The anchor discovery may be the best challenge yet to orthodox American historians. For years, they have refused to believe that ancient Europeans and Africans had visited America before A.D. 1000, despite the Celtic stone cairns, Roman coins, and Phoenician urns that keep being uncovered on the New England coast. Now, from America's western shore, comes a new affront to the continent's "official" history: some doughnut-shaped stones tossed into the ocean two thousand years ago by Chinese sailors wrecked on the wave-lashed shores of Palos Verdes. It may take another generation for our school history books to catch up.

Lompoc: Land of the Giants

The Bible's book of Genesis, chapter 6, verse 4, tells us, *There were giants in the earth in those days.* This puzzling statement took on new meaning for a group of Mexican soldiers stationed in Lompoc in 1833.

The soldiers were digging a powder-magazine pit on the old Lompoc Rancho one morning when they unearthed a human skeleton. Not unusual, except that this skeleton, lying beneath a layer of cemented gravel, was twelve feet tall. The giant had double rows of teeth on its upper and lower jaws and was surrounded by burial offerings: carved shells, huge stone axes, and porphyry blocks covered with hieroglyphic symbols.

Local Indians heard of the find and panicked. They insisted that the skeleton was an evil omen, so authorities, anxious to head off trouble, reburied the mammoth remains and the strange trinkets somewhere on the rancho.

Lompoc Rancho's behemoth bones weren't unique. Giant skeletons surfaced all over America during nineteenth- and early-twentieth-century archaeological and mining projects. Excavations at such places as Lovelock, Nevada, and the mound country in central Minnesota were said to have yielded dozens of the oversized remains. Indians in these areas were familiar with the giants, and spoke of them with fear and hatred. They said that their distant ancestors were menaced and harassed by these gargantuan humanoids and fought great bloody wars to drive them out of their territories.

Virtually all of the giant remains have been lost or destroyed due to the sloppy record-keeping and storage practices of the times. Subsequently, modern archaeologists have mostly written off reports of the findings as hoaxes and the Indian legends as fantasy.

But we can't be too sure. Someday, a spade or earthmover excavating the hills around Lompoc may again uncover a twelve-foot, double-jawed confirmation of Genesis 6:4.

Mu—Lost City of the Lemurians

On the western edge of the Santa Monica Mountains National Recreation Area, not too far from the beach houses of Malibu, lies what one researcher believes may be the most spectacular hidden archaeological site in North America.

Robert Stanley, a journalist and publisher of *UNICUS* magazine, has traveled around the world in search of ancient mysteries and lost ruins. But he never suspected that he'd find the remnants of a lost world literally (almost) in his own backyard, on the slopes of these chaparral-covered mountains that bisect the Los Angeles basin.

In 1985, Stanley was hiking through the Santa Monicas when he began to notice odd and unnatural-looking formations around the Los Angeles–Ventura county line. He noted gulches that looked like sculpted ramparts, stone walls on rocky hills never occupied by houses or livestock, and floorlike flat surfaces at the tops of windswept peaks. There was also a huge rock outcropping that resembled the outline of a human face staring out to the Pacific, which Stanley dubbed the Sphinx.

Researching the history and lore of the area, Stanley found a local Chumash Indian legend of a "First People" who had lived in the mountains long before the Chumash arrived in around 3,000 B.C. The Chumash said that these mystery people were long gone, but some of their artifacts—crystalline sculptures of strange animals and the like—could be found in certain mountain caves. As with the Anasazi ruins of the Southwest, the First People's remnants were avoided by the local Indians.

What was most intriguing about the Chumash legend was the story of the First People's demise. The Chumash claimed that the civilization had been called Mu and had been wiped out in a catastrophic flood. This exactly paralleled the legend of Lemuria, the Lost Continent of the Pacific.

Geologists and oceanographers believe that at the end of the last Ice Age, the Malibu sea level was at least two hundred feet lower than today. This would have made the Channel Islands a far-western extension of the Santa Monicas and allowed for a large lowland region—the Mu of the legend—to exist in what's now the California coastal shelf of the Pacific Ocean. That prehistoric peoples lived in this area is beyond dispute. One of North America's oldest human remains—the 13,000-year-old Channel Islands Woman—was found on Santa Rosa Island, twenty-five miles west of Malibu.

Stanley thinks that Mu's lowlands were wiped out by the rising post–Ice Age sea levels. The higher regions of the civilization, whose traces he says still exist in the Santa Monicas, may have been destroyed by a tsunami—a fast-moving, powerful tidal wave. Such a wave would have devastated coastal hillside settlements and left countless tons of silt and debris in its wake.

Mu may be the Californian equivalent of underwater archaeological sites like Japan's Yonaguni, Egypt's Alexandria, or Wisconsin's Rock Lake. Robert Stanley has become an expert on the Mu site and has involved both professionals and laypeople in explorations of the area. However, he has not revealed the exact locations of the area's most peculiar features, fearing their destruction by vandals or curiosity hunters.

Which Came First, the Spark Plug or the Rock?

Debate has raged for over thirty years about a twentieth-century artifact discovered in a half-million-year-old rock. Skeptics and believers are still arguing about it more than forty years after it was found in the Coso Mountains.

On February 13, 1961, Wally Lane, Mike Mikesell, and Virginia Maxey made one of the strangest and most inexplicable archaeological finds in California history. While hunting for geodes, one of the three picked up a brown rock near the top of an unnamed 4,300-foot peak, twelve miles southeast of Olancha. Geodes are generally round (sometimes cigar-shaped) rocks with a hollow interior studded with mineral crystals. They are highly prized by collectors and dilettantes alike, and specimens that contain amethyst are worth many hundreds of dollars. The three rock hunters had set out to find some specimens for their store in Olancha and were targeting a peak in the Coso Mountains just six miles northeast of their shop.

After a good morning's collecting, the trio dumped their finds into a sack that Mikesell was toting and headed home. The next day Mikesell pulled a likely-looking, fossil-shell encrusted specimen out of the bag and went to work with a diamond saw. After the blade was nearly ruined, the rock split apart, revealing what looked like a porcelain cylinder surrounding a shiny metal rod. It also contained what looked like a washer and a nail.

The trio sat on the discovery for a while, but early on, Maxey spoke to a geologist who informed her that the rock encasing the apparently artificial object would have taken 500,000 years to form. Maxey was at first quoted as declaring the find "an instrument as old as Mu or Atlantis. Perhaps it is a communications device or some sort of directional finder or some sort of instrument made to utilize power principles we know nothing about."

To this day, the bizarre artifact defies explanation.

The few who have tried at all say it's a clay-coated piece of mine machinery debris; this is unlikely, since the "Coso Geode" was found several miles from the nearest mine shafts. At any rate, clay concretion processes don't happen in dry, rocky desert regions like the Coso range.

Sometime in the mid-1960s, Ron Calais, a scientist with a heavy creationist bent, was allowed to examine the Coso Geode. He took pictures and X rays of the cut halves, which was a great stroke of luck when the object later went missing. The X rays showed a cylindrical structure with a metal ring at one end and a flared metal cap at the other. A threaded, screwlike area topped the assemblage.

In 1969, International Fortean Organization (INFO) journal editor Ronald Willis published a careful and thoughtful article on the Coso artifact. In the article, Willis followed the skeptical but interested style of Charles Fort, an early-twentieth-century chronicler of the unexplained.

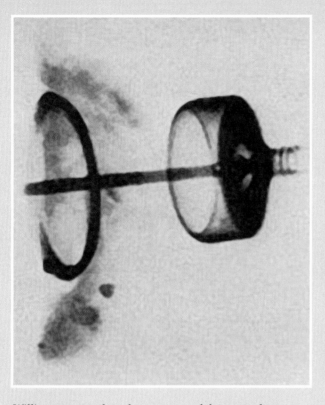

Willis commented on the structure of the anomalous object, but stopped short of calling it an advanced piece of technology from a lost age. He simply wrote that the object was "the remains of a corroded piece of metal with threads." He finally went out on a limb and guessed that the thing might be a spark plug.

Creationists soon latched on to the find, since if authentic, it calls into question the ordered pageant of history that mainstream science has presented to us. It was a prime example of an OOPArt (Out Of Place Artifact) such as the Crystal Skull and what appeared to be an ancient battery discovered in Iraq in the 1950s.

In the late 1990s, various organizations reopened investigations into the Coso artifact. They looked at the claims of researchers such as Donald Chittick of the Institute for Creation Research, who started with the premise that the rock was in fact a bona fide geode. Skeptics pointed out that just because the original rock-hunting trio was looking for geodes did not necessarily mean that they found one. Since there were other modern objects (the nail and washer) embedded in the surface, along with fossil shells, this indicated that the rock may have been covered with mud sometime between 1910 and 1930, picked up hitchhikers, and finally hardened in the desert sun.

Pierre Stomberg, a skeptic, contacted the SPCA (that's the Spark Plug Collectors of America) and asked them to look at the X rays. President Chad Windham responded with a letter and two examples of Champion spark plugs from the 1920s. Everything matched up, allowing for corrosion of the metal and other components. The creationists responded that certain parts of the "spark plug, particularly the spring or helix terminal . . . do not correspond to any known spark plug today." However, many readers of the Creation Outreach Web site tended to agree with the skeptics. So much for faith.

There are plenty of other OOPArts to keep the revisionists busy, many of which are much harder to explain. That's fortunate, because the spark-plug-in-a-rock is no longer around for investigation. Perhaps it has returned to the space-time transient realm from whence it came. The Coso artifact was on display for a while at the Eastern California Museum in Independence, but was reclaimed by its owner in 1969. After forbidding any further dismantling or examination of the relic, he tried to sell it for a reported $25,000, but couldn't find a buyer.

Recent attempts to trace the owner, the original finders, or the geode have been unsuccessful. All that's left of this strange archaeological anomaly are a few photographs, yellowing accounts in some obscure journals, and a tantalizing archaeological mystery that may never be resolved to anyone's satisfaction.

Not all the buried artifacts from antiquity are the remnants of long-lost civilizations. Sometimes they just look that way!

Buried Egyptian Temple, Guadalupe

"You are here to please me. Nothing else on earth matters," said Cecil B. DeMille to his expectant crew as they sat in the sand waiting the start of production on his biggest extravaganza to date. The film was to be the first incarnation of *The Ten Commandments* (DeMille remade the epic in 1956 with Charlton Heston). The legendary director with the outsize ego had a massive complex built for the initial part of the story, portraying Hollywood's idea of ancient Egypt. The year was 1923, and the sleepy town of Guadalupe, on the central California coast, was suddenly neighbor to a

bustling metropolis of over five thousand souls just a few miles away on the Nipomo Dunes.

The sheer size of the set dwarfed anything yet produced on film. DeMille was a stickler for reality. In a scene he had directed years earlier, he once used real bullets when actors had to shoot their way through a door for a western. He spared no expense for his *Commandments*. Parts of the film were shot in the new two-strip Technicolor process to show off the elaborate Pharaoh's Palace. In addition to its skyscraperlike height, the palace was 720 feet long and featured an Avenue of the Sphinxes, with twenty-one five-ton statues lining the royal road. There were also four statues of the pharaoh, all over thirty feet high. The "city" was surrounded by an 80-foot-wide, 120-foot-high wall covered with hieroglyphics modeled on those unearthed just the year before in King Tut's tomb.

At the close of production, the director had workers tear down the set and bury the whole thing. Apart from any egocentric issues he may have harbored, DeMille was protecting his creation from interlopers: It was then common practice for low-budget companies to use sets that the major studios had left behind.

The plaster and wood detritus lay partially buried under the shifting sands for almost sixty years, until a few film buffs, armed with cryptic information from DeMille's posthumously published autobiography, began to search for the buried city. They found it soon enough but have been hamstrung since the mid-1980s, lacking funds to finish the excavation. Expected help from the Hollywood community has not come to pass, despite an initial $10,000 donation from the Bank of America, one of the original financial backers of the film.

The dunes shift a few feet a year, alternately revealing and covering up sphinx noses and

pharaohs' toes. The plaster props have the consistency of blue cheese and require a soak with hardening preservative before they can be moved. Coins, bits of costumes, and even an empty bottle of the cough medicine favored during Prohibition for its high-proof punch have been excavated. The Nature Conservancy has stewardship of the area, now called the Guadalupe–Nipomo Dunes Complex, and plans to leave the artifacts in place until more money is donated to mount a systematic dig. Ground-mapping radar has revealed at least twelve of the sphinx statues.

Some of the plaster pieces are on display in the Dunes Visitor Center on the main drag of Guadalupe and, curiously enough, in the local auto parts and hardware store up the street, where owner John Perry easily slides into his role as self-appointed civic booster. His store is a homegrown version of the official exhibit, featuring books, other pieces pulled from the sands, and a phalanx of glass cases to hold it all. Perry will give exact directions to the main ruin area, although there is not much to see. The views from the Nipomo Dunes nature road give little hint of what lies below. A scattering of lumber and a rounded plaster fragment emerging from a massive hill were all that was visible in May 2005. Cecil B. DeMille's temple sleeps beneath the shifting sands, as it has done for almost three quarters of a century, waiting for a rebirth that Hollywood bigwigs have so far failed to provide.

Guadalupe is located along Highway 1 in Santa Barbara County, eight miles east of Santa Maria and the 101 Freeway. The Nipomo Dunes are due west, approximately six miles from town on West Main Street.

Frenchman's Tower: Palo Alto

My friend's family has lived in the area of Palo Alto for generations and showed me Frenchman's Tower, something only locals know about. It was built in 1875 by Peter Coutts, a mysterious Frenchman whose farmland is now most of Palo Alto and Stanford University. It's located on Old Page Mill Road in Palo Alto, on a quiet, one-lane residential street. As you drive past the goats and trees, you suddenly find a red brick tower to your right.

I would say it is about 30-feet-tall, and only 5 feet or so from the road. You have to climb over a barbed fence that is obviously bent from previous explorers. My friend's mom told me that in the 1970s the daughter of the Stanford Athletics Director was kidnapped, and they found her body there.

The weirdest thing about Frenchman's Tower is that nobody knows why it's there. Most people think it was meant to be a base for a water tower, but the windows suggest otherwise. Others think it was part of a network of secret tunnels, a weapons cache, or a prison for the mad Madame Coutts.

According to the nearby plaque, it was begun in 1875 as a part of Peter Coutts' irrigation system. HIS REAL NAME WAS PAULIN CAPERON AND HE WAS A WEALTHY NEWSPAPER PUBLISHER WHO WAS BANISHED DURING THE FRANCO-PRUSSIAN WAR. HE FLED TO CALIFORNIA IN [1874].

The historian at the Palo Alto library believes it is a "folly," a decoration to mark the boundaries of properties and provide interesting scenery. Whatever it was originally built for, it became very popular for people to visit and carve their names and years on the outside bricks (the dates go back over 100 years, and some people returned decades later to carve it again).–*Jocelyn Laney*

Some of the more curious ancient features of the California environment are unquestionably natural, yet somehow this does not diminish their mystery or allure. Take for example sand dunes that sing, stones that race across the parched desert floor like pucks in some time-warped game of shuffleboard, and briny waves that can be made to sound like the beating of distant drums. While these may all be natural occurrences of the California landscape, because of the strange sensations they evoke in those who experience them, we like to refer to these beguiling environmental anomalies as "unnatural wonders."

Singing Sands and Booming Dunes

It sounds like some kind of tall tale, but the phenomenon of "booming dunes" has been documented in scientific journals since at least the 1960s, and in oral histories from the Middle East and Asia for thousands of years. The sounds have been variously described as roaring, booming, squeaking, and singing. Some have been compared to such musical instruments as a kettle drum, zither, tambourine, bass violin, and trumpet. The amazing thing is that the sound is felt, rather than heard, and seems to come from everywhere and nowhere.

The phenomenon of *nad,* a Sanskrit term signifying transcendental, astral, psychic, or paranormal music, may have some of its origin in the occurrence of these dune tunes. We heard about this phenomenon years ago when a friend reported mysterious "harplike" music he heard over the wind late at night during a solitary desert camping trip. He had no idea where the ethereal sounds were coming from.

Only seven places in the continental United States are permanent home to the singing-sand concerts, and one of these is in the Mojave Desert on the way to Vegas. Two others are in the far reaches of Death Valley National Park. All the locations have been closed to dune buggies and other assorted sports for many years. The only way in is to hike.

For plain old sand to emit unearthly sounds, the scientists tell us that several exacting factors need to be present: The grains have to be round and between 0.1 and 0.5 millimeters in diameter, the sand has to contain silica, and a certain stable humidity must be present, typically less than 0.1 percent, depending on the size of the grains. The farther the material has traveled to its present home, the better, since as a result of wind and buffeting action against the ground and other sand grains, the individual grains are usually more uniform.

Kelso Dunes, about thirty miles south of Baker, is perhaps the quintessential singing-sand hangout, certainly in California and possibly in the world. On a drive south from I-15, the landscape is typical SoCal desert, with Joshua trees and the usual scrub stretching to the horizon. Eventually, the land begins to slope downward, and the dunes heave into view. About eight miles after the town of Kelso (a seemingly uninhabited place with an incongruously large railroad yard), signs indicate the turnoff to the dunes. Don't speed on the washboard gravel; nearly invisible but deep, dry creek beds cutting across the road will total the suspension of the hardiest vehicle.

The main sand hill, six hundred and fifty feet high, is visible from the road and is a strenuous hike from the last turnaround. There are a few methods to get the sand to perform, but a 1979 report by Caltech scientist D. K. Haff probably gives the best instructions: "[T]he most spectacular and enduring vibrations were produced by the movement of large quantities of sand. This could be initiated by vigorous kicking at the sharp dune crest in order to dislodge a metastable surface layer on the lee slopes." English translation: "Go to the top of the dune and kick sand down the steep side." Make sure the day is calm, since wind will not only mask the sounds, but also tends to make for unstable conditions that keep the sand from cascading evenly. On a recent expedition, we discovered that just walking along the crest of the highest dunes will elicit a sound not unlike a tuba, making each step a musical experience.

Panamint Dunes, a mere three-mile hike from the dirt road, is located in the Panamint Valley, just over the mountains west of Death Valley on Highway 190. This dune field has the least amount of reward for the singing-sand tourist, likely due to the shape of the grains and the presence of underground water close to the surface.

Eureka Dunes, however, beats out Kelso in a photo finish. Eureka is at the end of a bone-jarring forty-four-mile drive over a graded dirt road. This dune field features all the booming activity found at Kelso, albeit with less volume, but the best chance for solitude, which may be the most important thing.

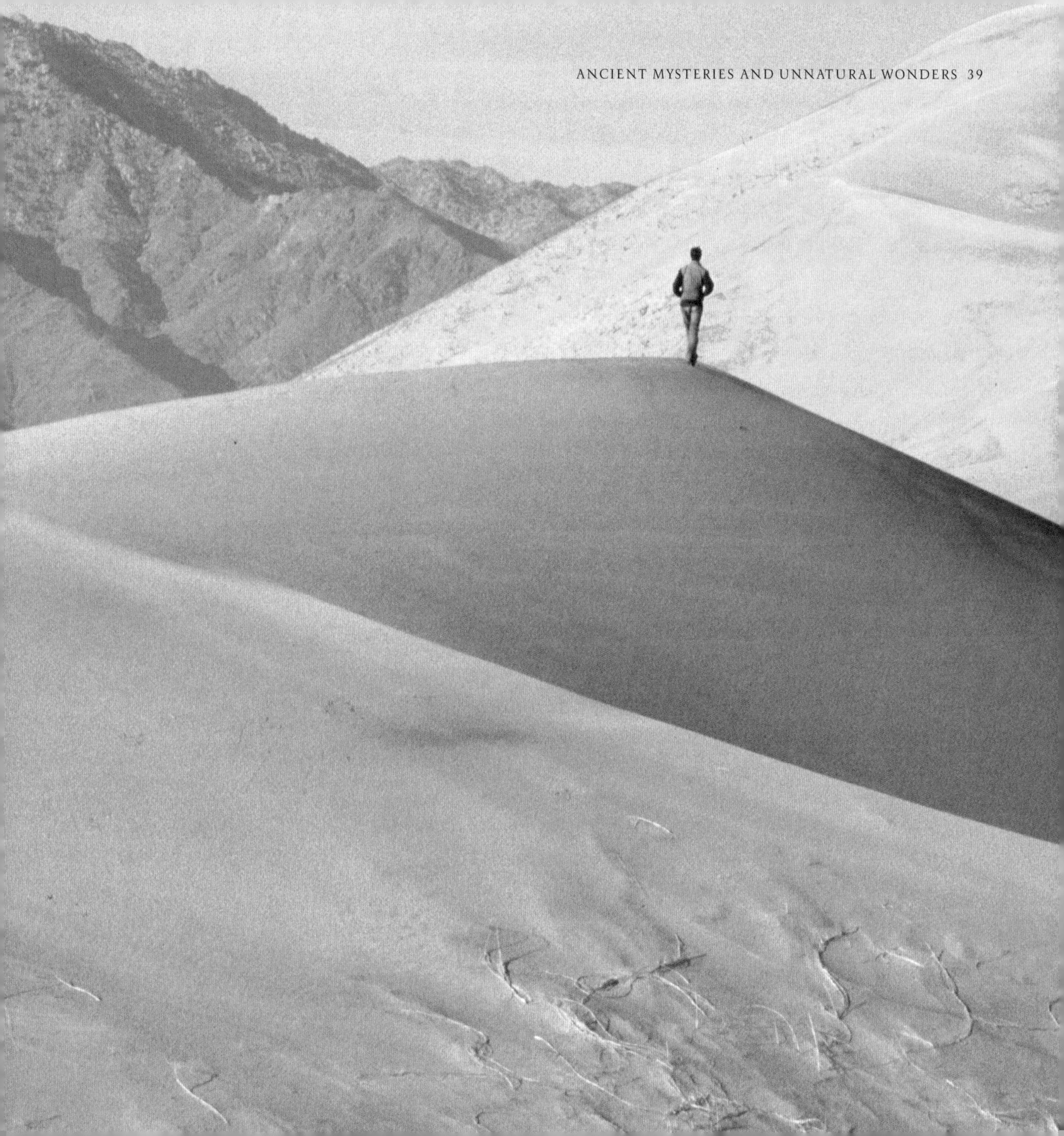

The Place Where the Rocks Move

When you're tired of sand dunes, dangerous abandoned mines, and yet another interpretive sign, there's only one place left to go in Death Valley: The Place Where the Rocks Move. A few rough miles from the end of the paved road lies one of the most weird and beautiful locales in this most desolate of national parks, and it is complete with rocks that "race" each other, leaving tracks of their otherworldly movement behind for passersby to marvel at.

Most packaged tours and the blue-haired crowd stop at the spectacular Ubehebe volcanic crater at the north end of the valley. Just before the start of the short loop that leads to the lip of this quarter-mile-deep hole, a track cuts off through the lava and recedes to the southwest. An unassuming sign posted at the intersection reads THE RACETRACK—27. We're talking racing rocks, and they're twenty-seven slow miles away. About an hour of bad washboard gravel road rewards your vibrating eyeballs with the sight of a beige smear along the bottom of a huge valley. There is no camping allowed in the Racetrack Valley, so this is a day trip or a very dangerous drive out in the dark.

Your highly developed aesthetic sense thrills at the simplicity of the scene. A sizable conglomeration of uplifted bedrock called the Grandstand juts up from the center of an ancient dry lake, which stretches to the base of the bare mountains that surround it. Step onto the dried mud and look at it closely. The floor of the valley is covered with countless fingers of tiny cracks, stretching to the horizon. You could follow one of these infinite clefts anywhere on the playa without stopping. Be thankful you're not on psychedelics, or this would be sensory overload.

It's about a ten-minute walk from the first pullout area and ubiquitous Park Service information sign to the Grandstand. The blackish brown outcropping, about 100 by 500 feet, still resembles the island it once was. The demarcation between dry mud and hard rock is gradual, and rings the formation like a soft halo. Climb up the hundred feet or so to the top and have a look around. The dark, rough rock is stippled with a beautiful pattern of lighter reflective strips of some micalike compound. It's positively hallucinatory.

Don't look for the traveling rocks here. This is just the prelude.

The hearty might want to make the two- to three-mile walk to the southeast end of the racetrack to see the main attraction. Laziness (or heat—in the summer months) draws others back to the car and a short hop south to the next pullout sign. Walk almost due east for fifteen or twenty minutes across the lake bed until the floating, shimmering black dots on the horizon resolve into hundreds of very dark, scattered rocks.

The mysterious rock race apparently moves at glacial speeds, and no one has ever witnessed it actually happening, but the evidence is clear. Smeared depressions all end at a rock. Some of the tracks are hundreds of feet long. It's as if some spectral hand decided to use the mud as a doodling pad. A few of the tracks are ramrod straight; others curve, zigzag, and even turn back on themselves. It's creepy and exhilarating at the same time. Many of the rocks have even pushed up a lip of dried mud in front of them, which blows away the "rocks-move-by-wind-pushing-across-frozen-surface" idea. The nail in that coffin is the fact that only a very few appear to have moved in the same direction. Selective winds? How the hell did these things get out here anyway? Some are at least a half mile from the nearest mountain. Perhaps they have been traveling for millennia.

In his excellent book *The Rebirth of Pan,* author Jim

Brandon remarked that the mud flats are honeycombed below ground with abandoned mine tunnels and theorized that some kind of force is present in such places (there are at least three other "racetracks" on other dry lakes), and he delights in the apparently pointless lark of moving rocks when no one is looking. There are rumors that there have been attempts to photograph the rocks in time-lapse, but we could find no evidence of such a study. The rangers hadn't heard of such a project.

Some of the tracks stop in mid-slide, with no rock to be seen, which suggests stupid human activity. Apparently, someone has moved a number of the rocks. Don't spoil the fun for the next tourist. And, if the ranger catches you, there is a very heavy fine. Riding a bike on the dry lake is also a big no-no. No mechanized transportation is allowed in the designated wilderness. Rangers hide in the hills and appear out of nowhere to ticket scofflaws, so behave!

Wave Organ—San Francisco

It's a truly unique audio experience, something like listening to the world's largest seashell. Some say it sounds like distant drums, others refer to it as quiet thunder, and the fifty-something-year-old hippie standing next to us, with the tie-dyed bandana covering up a huge bald spot on what was probably once a magnificent head of free-flowing hair, says it sounds "soooooo cooool," between tokes of his specially rolled cigarette.

The visual experience is none too shabby either. Located at the very end of a jetty in San Francisco's Golden Gate National Recreation Area, amid the panorama of the Golden Gate Bridge, Alcatraz Island, and the city skyline, sits a little-known place of interest: the Wave Organ.

Created in 1986 by artists Peter Richards and George Gonzales, the Wave Organ is a "wave-activated acoustic sculpture." There is an undeniably otherworldly, ethereal quality to this very impressive work of auditory physics. That may be because many of the granite and marble stones used to create this monument to the ocean's reverberations came from a cemetery that dates back to the gold rush.

Dozens of long PVC pipes are situated at various locations and elevations along the edge of the small peninsula. The listening ends of these pipes are positioned all along the isthmus and inside a specially constructed stereo booth. When the waves crash against the open ends of the pipe and the consequent interchange of the bay water flows in and out of the tubing, a wonderfully calming and natural piece of music is produced.

It is best to visit the Wave Organ at high tide, and that can be odd hours, depending on the time of year. But odd hours in San Francisco are never dull hours; we're sure you'll find something to do while waiting for the tide to come in.

Fabled People and Places

Throughout history, adventurous explorers have set out to find mythic lands and mysterious peoples. Here at *Weird California* we too are on a quest to discover fabled locales and elusive populations, the tales of which have been passed down to us through the generations. As medieval knights searched for the Holy Grail or the Spanish conquistadors sought the Fountain of Youth and El Dorado, we endeavor to find storied lands, where enclaves of retired Munchkins lead reclusive lives or Lizard People roam the underground just beneath our feet. We venture to the lofty summits of Mount Shasta and charge into the Valley of Death itself to discover if the center of the world can really be found right here in our own Golden State. Do wooden ships laden with incalculable treasures lie just beneath the shifting sands of our southern deserts? That's what we want to find out!

So we look for clues that might lead us to places we have heard tell of, without any real hard evidence that such places ever actually existed. No matter. We continue to seek to satisfy our curious nature, for we have faith that there is more to our wondrous state than just prefab strip malls, sprawling suburbs, and grey stretches of highway. We forge ahead undaunted on our expeditions with all the fervent conviction of Don Quixote going forth to face the windmill giants. We keep an open mind, just in case these fabled people and places are like Brigadoon and must be believed to be seen and not the other way around. For we want to believe in them, even though we know these things we search for may exist only in our own collective imagination.

Munchkin House

There used to be several Munchkin houses in La Jolla, but recent developments and developers have wiped out all but one of these diminutive domiciles. While we were searching for the elusive locale, a local jogger related the accepted legend: After production wrapped on *The Wizard of Oz* in 1939, a few of the actors who had played Munchkins, their pockets bulging with MGM cash, decided to move down south and build themselves a tiny town of their own in the tony burg of La Jolla, just north of San Diego. They chose the north slope of Mount Soledad, high over the Pacific

Ocean, and retired to obscurity with a million-dollar view of the breakers and coastline stretching to the horizon.

Unfortunately, this movieland tale is based on nothing but rumors. Some of the stories may have stemmed from the fact that local author L. Frank Baum wrote much of *Oz* at his home here and while partying at the nearby Hotel Del Coronado. Beyond this, there is little or no evidence that movie midgets had anything to do with the teeny-scale houses here, and there is no evidence that a Lollipop Guild suddenly opened for business in 1940s San Diego.

The model homes were designed by famed architect Cliff May and built in the late 1930s to show off his new California ranch and mission-inspired ideas. They appear to have been sporadically occupied since then, presumably by very short people. A woman whom no one seems to know much about bought the land and homes a few years ago. Over protests from area residents, she demolished two of the original three houses and built an ostentatious,

mansionlike monstrosity that now hugs the hill and completely overshadows the little house on Hillside Drive.

Some think that the house only looks Lilliputian because of the way it is built on a steep slope. The front is on the uphill side, giving the illusion that the place is smaller than it really is, but a six-foot-tall man would bump his head going through the front door. No one is living there now, so we went out back to see for ourselves. The roof is so low that almost anyone can touch it. Unless you actually are a Munchkin, the ceiling would probably be only a couple of feet overhead. The kitchen sink is at mid-thigh. The aforementioned six-footer would need to duck through interior doorways.

With newfound riches flowing into the bank accounts of latter-day stars of dwarf-tossing competitions, perhaps this last home can be saved after all and live up to its reputation.

Following the Yellow Brick Road to Munchkinland

Munchkinland is true. My girlfriend and I found it by accident one night driving around in La Jolla back in 1973. We did not believe what we saw to be true so we went back in the daylight and discovered it was absolutely true. I walked up to a house and knocked on the door pretending to be looking for someone. The door was chin-high (I am 5´6˝). The woman who answered the door was a midget and was really quite nice, amused by my curiosity. The homes are located near Mount Soledad in La Jolla. If my memory serves me well, you will run into the small community by turning left onto Hidden Valley Road from La Jolla Valley Parkway.—*Bambi from San Diego*

We're Off to See the Midgets

There are several alleged locations of Midget Town, all of which are in the Bixby Knolls area of Long Beach. There are many private residential areas in this neighborhood that one can easily attribute to a midget colony. The most convincing one lies adjacent to the Virginia Country Club at the end of a long, dead end street either called Virginia or Country Club. As you drive down this street you will see all kinds of DEAD END and NO TRESPASSING signs designed to deter the casual observer. You will reach a checkpoint with a wooden gate and a small button on the left hand side. Despite the threatening signs, all you have to do is push the button and the gate will automatically open.

If you drive inside, you will notice that the first house on your left is equipped with a giant front door and doorknobs that look no taller than three feet high. The rest of the houses appear normal. If you continue driving, you will reach another gate, which cannot be opened by nonresidents, followed by a third gate which can only be seen in the distance (I have never reached the third gate). Make sure you're in and out of there pretty quick, because the residents will call security. On your way out, turn right on the first street and go about five or six blocks and you will see the house from the movie *Ferris Bueller's Day Off*. Seeing the house almost makes up for the fact that you got nothing out of this journey other than seeing one house with very low doorknobs.

This is what I have experienced firsthand. Of course, it is nowhere near the stories I have heard about midgets throwing bricks at you or shooting BB guns. The strangest part to me is that everyone in Long Beach (and beyond) knows about it. Even my friend said that he and his buddies used to go looking for Midget Town when they were young. I've also heard of Midget Towns in both Irvine and San Diego (allegedly the one in San Diego has its own McDonald's).—*Randy Mills*

Midgetville in SoCal Is So Cute!

There is a Midgetville in San Diego. It is located on Mt. Soledad, but I couldn't give you directions—we found it by accident. It is really something to see, small houses and mailboxes, it's amazing. I can tell you that even though the people that live on this very prestigious mountain deny its existence, it is absolutely there and I have seen it!

The mountain has a large white cross at the top of it. There is a little section where the houses were so small and the doors are small and the mailboxes and everything was so much smaller. You can stand by the houses and almost be as tall as they are. It is so cute! —*Teresa*

Midgets Up the Mountain

About Midgetville in San Diego, it is definitely on Mt. Soledad. I lived in San Diego back in '96 and went there many times at night. It's relatively small, only four or five houses, and it's on an upward slanted road so the small gates and doors are hard to recognize from the street. I can't remember the street name anymore, but if I was there I'm pretty sure I could find it.—*Brian*

Midget Houses Are Pretty Dang Nice

There's a dwarf community in San Diego, somewhere in Coronado. The houses all look normal except the windows are low and the doors are small. Pretty dang nice houses too!—*Anonymous*

Midget Town's in a Dangerous Hood

There is supposedly this house in Long Beach where this butler killed and hung two children of the house out the back window. The cops later boarded up the windows, and the window which the kids were hung out of is facing an alley (Egor's Alley).

Legend has it that if you drive down the alley at night, you can still see the blood dripping down the window and wall. This is located pretty close to another legend: Midget Town by Virginia Country Club. It's off of Carson, past Atlantic.—*Brad Z*

Fear and Loathing in Midgetville

The Midget Village was off of Clay Street near Goldenwest St. We went there one night very late and got so spooked by it that I thought we were going to be chased by "little people." We took off and never returned. Scared the hell out of us.
—*Tim Harvey*

A Little Village by the Bay

There is a Midgetville in the Bay Area. I have been there but cannot recall if it was San Leandro or where it was. One whole street was little houses. Some Victorians, some bungalows. Just scaled down. You would never really notice unless someone told you. Not like they are four feet tall or anything. Still got the creeps and just wanted to leave.—*LMK*

Center of the World

The center of the world is not New York City, home of the United Nations and a hub of world finances. And it's not Washington, D.C., where a small group of power brokers make decisions that affect people around the world. And it's not Jerusalem, where landmarks from many of the world's major religions reside. No, believe it or not, the real center of the world is located in the middle of a sleepy desert in Felicity, right here in California.

Felicity was founded in May 1986 by Jacques-Andre Istel, who wrote a children's book entitled *Coe the Good Dragon at the Center of the World*. He became mayor of the town he founded, outfitted it with a number of spectacular displays, and had it legally certified the official Center of the World. Istel still lives in the town, which he named after his wife, promoting it and selling Felicity perfume to supplement his income.

The logical among you may be thinking, The world is spherical. Therefore, any random point on its surface can technically be the center of the world. What makes this spot different from any other dot on a map?

Well, Felicity has gone above and beyond in its efforts to be the actual center of the world. First and foremost, it has a pyramid, with a plaque inside proclaiming the town to be the Center of the World. Visitors are encouraged to stand in this spot and make a wish. They are then granted documentation, signed by Mayor Istel himself, certifying that they have stood at the center of the world. In 1985, the pyramid was legally recognized as the Center of the World, after the sixth printing of Istel's book. In 1989, the French government recognized the site as well. We have no idea why.

The town also features a flight of stairs formerly

part of the Eiffel Tower, a checkerboard-field of flower combinations, a sundial featuring a facsimile of Michelangelo's *Arm of God* sculpture, and several other strange attractions and sculptures.

Among these are a number of granite blocks placed in the desert. The most interesting of these is the *Wall for the Ages,* which is engraved with the names of people who have visited Felicity. Other similar walls are engraved with the story of the birth of aviation, the history of the Foreign Legion, and a number of other notable tales.

What it all boils down to is that the center of the world is not fast-paced, full of wealth, or a seat of international power. No, instead, it's in the middle of a desert, home to only a handful of people, and is just about as far removed from the center of worldly activity as one town can get.

Cosmic Thrills at Rosicrucian Park

The brochure reads, "The Rosicrucian Order is a worldwide philosophical and initiatic tradition that offers time-tested techniques for re-discovering the wisdom, compassion, strength and inner peace that already reside within each human being."

That all sounds good, but the message would seem a lot more serious if there wasn't a statue of a saggy breasted hippopotamus in a pharaoh's hat outside the doorway to this establishment of enlightenment in San Jose.

One does not need to be searching for mystical, spiritual, or scientific answers to enjoy the serenity of the Rosicrucian Park, though the Rosicrucian Order does claim it can help you on those quests. The park takes up a full city block, and the combination of Egyptian and Moorish architecture and landscaping is undeniably both mysterious and striking.

Sphinxes, pyramids, planetariums, and grand temples all seem strangely out of place on Naglee Avenue, but once you are inside the grounds of Rosicrucian Park, modern San Jose suddenly feels out of place.

In 1915, businessman and occultist Harve Spencer Lewis announced to the world that Pharaoh Akhenaton's secret society was now taking applications. The society was known as the Ancient and Mystical Order Rosae Crucis (AMORC), or the Rosicrucians. Lewis was its Imperator, or head.

AMORC claimed to have been founded by the ancient Egyptian ruler Akhenaton, generally credited as the first monotheistic sovereign. From there, it worked through Western history in 108-year cycles of public and private activity, making an especially strong splash in the Renaissance, when the followers of the legendary Christian Rosenkreuz antagonized the Catholic Church with their faith in reason, personal enlightenment, and a coming new age. Many great men in history have allegedly been members of the secret society. With the twentieth century under way, the group's leaders had apparently decided it was once again time to resurface.

There were already several Rosicrucian groups in existence in 1915, and many of them disputed Lewis's group's claims to antiquity and authenticity. AMORC did well, nevertheless, dispensing its "ages-old wisdom" by mail to dues-paying members. Their ads still appear in countless magazines, promising the secrets of "cosmic consciousness" to sincere seekers.

AMORC's international headquarters occupies the city-block-size compound in San Jose. All the buildings have been designed to look like Old Kingdom shrines and temples, reflecting the Rosicrucian love of things ancient Egyptian. The park's elaborate fountains, tiled walkways, gardens, and statues also faithfully evoke the Land of the Pharaohs. Not surprisingly, the park's biggest attraction is the Rosicrucian Egyptian Museum, the largest collection of ancient Egyptian relics in the western United States. The museum displays relics, mummies, and a life-size replica of a rock tomb, along with several multimedia exhibits depicting daily life in ancient Egypt.

Next door the planetarium presents AMORC's vision of the universe and the future. It contains a "star projector" that can project over 2,100 stars, planets, and other extraterrestrial wonders. It has the ability to modify the sky forward or backward in time 13,000 years. There is also a Foucault Pendulum inside, and everyone loves a Foucault Pendulum. Especially Foucault.

Closed to public eyes, there are other grand Egyptian-style buildings. There's the Research Library, which houses thousands of rare books on mysticism. Rose-Croix University is here as well, along with the massive, secretive Supreme Temple.

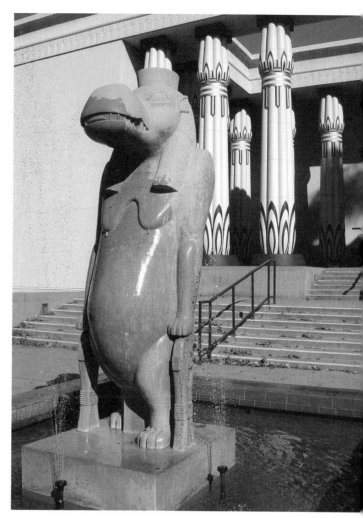

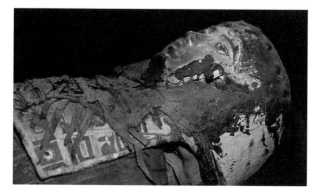

The Rosicrucians do not claim to be a religion, but rather a mystical association. If that sounds to you like they sell literature and accept a "small fee" from students, then you are already well on the path to metaphysical oneness. (A sophisticated Web portal at www.amorc.org points Internet surfers to Rosicrucian readings, activities, and merchandise.) But don't let the hint of commercialism prevent you from enjoying the park. It really is an interesting and peaceful place.

Utopian Communities

"A map of the world that does not include Utopia is not worth even glancing at, for it leaves out the one country at which humanity is always landing."
— Oscar Wilde

Human utopia seems always doomed to failure. Hundreds of planned versions of heaven on earth litter the North American landscape with their silent carcasses. Among the many dreams that have drawn people to these places is the most noble of all, a perfect society where all problems are solved and life is lived in harmony and true happiness. At one time or another, some twenty or more locations in California have sheltered the hopes of various seekers of such an existence. Most functioned as political or religious experiments, or some mingling of the two. Spiritualists bought up land south of Santa Barbara in 1883 and called it Summerland after the traditional name for the Nordic Happy Hunting Ground. Holy City, which flourished for a surprisingly long stretch near Santa Cruz, from 1918 to the early 1950s, would have done the Ku Klux Klan proud, with its racist and misogynistic creed. Most of the Californian utopias, however, were built on socialistic or peaceful Christian principles.

It is always easier to be a holy man in a cave than in civilization. The cities and society in which the utopian colonists lived tempted them with desires as strong as Eve's when she gave in and ate that apple. As a result, many of the utopian communities were done in before they had much of a chance. Others simply ran out of money or could not survive after the death or change of heart of a strong-willed founder. Today, most of the utopias of California lie in ruins or have been overtaken by raging urbanity. One of the few exceptions to this de-evolution still exists, albeit under different auspices.

Home of the Theosophists

On a sunny February afternoon in 1897, Katherine Augusta Westcott Tingley presided over an elaborate dedication ceremony on a commanding piece of property overlooking the Pacific in San Diego. The Universal Brotherhood and Theosophical Society had recently acquired the prime piece of real estate at Point Loma and intended to show the world that a community based on the principles of Madame Helena Blavatsky would point the way to a new golden age. Tingley solemnly sprinkled corn, wine, and oil on a stone, lowered a metal box into an opening on the top, sealed it in with mortar and a silver trowel, and intoned, "I dedicate this stone, a perfect square, a fitting emblem of the perfect work that will be done in the Temple for the benefit of humanity and glory of the ancient sages." The group planned for the site to be an international head-quarters of theosophy, that "knowledge of the divine" that Blavatsky had learned in Tibet. It would be complete with living quarters, a school and college, and a center for arts and sciences. Tingley's rule was autocratic, but successful, and the group became part of the cultural framework of San Diego for nearly fifty years. The Theosophists produced Greek dramas and other plays in an outdoor

amphitheater on the grounds, as well as other places in the city. Tingley traveled the world, preaching the virtues of theosophy and founding many local chapters. She also spearheaded a host of humanitarian efforts, one of the more notable a mission to Cuba after the Spanish-American War in 1899. Tingley developed a special love for Cuba and actually moved seventy-five Cuban orphans to the compound to be raised in the theosophical way of life. This action would come back to haunt the settlement when muckraking writers from the *Los Angeles Times* leveled charges of endangerment and mistreatment. Tingley sued for libel and won.

The colony continued to grow and prosper even after Tingley's death in 1929. But the Brotherhood was finally forced off its original property by the advent of the Second World War and the attendant demands for military facilities with a commanding view of the Pacific. They were paid a fair-market value for the compound and moved to Covina. Today the Church of the Nazarene's university owns the property on the bluff. The university is well aware of the history of the place and has made efforts to return the grounds and buildings to their former glory. The outdoor Greek amphitheater is now used for performances and commencements, and some of the original round theosophical structures, topped with turquoise-and-lavender faceted globes, now house administrative offices. The surviving remains of Katherine Tingley's theosophical paradise might make her smile.

A Utopia Spelled Z, Z, Y, Z, X

The enduring legacy of Zzyzx Mineral Springs and Health Resort is a testimony to the strange vision of a self-proclaimed evangelist and health guru who moved out to the end of nowhere in the Mojave Desert and proceeded to make a utopia in his image—part high-minded religion and part hucksterism. Ingenuity and a lot of fast talk burnished up this spot on the shore of a dry salt flat, and for a while made the post office in nearby Baker one of the busiest in southern California.

Millions of travelers on Interstate 15 have passed the exit for Zzyzx a few miles west of the Death Valley highway, possibly noting the unusual name, but most were too busy getting to one Sin City or another to bother with it. Four and a half miles south over a gravel road lie the ruins of the dream of one of the desert's most legendary characters.

Curtis Howe Springer had made a name for himself as a radio evangelist in the 1930s, beginning at radio station KDKA in Pittsburgh. Like many of his ilk, he eventually pointed his crusade toward the West Coast, where spiritual fads and miracle cures were starting to find a willing and gullible audience. Like his predecessor, Sister Aimee Semple McPherson, Springer put down new roots in fertile soil and set about expanding his vision.

Springer was no amateur when it came to managing vacation retreats. He had founded and/or managed six resorts in other states before he and his fiancée, Helen, with their (gasp) daughter in tow arrived at what he called "a mosquito swamp" in the eastern Mojave in 1944. He filed a mining claim on twelve thousand acres and began building his base of operations. Three days a week he lived in a hotel suite in Los Angeles, where he made tapes for his national broadcasts and conducted other business. He would then board his crusading bus and round up derelicts on skid row, offering them meals and shelter in exchange for construction work with his new desert outfit. Some of them left immediately when the no-alcohol policy was revealed, but many stayed, some for years and a few for the rest of their lives.

When Springer was done, the new town at the foot of Soda Mountain boasted a chapel, a cross-shaped pool with soaking tubs, an artificial lake, a two-story sixty-room hotel, and even an airstrip, which he named Zyport. With some assuredly highfalutin wrangling, Springer managed to buy an old seagoing freighter and dismantled it for parts to add to his growing compound. A launch or lifeboat from the project still sits at the site, high and dry and rusting, but so far preserved in the desiccating desert sun. The main drag was dubbed the Boulevard of Dreams.

Springer then went into high gear, promoting his new retreat on his international radio sermons. People calling his Los Angeles phone number heard a recorded voice beckoning them with, "Hello, this is your old friend Curtis Springer coming to you from Zzyzx Mineral Springs out in the heart of the great Mojave Desert." He touted the place as the last word in health and vitality. Free bus rides left every Wednesday from the Olympic Hotel on Figueroa Street in L.A., ferrying the hopeful out in droves.

A day at Zzyzx included a hearty breakfast of goat milk and Springer's popular Antedeluvian Tea, said to prolong life. Though he tried to be relatively self-sufficient, the only livestock that could be sustained on the alkali flats except for goats were rabbits, which formed the bulk of the meat served. All of the veggies were trucked in a couple of times each week. Guests stayed for a reasonable sum, but were heavily encouraged to make free-will "donations" to the Springer Foundation. They were also subjected to rousing sermons delivered twice daily by Springer over a booming PA system.

The evangelist's miraculous cures were big items at the

retreat, including the aforementioned tea and a $25 do-it-yourself hemorrhoid cure kit. One of his most successful remedies was Mo-Hair—a baldness cure. The folksy Springer instructed the soon-to-be-hairy to rub the concoction vigorously into the scalp, then to double over and hold their breath for as long as possible. The resulting flush to the cheeks and scalp was proof, he said, of the virtues of his discovery. One man who took Springer to court over his continued baldness after extensive use of Mo-Hair watched in astonishment as the preacher reached into his pocket and peeled off the $2,500 fine "as casually as if he was taking care of a $2 traffic ticket."

Well after Zzyzx was established, Springer began to offer lots for sale on the adjacent property—which he had neglected to buy—so that the well-to-do faithful might take twenty-four-hour advantage of his healing waters and lifestyle. This act, along with occasional complaints to the authorities about his "cures," eventually focused government attention on his operation. In 1974, the Bureau of Land Management (BLM) informed Springer that he could not sell land that he didn't own, and he was evicted from the property, along with a few hundred followers. Curtis Howe Springer died in Las Vegas in 1986 at the age of ninety, after he had served several jail terms for sundry felonies.

Today California State University's Desert Studies Center occupies the site. Zzyzx was finally entered as an official geographic name in 1984, proving that Curtis Springer did indeed have the last word. To get to the place he dreamed up, take the Zzyzx Road exit—eight miles west of Baker on Interstate 15, then south on a paved road, which soon ends at a graded gravel road.

The Dark Watchers of the Santa Lucias

These lovely rugged mountains that run southeast from Monterey all the way to San Luis Obispo are the home of the eerie Dark Watchers—black, humanlike phantoms who stand silhouetted against the sky on the ridges and peaks of the Santa Lucias. Nobody knows what they are, where they came from, or why they haunt these mountains. Nevertheless, they've been seen many times over the years, with stories about them dating back to Chumash Indian legends. They are said to appear most often around twilight, seemingly staring into space from their hilltop posts.

The Dark Watchers have been immortalized by Monterey County's two greatest literary figures. Nobel prizewinning author John Steinbeck, in his short story "Flight," told of the hero seeing "a dark form against the sky, a man standing on top of a rock" in the Santa Lucias. And the iconoclastic poet Robinson Jeffers wrote of the mountains' "forms that look human . . . but certainly are not human" in his poem, "Such Counsels You Gave to Me." (Whether the two writers ever actually saw the dark phantoms or were just drawing on local lore is not known.)

More recently, a local high school principal was on a hunting trip in the Santa Lucias when he spotted a dark figure in a hat and long cape, standing on a rock across a canyon and slowly surveying the surroundings. When the principal called out to the other hunters, the phantom vanished, and the man was left wondering who the strange figure was.

Weirdness Abounds at Mount Shasta

No place in America is the subject of as many occult legends and stories as the majestic snow-capped dormant volcano now called Mount Shasta. Rising 14,162 feet above sea level in the Cascades and visible for over one hundred miles in the magnificent north of the state, the mountain has been famed in folklore and metaphysical speculations for centuries.

Shasta's story ties in disparate elements including white-robed phantoms, the fabled Lost Continent of Lemuria, underground cities, gold-bedecked tombs, and a host of the most colorful dreamers, holy men, and prophets this side of Tibet.

The Shasta mythos begins, appropriately enough, in Indian times. Hopi legend says a race of Lizard People built thirteen underground cities along the Pacific Coast region thousands of years ago. One of these settlements was supposed to be beneath Shasta. The Lizard People might have survived into modern times; in 1972, a San Jose resident hiking on the mountain swore he saw a "reptilian" humanoid in shirt and trousers walking along the slopes.

The Siskiyou and Miwok nations, who considered the mountain holy, had a legend about an invisible race of beings who dwelt there. The natives were so afraid of offending these spirits that it was taboo to climb the mountain above the timberline. One old Indian told of how, when his father had approached the forbidden zone, he had suddenly heard "the laughter of children" echoing across the deserted slopes.

The Lost Continent of Lemuria

When whites arrived in the region, they began to create their own legends about the strange peak. One came from Frederick Spencer Oliver, a teenager who lived just south of Shasta. Oliver spent most of 1883 and 1884 dictating a book whose contents he claimed he received from an entity that called itself Phylos the Tibetan. Titled *A Dweller on Two Planets,* the book was first published in 1886 and is still in print, a classic of what is now called "channeled" material.

Dweller is largely about Phylos's life on the continent of Lemuria, the Pacific's equivalent to the lost continent of Atlantis. Lemuria is a favorite subject of occult writers, who claim the continent once housed a highly advanced civilization. A massive cataclysm around 12,500 B.C. destroyed the Lemurian world, they say, and the land sank beneath the Pacific Ocean. However, some Lemurian sages escaped the disaster. They burrowed into tunnels and secretly lived on into modern times.

Phylos had been through several lives in both Lemuria and Atlantis, as well as in more recent times. In one account, he revealed a strange secret about Mount Shasta.

Incarnated as Walter Pierson, a California gold miner, Phylos was reintroduced to his mystic heritage by Quong, a shadowy Chinese man. Quong took him to one of Shasta's canyons, where a hidden tunnel led to the secret meeting hall of the mysterious Lothinian Brotherhood deep within the mountain. Marveling at the vision of this hidden temple, Phylos described "the walls, polished as if by jewelers, though excavated as by giants . . . ledges . . . exhibiting veinings of gold, of silver, of green copper ores, and maculations of precious stones . . . a refuge whereof those who 'Seeing, see not,' can truly say: 'And no man knows . . . / 'And no man saw it e'er.'"

But one man did know and claimed to have seen the secret tunnel. The man was J. C. Brown, a prospector for

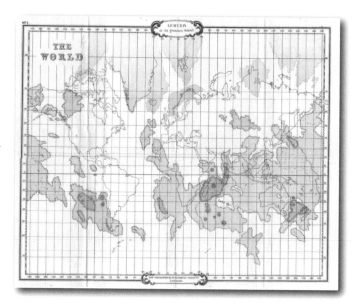

the British Lord Cowdray Mining Company.

Brown was prospecting near Mount Shasta in 1904 when he came upon a partly caved-in tunnel in a mountainside. After clearing the opening, he found himself standing in a long, narrow room whose walls were lined with tempered copper and decorated with shields and wall pieces. Exploring farther, Brown found more rooms filled with gold and copper treasure, much of it covered with strange, undecipherable hieroglyphics. The rooms' floors were littered with enormous human bones, the remains of a race of giants.

This already unlikely story takes an even more unlikely turn. Instead of carting off any of this amazing treasure, Brown quietly returned to civilization and kept the find a secret. Little was heard of him for thirty years. Later on, it was found out that he spent these years studying legends about Lemuria and the occult history of western America. Brown was especially interested in Los Gigantes, a legendary race of giants who had inhabited prehistoric North America.

The old prospector eventually surfaced in Stockton,

thirty years after his adventure in the Cascade Mountains. Then seventy-nine and living off an unexplained private income, he joined forces with John C. Root, a retired printer and student of the occult. Root was fascinated with Brown's tale, and the two men organized an eighty-man expedition to search for the lost tunnel. On the eve of the expedition's departure, the explorers assembled at Root's house, and Brown told them that he would have a "surprise" for them the next morning. And surprised they were when Brown failed to show up the following day. He was never seen or heard from again.

Police investigating the disappearance were puzzled by Brown's complete lack of motive for flying the coop. He'd never taken a cent from the explorers, and had always seemed totally sincere in his desire to relocate the tunnel and its fabulous relics. The case remains unsolved, and the tunnel, if it ever existed outside Brown's imagination, was never found.

Beings with Three Eyes

Around the time Brown had been reading about lost continents and giant prehistoric men, astronomer Edgar Eugene Larkin was in the Cascade Mountains, testing a new telescope. When he trained it on Mount Shasta, he was astounded to see three gold-domed marble temples on one of the slopes.

Larkin had never heard of the Lemurians or their secret city, so he soon began to ask locals about the strange temples. Townspeople were only too happy to answer him.

They claimed that tall, long-haired, white-robed people were sometimes seen around the mountain roads and paths. The strange beings wore headbands, they said, to cover the pineal "third eyes" protruding from their foreheads. Sometimes the white-robed creatures appeared in local towns, furtively trading gold dust and nuggets for supplies. When people tried to follow or photograph the beings, they would disappear into the shadows or simply fade into nothingness.

Rosicrucian author Harve Spencer Lewis, writing under the pen name of Wishar Cerve, spoke of these entities in his *Lemuria, the Lost Continent of the Pacific.* He said that they sometimes chased trespassers away from Shasta's eastern slope, a wilderness area reputed to be their stronghold. There, the white-clad phantoms held eerie midnight ceremonies, chanting as they stood encircled around a fire that cast beams up to the clouds. Lewis also claimed that inexplicable light beams stalled cars along the region's roads and that UFO-like "boats" often flew high in the skies over Shasta.

Magic Dwarfs and Other Weirds

As more seekers of mystery and enlightenment came to Mount Shasta, the strange yarns and legends multiplied. One tale emerged about a race of dwarfs living inside the mountain who possess magic bells that are sometimes heard ringing from above the timberline. Another story tells of a huge boulder called Sphinx Rock, on Shasta's south slope at around eleven thousand feet, sculpted into a human form by persons unknown. Bigfoot has made a few appearances at Shasta as well. In 1963, a Sasquatch allegedly carried an injured hunter to safety just north of the mountain.

In recent years, the volcano's reputation as a place of mystery and revelation has become stronger than ever. During the 1987 Harmonic Convergence, a worldwide event intended to mark the beginning of a new age of peace and enlightenment, Mount Shasta's snowcapped slopes appeared on television screens around the world as a symbol of the movement. Aquarian prophets proclaimed the peak a prime "power spot" on the planet and a key place for the great gathering.

Thousands showed up at Shasta on the big day, August 16. But despite the masses' meditating, praying, chanting, humming, and sage-burning, not so much as one white-robed, three-eyed Lemurian showed up to greet the assembled celebrants. Perhaps these wise beings feel they've created enough mysteries and are keeping to themselves for now.

Lost Ships in a Desert Sea

The more one looks at the Salton Sea, the more remarkable it becomes. It is an incongruously large body of salty water, landlocked in a barren desert mere miles from the Mexican border and growing ever saltier. It should have dried up long ago, but it lives on, with a history of recurring inundations and dry spells going back hundreds, even thousands, of years.

There was a time when the Colorado River boasted an extensive delta system. That was before the arrival of the twentieth century and the Southwest's thirst for water and lust for energy shrank the river to the mere trickle that now limps to the ocean some one hundred miles south of the Mexican border. The most recent catastrophic flooding of the delta may have occurred in the seventeenth century, making it possible for a sizable ship to sail as far north as the present-day Salton Sea.

Legend has it that a Spanish galleon laden with a cargo of pearls made its way through the Sea of Cortez and up the passage in the late 1600s (possibly on a tidal surge) seeking an eastern passage to the open Pacific. Consulting their maps, the conquistadors thought that California was an island. Unfortunately, existing historical accounts lack sufficient detail to give us the whole story.

Reports also tell of a Spanish pearl ship, captained by Juan de Iturbe in 1615, that sailed farther up the gulf than any had previously done, went through a narrow strait, and found a large inland sea. They were forced to beach the boat when, after weeks of exploring, the passageway through which they had entered seemed to have disappeared. The captain and crew took what provisions they could and trekked on foot across the desert. Months later they arrived at a Spanish settlement in Mexico. The accounts of the ordeal, if any still exist, are buried in official records in Madrid. Did the ship run aground in the Imperial Valley, somewhere in the vicinity of the present-day Salton Sea?

Probably the first mention of the discovery of a stranded ship was by a man known as Manquerna, from Sinaloa, Mexico. Working in 1775 as a scout in the initial land explorations of California, Manquerna traveled by night to avoid the heat. On one of these nocturnal treks, he encountered what looked like a Spanish ship that seemed more than a hundred years (and more than a hundred miles) out of place. He climbed aboard to discover that it was loaded with pearls. He took what he could safely conceal and made note of the ship's location. After his tour of duty, Manquerna recruited a small cadre of soldiers and set out for the rest of the treasure. The trip was a bust, but greed-stoking stories began to circulate.

In 1891, a prospector reported what appeared to be a strange shipwreck on the west side of the Imperial Valley. This was after an excursion during which he became lost, ran out of water, and suffered symptoms of heat exhaustion and delirium until rescued. This possibly hallucinatory account and that of Manquerna alone at night in the desert raise doubts, but the memories are from the same area and the descriptions of the wreck seem to match.–*Robert Larson and Greg Bishop*

The Underground City of the Lizard People

Deep beneath the heart of Los Angeles's financial district lies another city remembered only in obscure Indian legends, an underground world built by a strange race that vanished five thousand years ago.

At least that's what mining engineer W. Warren Shufelt claimed in the January 29, 1934, edition of the *Los Angeles Times.* According to reporter Jean Bosquet, Shufelt was ready to dig up downtown L.A. in search of this ancient subterranean civilization.

Shufelt had first heard of the city in a Hopi Indian legend. The Lizard People were an ancient race that had nearly been wiped out after a meteor shower rained down on the Southwest back around 3,000 B.C. To shelter their tribe from future disasters, they constructed these subterranean settlements, which housed a thousand families each, along with stockpiles of food. As the story had it, the tribe used a "chemical solution" that melted solid bedrock to bore out the tunnels and rooms of their subsurface shelters.

Along with housing people in the event of a disaster, the tunnels were also constructed to hold a trove of golden tablets that chronicled the tribe's history, the origin of humankind, and the story of the world back to creation.

A Hopi chief named Little Green Leaf told Shufelt that the vanished race's capital city was located under present-day downtown Los Angeles. In 1933, after surveying the area, Shufelt occupied the Banning property at 518 North Hill Street and sank a 350-foot shaft straight down, digging for what he said was a "treasure room" directly underneath. Shufelt said that he had located gold in the catacombs below with the aid of his "radio X-ray." This peculiar instrument, which was sort of a tricked-up dowsing rod, had also helped him map the location and extent of the underground tunnels.

Shufelt said that the subterranean city was shaped like a giant lizard, with the head in the vicinity of Chavez Ravine (the present location of Dodger Stadium), and the tail tapering out beneath the Central Library. The "key room," the chamber that contained the map of the city and the directory to the gold tablets, lay several hundred feet under the present site of Times-Mirror Square. Shufelt also said that ventilation tunnels extended westward, opening at the Pacific Ocean.

Despite his extensive mapping of the treasure-filled underground city, Shufelt never actually found it. Shortly after the *Times* story appeared, the project, which, amazingly enough, had been authorized by the city council, suddenly ceased. Shufelt and his cohorts disappeared. The whole mysterious, improbable business was written off as a hoax and quickly forgotten. Since then, mysterious tunnels have been unearthed in downtown Los Angeles, but they've usually been explained away as the work of smugglers hiding illegal Chinese laborers in the nineteenth century.

There's a postscript to this strange little tale: the vision of Miss Edith Elden Robinson of Pico Rivera, which appeared in the highly respected American Society for Psychic Research's journal.

On the evening of December 22, 1933, five weeks before Shufelt's excavations hit the pages of the *Times,* the clairvoyant Miss Robinson envisioned that under Los Angeles lay "a vast city . . . in mammoth tunnels extending to the sea-shore." She said that the tunnels had been constructed by a vanished race to protect themselves from danger and to provide access to the sea.

Who knows? Maybe this fabulous subterranean city really existed. Perhaps it's even populated with contemporary Lizard People who live below modern-day Los Angeles, emerging only furtively to watch the twenty-first-century barbarians slowly strangle their surface-level civilization with smog, traffic, and urban sprawl.

Vikings in California?

Evidence of pre-Columbian exploration of the Southwest by Chinese and even Japanese adventurers has been hotly debated for years, but how about red-haired, mead-swilling Vikings? In his 1959 booklet *Lost Ship of the Desert: A Legend of the Southwest,* Harold O. Weight featured several stories going back as far as 1870 about the remains of a Viking longboat being seen in the Anza-Borrego region. While the legend of the Viking ship may not have much going for it historically, it does score high on the tall tale hit parade.

Louis and Myrtle Botts were on a camping and wildflower-hunting trip in the area in 1933 when they met a prospector coming out of the wilderness. He told them about a ship he had seen sticking out of a canyon wall, and reportedly even pulled a couple of deteriorating photos out of his wallet to show the couple. The next day, following the old-timer's directions, they were startled to see the gracefully curved prow of a longboat protruding from high up on a shale cliff. The thing had circular marks along its sides as if shields had been attached to its hull. Just after the Bottses returned to

camp, a huge earthquake hit. When they attempted another foray a week later, they found the canyon blocked by a massive landslide, which effectively sealed the entrance and conveniently buried the relic under tons of broken rock, foiling their plan to bring back photos.

The story of the stranded Viking ship may be bolstered by reports of blue-eyed and fair-haired Native Americans still occasionally born among the Mayo tribe of northern Mexico. If Norsemen were able to sail through the Bering Strait in an earlier period of global warming, then the Mayos' legends about "Come-from-Afar-Men" may hold water. The Lost Viking Ship of the Anza-Borrego awaits an excavation.

Deep into the Valley of Death We Go

Perhaps Death Valley's name is what gives the land its sinister, otherworldly reputation. Certainly, the searing heat and the moonscape panoramas also contribute to the mystery that surrounds the park.

And of course there are the legends. Tales tell of rotting wagons and gingham dress–clad skeletons half buried in the shifting sands, of the fabulously rich Lost Gunsight Mine and Breyfogle's elusive gold vein.

A more macabre mythology has taken hold in the wake of serial killer Charles Manson's capture here in 1969. Manson retreated to Death Valley with his gang of killer flower children after two bloody nights of slaughter that he hoped would set off a cataclysmic race war. An adherent of a variety of occult doctrines, Manson believed that Devil's Hole, a deep, water-filled cavern on Death Valley's Nevada side, was the portal to an underground world where he and his followers could wait out the apocalypse, reemerging as leaders of a purified world. But he was arrested before he could figure out how to get his band through several hundred feet of hot, salty water that had drowned two skin divers just a few years earlier.

Manson may have learned of the underground world from the story of Tom Wilson, a Cahroc Indian who was a Death Valley guide in the 1920s. Wilson said that when he was a boy, his grandfather told him that he had found a tunnel that extended for miles beneath the valley. Walking its length, the man ended up in an underground chamber where a race of fair-skinned people dwelt. The people spoke a strange foreign language, wore clothes made of a leatherlike substance, and illuminated their home with a pale greenish yellow light of unknown origin.

The Indian eventually resurfaced and returned to his people, who were skeptical about his adventure. But Tom Wilson believed that the old man hadn't lied, and he spent the rest of his life searching for the entry to this underground world. At one point, he teamed up with a prospector named White, who claimed that he too had found strange underground dwellings in Death Valley.

White's story was that he had been exploring an abandoned mine in Wingate Pass when he fell into a hidden tunnel that led to a series of rooms that were filled with leather-clad human mummies. Gold bars and other fabulous treasures were stacked in piles around them. There was a passageway leading beyond the rooms as well, lit by an eerie greenish yellow light. White dared not explore any farther, fearful of what might lie beyond.

He visited the rooms three more times, once with his wife and once with another prospector. But he was unable to locate the cavern later, when accompanied by Wilson and a group of archaeologists. The area around Wingate Pass was eventually absorbed into the China Lake Naval Weapons Center and is now closed to the public.

But other mystery sites in Death Valley are still accessible. One is the Amargosa Mountains, in the southeast corner of the valley. Years ago a desert rat was driving through this range in his Jeep when he came to a group of boulders blocking the road. He parked his vehicle, found a narrow pass between the rocks, and walked down into a sandy valley, where he saw about thirty wooden buildings half covered by sand dunes and laid out like a planned community.

The explorer went inside some of the buildings and found wooden tables set for meals, brass candlesticks, scraps of cloth, and even an empty picture frame on the wall. There were no human remains, and no signs of violence or natural disaster.

No ghost towns were known to exist in these arid mountains. Whether the unnamed explorer had really located a lost community or was just spinning a tall tale has never been determined.

Unexplained Phenomena

*C*harles Fort *(1874—1932)* is sometimes referred to as "the father of strange phenomena." A complex and odd fellow in his own right, Fort would scour newspapers and magazines, looking for stories of strange and extraordinary events. He would spend hours at the New York City library, writing notes and collecting what he considered "weird observations." He traveled with his wife, Anna, seeking out these strange stories, and published several articles and books on his findings.

Today, more than seventy years after Fort's death, there are numerous societies and publications dedicated to Forteana, a modern-day term used for anything that is classified as unexplained. These groups attract scientists and scholars, as well as deranged crackpots and the occasional visitor from Mars. But as we like to say here at *Weird California,* "Keep an open mind and anything is possible."

Like Charles Fort, we have discovered that our home state has its share of unexplained phenomena cropping up in every corner. Through our research, we've gathered some amazing accounts of California's truly odd hot spots. But unlike some pseudoscientific organizations geared toward trying to solve or, worse yet, debunk these claims of unexplained activity, we prefer to simply record the events and report our findings. We will leave it to you, the reader, to contemplate the staggering possibilities and draw your own conclusions about these baffling events. Can strange and mystifying occurrences, such as antigravity vortices, curious floating lights, and stones falling from the skies—which really do happen all across California—be proof of supernatural activity? Or is there a logical reason for their existence? Whether you're a true believer or a diehard skeptic, we're sure that you will agree that the anomalous happenings around our state are not so easily explained away.

The Battle of Los Angeles

With Pearl Harbor fresh in the nation's mind and war jitters at a fever pitch, Los Angelenos were jarred out of their comfy beds shortly after two a.m. on the morning of February 25, 1942, by the sound of air-raid sirens and antiaircraft fire. It was the first time in history that an airborne enemy had been engaged in the continental United States. But just which enemy was it? Officials and civilian witnesses were never entirely sure what they had seen. Nevertheless, defense batteries opened up from their bases in Inglewood and Santa Monica and other south bay locations that were never pinpointed, since "loose lips sink ships." Shrapnel and a few unexploded shells fell from the skies, smashing into sidewalks, driveways, and even a few homes. Miraculously, only five deaths were reported, and all but one of those were due to traffic accidents and a couple of heart attacks.

Although newspapers continually referred to the invaders as planes or possibly blimps, no one could agree on their size or even the number of targets. Reports ranged from one object to perhaps fifty. At two twenty-five a.m., a general blackout was ordered and lights began going off from northern L.A. down to the Mexican border. Though residents were asked to stay indoors, many could not resist the show and crowded outside onto sidewalks and balconies. There was even a "blackout murder" as one killer took advantage of the darkness to beat a forty-year-old woman to death in a rooming house.

Army observers looking at the celestial fracas through binoculars from atop a tower in Culver City thought they saw a group of silvery objects, which they assumed were airplanes. All witnesses agreed that the things came in from the northwest (probably from the ocean) near Santa Monica and moved southwest in a leisurely fashion until they disappeared somewhere south of Long Beach. Because all lights in the city had been turned off, stars shone on the moonless night with an intensity most Angelenos had never seen.

Just before the firing started, a woman identified only as Katie said that she received a call from the local air-raid warden at her home near Santa Monica, telling her to look out the window and see if anything unusual was there. There definitely was. What Katie saw was some huge object in the early morning sky. Jeff Rense reports on the sighting in *The Most Incredible Mass Sighting Of All? 1942 "Battle Of Los Angeles"* (http://www.rense.com/ufo/battleofla.htm): "It was just enormous! And it was practically right over my house. I had never seen anything like it in my life!" she said. "It was just hovering there in the sky and hardly moving at all. It was a lovely pale

orange and about the most beautiful thing you've ever seen. I could see it perfectly because it was very close. It was big!"

When the "attack" began, powerful searchlights lit up the sky, converging on the object (or group of objects) so that the gun batteries could get a good bead on the thing. The UFO never changed direction or speed, even with the combined firing of hundreds of antiaircraft guns, many of which scored direct hits. The whole thing lasted for about a half hour, as the mystery planes took their sweet time traveling twenty or so miles across the night sky.

Optical physicist Bruce Maccabee performed a detailed analysis of one of the dramatic original negatives from the *Los Angeles Times*. Taking into account the size of the searchlight beams, the angle of incidence from the ground, and the reported altitude of the target, he estimated that the UFO measured anywhere from one hundred to three hundred feet from end to end. (Check out his findings at http://brumac.8k.com/BATTLEOFLA/BOLA1.html.)

The strange thing about contemporary news accounts is the glaring lack of any concrete guess as to what exactly was floating over a metropolis of three million people that night.

William Randolph Hearst's L.A. *Herald Express* summed up the strange happenings of the early morning hours of February 25, 1942, with this jingoistic feature.

WAS IT A RAID?

An analysis of the first report on the firing in the Los Angeles area early today fails to give convincing proof that any enemy planes were over Los Angeles during the disturbance. It is significant that "no bombs were dropped and no planes were shot down." It may be also stated that persons equipped with powerful glasses failed to discern a plane or planes at the apex of the searchlight beams where many people feel sure they saw a moving object or objects under the fire of our batteries. If a moving plane or object was caught in the light beams, it seemed to move too slowly across the sky to have the speed of a modern air-

plane, such as our own planes which flash across the sky so rapidly. This newspaper, at this time, is unwilling to hazard even a guess on exactly what transpired in the skies above Los Angeles last night, but certainly the city was given a splendid practical lesson on what to do in case of attack.

Hearst's editors also reported a "rising chorus of demands that the United States Government immediately evacuate from Southern California all Japanese-alien and American-born alike." Curiously, the only quotes from the "chorus" were attributed to two Congressmen from Santa Monica calling for "concentration camps." This of course actually happened a few months later.

All Eyes Are on the Skies over Topanga Canyon

Topanga Canyon, just outside Los Angeles, is the site of one of the most active UFO flaps in history. Huge objects have been reported gliding silently in the steep ravines, structured craft hover over isolated cabins and homes, and a rash of abductions have startled researchers. Strange, unearthly animals have been sighted. The Topanga *Messenger* even featured a story on a local family who had been harassed by a huge "ship" with bright lights.

I lived in Topanga Canyon for four years, right at the height of the UFO sightings. Often, while driving home from work at two a.m., I got the uneasy feeling that something was watching me and had plans to land in the road before pulling me out of the car. I put the jitters down to an overactive imagination from reading one too many UFO books, but upon arriving home, I always checked my watch to make sure there was no "missing time."

Early one morning while driving Topanga Canyon Road in a thick fog with a friend, we saw a blinking yellow light that seemed to come from everywhere. It was so bright that we could see the outline of sagebrush crowning a hill ahead of us. We braced for our long-awaited encounter. As we rounded a corner, the glow became almost blinding. I slowed the car to a crawl until we saw the light coming from behind a tree near the road. We shielded our eyes and peeked out between our fingers at . . . a beer sign that had been left on at the local bar.

And the rest of the time I lived in the canyon, I didn't see a thing. But plenty of other people did. Topanga became known as such a hot spot for saucer spotters that it began to resemble scenes from *Close Encounters.* Most of the sightings tended to cluster near the town center or the state park area just up the hill. Author and investigator Preston Dennett wrote a book on the period entitled, appropriately enough, *UFOs Over Topanga Canyon,*

published in 1999. He described hundreds of sightings and closer encounters that began in June of 1992 (barely two months after I moved out) and continued unabated for almost two years. One couple had so many visits over the period that they could just about predict when what appeared to be a craft would show up across the street from their home, hovering over a field of scrub brush. Strangely moving lights would dart around the canyon almost nightly. Dennett led a television crew out to the state park area one evening, accompanied by a group who claimed to be able to summon UFOs at will. They shined flashlights and even a laser beam heavenward and waited. Some in the group became excited and called attention to a slow-moving, amber light that appeared across the valley. The TV crew managed to get a few minutes of footage before the enigmatic object sank lazily out of sight below the ridgeline. Residents also reported military-type helicopters searching the area after UFO sightings.

Why would flying saucers take such an interest in Topanga Canyon? Dennett has his own theory: "I looked at other UFO hotspots, like Hudson Valley, New York, which is a rural area next to a large city. Like Topanga Canyon it's isolated there: deep canyons, lots of wilderness. . . . I think that UFOs use the area as a base. They hide there and study the population like hunters using a 'blind,' so that they can observe and be concealed by the local topography."

Sometimes, maybe, the inhabitants of the strange floating objects came out for a closer look around. In his book, Dennett reports the experience of Mimi Smith, who was driving in the area one night in November of 1994 when she stopped to watch what looked like a sheep crossing the road. "It was shaped like a sheep," she said later, "and its head was round and placed lower on its body, and it appeared almost as if it had waggled on some kind of spring. . . . It moved like it glided along. As I

looked at it, I saw that its eyes . . . were like holes with nothing there. You could see through. If you looked at the thing's eyes, you could see the fence posts in back of it." Smith saw the same unnerving specter a few months later in the same location.

Dennett says that sightings continue in the canyon, but don't run out there with a lawn chair. The UFOs are not as predictable as they were in the early '90s.—*GB*

The Cursed Devil's Gate Reservoir

This dry, brush-filled flood channel in Pasadena is the scene of some strange and possibly diabolical events. The chilling story begins when two young victims, still unaccounted for, disappeared here in the rough terrain of the San Gabriel Mountains under circumstances that defy explanation.

On March 23, 1957, eight-year-old Tommy Bowman was hiking on a trail above Devil's Gate with his family when he ran a few yards ahead of the others, rounded a corner . . . and disappeared.

Tommy's family searched the brush and repeatedly called his name to no avail. Soon a four-hundred-member search party was sent out, complete with helicopters, mounted patrols, bloodhounds, and professional wilderness trackers. After they scoured the entire area for a week, hacking through chaparral, and delving crevices and holes just off the trail, the search was called off. Rumors of kidnappers and child molesters were thoroughly investigated, and discounted. Tommy's disappearance has never been explained or solved.

Another child followed Tommy into oblivion just three years later. Six-year-old Bruce Kremen was on a hike with his YMCA group not far from where Tommy Bowman vanished when he began to tire and fell behind the others. Thinking the boy was winded by the exercise and the high altitude, the group leader told Bruce to return to the camp—in plain sight just three hundred yards away—and rest. The adult leader then watched Bruce walk the length of the wide, marked trail. When the boy was just yards away from camp, the man rejoined the other children.

But something got Bruce Kremen in those last few steps between the trailhead and the camp. He never made it back and was never seen again.

Again a massive search party tore the region apart. Again there was no evidence of kidnapping or molestation. And again the San Gabriels claimed a young victim, leaving no clues, no suspects, no remains—and no solution to the case to this day.

The eerie disappearances of Tommy Bowman and Bruce Kremen led some people to speculate that a curse or jinx hung over Devil's Gate Reservoir. Much of this speculation centered on the activities of one John Whiteside (Jack) Parsons, co-founder of the Jet Propulsion Laboratory and a resident of nearby Pasadena.

Parsons, a brilliant, self-taught rocket scientist whom Werner von Braun called the true founder of the American space program, was also a first-rank occultist. A devotee of Aleister Crowley's teachings, Parsons joined the infamous English occultist's *Ordo Templi Orientis* society in 1941, quickly taking over the group's Agape Lodge in Los Angeles.

Parsons's mansion on South Orange Grove Avenue in Pasadena became the center of southern California's occult bohemia in the 1940s and was for a while the home of ex-navy officer and science-fiction writer L. Ron Hubbard. Parsons saw Hubbard, the future founder of Scientology, as a natural magician and worked with him in a series of strange rituals designed to create a "moonchild"—a sort of anti-Messiah who would overthrow Judeo-Christian civilization and lead earth into a new eon.

The rituals, which took place in the southern California outback in late 1946, were said to have opened a portal to another dimension that's since been a point of entry for all sorts of strange entities. Some occult authors have hinted that the portal is in the Devil's Gate region and that the negative energies and beings that pass through it are responsible for the mysterious disappearances of the unsuspecting children.

It's as good an explanation as any for these tragic, tantalizing events and enigmas.

UFO Contactee's Headquarters—Mount Palomar

Ah, the flying saucer contactees of the 1950s. Such innocence. Such claims. So many personalities. So little room on the bookshelf but more in the wallet for their fascinating and rare books. There are many reasons to become infatuated with the study of the genesis of a modern, literally space-age, religion.

Again it's no surprise that a lot of this kind of thing winds up in California. Oppressed crazies have always moved ever westward toward the "frontier," until they ran out of room. The deserts of southern California became at first ground zero, and then the comforting womb, of the UFO contactee movement that began in the late 1940s.

Resolutely convinced that they were telling the truth (or at least trying to sound like it), the contactees told tales of meetings with space brothers and sisters who looked surprisingly like humans. They brought with them messages of brotherly concern and other beliefs that actually foreshadowed the values of the youth movements of the 1960s. In an era of McCarthyist politics, the movement was considered enough of a threat to arouse the U.S. government's attention and concern. Many of the believers spouted dangerously leftist sentiments, communicated to them, they said, by these aliens from other worlds.

One of the first to hop on the spaceship was a Polish immigrant who had fought for the United States in World War I. In the 1930s, he took up residence in a hotel in Pasadena and started handing out cards that read:

PROF. G. ADAMSKI

SPEAKER AND TEACHER OF UNIVERSAL LAW

AND THE FOUNDER OF UNIVERSAL PROGRESSIVE CHRISTIANITY,

ROYAL ORDER OF TIBET

AND THE MONASTERY AT LAGUNA BEACH

Adamski was well read in esoteric texts and primed, L. Ron Hubbard–like, for the best way to present his insight to the followers whom he knew would surely come if he just packaged things right. In 1949, he published a science-fiction novel, *Pioneers of Space: A Trip to the Moon, Mars, and Venus.* While UFO hobbyists and scholars debate the truthfulness of his encounters, one thing that is known for a fact is that all of Adamski's books were ghostwritten. His experiences, or what he said were his experiences, were rendered firsthand to Alice Wells—who along with Charlotte Blodgett and Adamski's lifetime secretary, Lucy McGinnis—penned all of his major books.

Momentarily down on his luck, he took up with Wells and moved into her rural campground called Palomar Gardens (at the base of Mount Palomar, not surprisingly), in northern San Diego County. Wells hired him as a burger flipper, but Adamski had bigger plans. While fiddling with one of his telescopes on the night of October 9, 1946, he and others saw a gigantic UFO hovering over the camp. A few months later he produced photographs of what he claimed were UFOs, which seemed to be attracted to the property and to Adamski himself.

With photographs and a bevy of sightings to his credit, Adamski needed the one push that would send him into superstardom, and he got it (or made a lot of people think he did). On November 20, 1952, McGinnis and five others were present at Adamski's first meeting with a spaceman. *Flying Saucers Have Landed,* Adamski's first saucer book, described this meeting in plodding detail.

For some reason, when the cigar-shaped craft appeared to them, Adamski asked the others to move away and had his first meeting solo with Orthon the Venusian. As he stepped out of his craft, Adamski "fully realized I was in the presence of a man from space—A HUMAN BEING FROM ANOTHER WORLD!" Orthon warned of the evils of wars and atomic weapons, and his new Earth friend in turn taught the Venusian to say "Boom boom."

While fiddling with one of his telescopes on the night of October 9, 1946, he and others saw a gigantic UFO hovering over the camp. A few months later he produced photographs of what he claimed were UFOs, which seemed to be attracted to the property and to Adamski himself.

PALOMAR GARDEN CAFE
PALOMAR MOUNTAIN
CALIFORNIA.

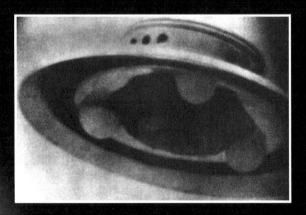

Buoyed by the favorable reception to *Flying Saucers,* Adamski set Blodgett to work on *Inside the Spaceships,* which was published in 1955 (later retitled *Inside the Flying Saucers,* probably due to the fact that by the time it was reprinted, people had actually been inside spaceships, the kind that are seen ascending from Cape Kennedy from time to time).

The space people's names were apparently the invention of Blodgett and, like many other alien handles of the time, sounded like ultramodern synthetic fabrics. In the first three pages, Adamski is willingly kidnapped from a hotel lobby in downtown Los Angeles by Firkon the Martian and Ramu, who hailed from Saturn. Later, he boards a scout ship, complete with one of those thrill-ride safety bars that come down over your lap, and flies off to meet more aliens, with monikers like Kalna and Ilmuth. These two were apparently space babes of the highest order. Adamski spares no detail in recalling their "draped garments of a veil-like material which fell to their ankles . . . bound at the waist by a striking girdle of contrasting color, into which jewels seemed actually to be woven." Apparently, Adamski didn't want to be one-upped by the likes of Truman Bethurum, whose 1954 book *Aboard a Flying Saucer* spoke of meetings with Aura Rhanes, a beautiful saucer captain from the planet Clarion, who was described as "tops in shapeliness and beauty."

Adamski went on wildly popular lecture tours and even claimed to have received an audience with Pope John XXII in 1963, although the Vatican has denied this. He died of a heart attack on April 23, 1965.

Palomar Gardens went through a series of owners and had fallen into partial disrepair when Larry Read and his partner Elizabeth Norris bought the property in 2001 and renamed it Oak Knoll Campground. All but one of the original buildings survived, the outhouse, appropriately enough. Read had no idea of the history of the place — that is until one day when he stood talking over plans for the property with the previous owner. "As we stood in the front drive, this busload of Japanese tourists pulled up and started taking pictures of everything," recalls Read. "We asked what was going on, and we were told, 'They're the Adamski people.' We had no idea what he was talking about, or what an Adamski was."

Read and Norris quickly educated themselves on the history of the place and its cosmically famous former resident. The Adamski Foundation contacted the two and proposed a tie-in. Oak Knoll now does a small side business in themed T-shirts and books by Fred Steckling, current director of the foundation. "We want to create a UFO-shaped museum to display the artifacts we've found on the grounds," says Read. He continues conspiratorially, "Some of the things are really surprising and tell us a lot about what was going on here when Adamski was around." So far, the only thing to be seen is the original metal PALOMAR GARDENS sign, painted over an older beer ad, hanging on a wall in the camp store. Read has also managed to locate the area where Adamski housed his fifteen-inch telescope, a miniature version of the more famous observatory at the summit of Mount Palomar. Adamski thought, correctly, that people would mistakenly associate his equipment with the one up the hill.

Interestingly, George Ellery Hale, the designer of Palomar's two-hundred-inch telescope, wrote in his memoirs that "elves" or "little people" would visit at night and routinely lend advice on improvements, but this is, of course, not emphasized by the present management at the Palomar Observatory. Oak Knoll is located just off Highway 76 at the Palomar Mountain turnoff.

The space people's names were apparently the invention of Blodgett and, like many other alien handles of the time, sounded like ultramodern synthetic fabrics.

The Integratron—Landers

It was a hot night in August 1953 when retired aircraft technician George Van Tassel lay dozing on the plot of land he had recently leased from the U.S. government. He planned to turn this out-of-the-way place in the desert town of Landers into a private airport and dude ranch and while away his autumn years in the southern California warmth.

Van Tassel had begun channeling what he claimed were friendly "space brothers" only a couple of years earlier, but the popularity of other UFO contactees like George Adamski and their thrill rides around the universe forced his hand. He needed a physical contact to establish his bona fides in the upper tier of saucerdom.

Fortuitously, his doze that night was interrupted by the shadowy figure of a man standing at the foot of his sleeping bag who announced, "I am Solganda, and I would be pleased to show you my craft." Van Tassel later wrote that he was led to a hovering UFO and stepped into what he described as a "butter colored" light emanating from the underside of the craft. He was taken on a tour of the ship and told that he had been chosen to bring a message of peace and interplanetary brotherhood to his fellow earthlings.

Thus anointed, Van Tassel began publishing *The Proceedings Of The College Of Universal Wisdom,* as he dubbed his new venture, a semi-regular newsletter sent out to the faithful. In return, they began to send in donations for a device that Solganda and his pals had instructed Van Tassel to build on his property in the high desert. Looking more like an insane astronomical observatory than a machine, it was supposed to enable humans to live well past the expected lifespan and give us a chance to evolve spiritually in this lifetime — without all that pesky reincarnation stuff.

By 1959, the forty-foot-high by fifty-five feet in diameter structure was nearly complete. Despite the homegrown construction and on again, off again schedule, the sturdy structure has survived nearly intact for almost fifty years, with only minor deterioration. Van Tassel erected a sign at the entrance which simply stated: INTEGRATRON: DEDICATED TO RESEARCH IN LIFE EXTENSION.

Vernette Landers, last relative of the Landers family, once sat in the Integratron for a free demonstration. Her only recorded comment was, "I felt a little better. It may have just been in my mind, but I don't think so."

In spite of some differences between his stories about the space brothers and those of his contactee contemporaries, Van Tassel never attempted to contradict his compatriots and went so far as to feature many of them at yearly conclaves, the Giant Rock Interplanetary Conventions. These were held annually from 1953 to 1977 and attracted thousands of attendees, who camped out for a weekend of listening to the latest messages from the galactic best-seller list. On sale were such treasures as Venusian Dog Hair as myriad hucksters vied for the hard-earned dollars of the saucer nuts in those glorious days. Giant Rock still sits as a monument to the era; it is a 2.5-mile drive north of the Integratron on a soft sandy road.

The spaced-out conventions ended for good when their freewheeling nature began to attract the less spiritually oriented — bikers and their ilk — not the gentle, new-age crowd Van Tassel catered to. "While it was going

on, it was a wonderful circus — thousands of people, each on their own wavelength, would come out there and camp," recalls UFO historian James Moseley. "He wouldn't charge them, except if they ate food at the diner he had out there. He didn't really make a lot of money on it, he was just a nice guy."

In 1958, Van (as his friends called him) produced a volume, *The Council of Seven Lights.* The introduction was succinct: "The information in this book is the result of a developed ability to awaken the nearly dormant consciousness to thoughts existing throughout time. Nothing can be thought of that has not been thought of before. . . . All of the principles of everything that can ever be already exist in the infinity of Universal Mind."

In a way, these musings were borne out by the work of the U.S. Army's remote viewing unit, which used "psychic spying" to gather intelligence on the Soviets, find lost planes and kidnapped officials, and probe the depths of space and time.

As the volume of checks from little old ladies started to wane, Van Tassel spent less time on the Integratron. In 1978, less than a year after the last Interplanetary Convention, he died in Santa Ana of a heart attack. His widow was left with taxes and bills for upkeep that she couldn't cover, and she sold the Integratron to a San Diego developer, who announced plans to turn it into a disco. Realization that no one would want to go to a disco in the middle of the desert was probably the main reason it was then sold to a group of Van Tassel supporters, who locked the gates until 1987. This didn't stop shadowy burglars from hauling off most of the center's remaining electrical equipment and records.

The property is now owned by two sisters, Nancy and Joanne Karl, who live there and have begun extensive restoration on the deteriorating Integratron. "We used to come out here and sneak into the Integratron when we were in college. We always loved the place, but had no idea we would eventually end up owning it," says Joanne. They have started a Web site and now give regular tours. "We try to follow in the spirit of George Van Tassel, which makes it difficult to buy paint and other things we need, since we can't use anything with metal in it." The space creatures apparently forbade the use of metal. Any wealthy potential patrons are encouraged to contact the Karl sisters through their Web site, www.integratron.com. With luck and a large chunk of change, the goal is to get the thing completely restored and working, as Van Tassel envisioned.

When we visited the Integratron, something sort of strange happened. We entered through a small door that opens to a lower level featuring exhibits on the history of the area, the Giant Rock Conventions, and Van Tassel himself. A sturdy and very steep staircase leads to the upper floor, where the parabolic dome rises some twenty feet overhead, capped by a massive concrete ring that holds the supporting ribs together.

The acoustics in the room are nearly perfect. Stand under the center of the dome, and sounds appear to come from everywhere. A whisper can be heard at any place in the room. This unique property inspired the owners to offer "sound baths," which consist of a series of haunting tones coaxed from an array of glass bowls specifically designed for the purpose. The patron sits in a comfortable hanging chair suspended from the top of the dome. The Karl sisters report that the auditory therapy has many adherents and verifiable benefits. A short demonstration of the bowls is certainly a meditative experience.

Left alone for an hour, we found it surprisingly easy to achieve a meditative state. It actually became difficult to keep up the mental noise that generally crowds the consciousness. It may have been just in the mind, but we don't think so.

It Rains Rocks in Chico—and Fish!

Something up there doesn't like this Sacramento Valley town. Years ago, for some unimaginable reason, Chico, in the northwest part of the state, was pelted by rocks, fish, and huge meteorites from on high.

The town's most celebrated round of mysterious falling objects happened in 1921. Late in that year an unexplained

plague of stones began to rain down on two adjacent warehouses standing at what is now the corner of Sixth and Orange. Chico marshal J. A. Peck and his deputies spent two months investigating the odd phenomenon, but were baffled. On March 14, 1922, Peck told the *San Francisco Examiner* that he had seen and heard the stones fall, and decided that some local prankster "with a machine" was responsible. Police kept a sharp eye on one suspect, but even when he was out of town the rocks kept falling.

By this time, crowds had begun to gather outside the warehouses to watch the peculiar hail. Witnesses noted that the rocks seemed to appear in midair and fall straight down, and that they were "warm" to the touch. A deluge on March 17 injured a bystander.

One observer was a local scientist who discovered some strange things about the rocks. Professor C. K. Studley of Chico State College recovered some of the stones and, after analyzing them, said that they were not of meteoric origin. Two of them even showed signs of cementation. Professor Studley also believed that the rocks were too heavy to have been thrown by any ordinary means, since one of his specimens weighed a full pound.

Fist-size stones weren't the first odd objects to rain on Chico. The *Chico Record* of September 2, 1878, reported that on August 20 of that year a huge number of small fish fell from a clear sky onto the town streets. They spread over several acres and completely covered one store's roof. Seven years later an iron meteorite weighing several tons plummeted to earth just east of town.

There is a place in California where the laws of physics just do not seem to apply. Here water flows skyward and people can actually walk up walls. So what do you do if you discover a site of such anomalous activity? You charge admission of course!

American mystery spots, like the one located in Santa Cruz, are a time-honored classic among roadside tourist traps. With wild claims of antigravity vortices and dizzying sensations, how could these places fail to entice the curious? Are they merely off-kilter rooms designed by highway hucksters to disorient the hapless tourist? Or are there really places that belie all that science has taught us about the way the universe operates? We can't really say for sure, but we're always willing to amble across any ceiling to find out for ourselves.

Visitors to the redwood-shrouded seaside resort and college town of Santa Cruz have often observed how . . . odd the local culture seems to be. They note the town's many peculiar characters, its eccentric civic politics, its vast array of bohemian subcultures, and—more darkly— its onetime status as the mass-murder capital of the world. And they wonder what makes this attractive beach town seem even more bent than its sister university city, Berkeley, fifty miles to the north, several times larger, and far more famous as a counterculture weirdness-incubator.

The answer might lie in a hundred-fifty-foot-wide patch of land just north of the city called the Mystery Spot. First discovered in 1939 and opened to the public a year later, this hillside lot is one of North America's most famous and visited "vortices"—sections of land where the laws of gravity, perspective, and even physics are suspended.

Originally, the land around the spot was slated to be a summer-cabin site. When surveyors attempted to chart the lot, goes the story, they found that their instruments wouldn't give accurate readings over one particular piece of land. People who visited this spot claimed that a force seemed to be trying to push them off-balance, making them light-headed and dizzy. Recognizing a good thing when they saw it, the owners abandoned their plan to develop the land. Instead, they opened up the site as a tourist attraction, claiming that strange forces were at play on the hill.

Visitors to the Mystery Spot are taken into a small hillside shack sitting over the vortex and shown a variety of bizarre and seemingly inexplicable sights. Plumb bobs hang almost parallel to the cabin floors, billiard balls seemingly roll uphill, and people look as if they are standing at impossible angles or dramatically change height when they move a few feet.

Various theories have been advanced to account for these odd phenomena. Some claim that the Mystery Spot is sitting on an electro-magnetic hot spot. Others say that unknown geophysical forces are at work here. The Mystery Spot's own Web site (www.mysteryspot.com) speculates about a powerful "guidance system" for UFOs buried beneath the land that bends and distorts the laws of gravity . . . and presumably, the local culture of Santa Cruz.

Writing in the May 1981 issue of *Omni*, psychologist Ray Hyman came up with a far more prosaic explanation for such "vortices." Investigating the Oregon Vortex, a tourist attraction virtually identical to the Mystery Spot, Hyman noted that the cabin wherein all the "phenomena" took place was an architectural funhouse. It was filled with horizons that weren't level, corners that weren't squared, and walls that weren't vertical, all of which distorted normal frames of visual reference and created a series of optical illusions that made it seem as if gravity was being violated right and left.

Whether a clever collection of optical illusions, a geophysical anomaly, or an interstellar GPS marker for the space brothers, the Mystery Spot has spent the last sixty-plus years as one of the area's most famous tourist stops. Part of this may be due to the fact that employees give every visitor a black-and-yellow bumper sticker, a free advertisement that can be seen emblazoned on autos across North America. A visit to this hillside cabin may not convince you that anything paranormal is happening there, but will provide entertainment and possibly some insight into Santa Cruz's ethos of eccentricity and illusion. The Mystery Spot is at 465 Mystery Spot Road.

Bizarre Beasts

Monkey-men, hairy malodorous bipedal giants, phantom panthers, and shadowy winged demons—could mysterious creatures like these really roam the California countryside? It hardly seems possible that they are lurking around in our forests or deserts without ever being captured or photographed. Could enormous sea serpents swim the dark waters of our lakes and oceans without ever being netted and hauled ashore? The notion seems just too far-fetched. Still, there are so many credible eyewitness accounts of such bizarre creatures that we must wonder.

Despite widespread development and the destruction of natural habitats, there remain remote areas of the state where sightings of unusual beasts are reported every year. Stranger still are the reports of mysterious animals that appear in the heart of densely populated urban areas. And think of this: Researchers suspect that only one sighting in every ten is ever reported, because most witnesses fear ridicule.

Cryptozoologists, who study unexplained species of animals, are constantly on the lookout for evidence of never-before-documented wildlife, and sometimes previously unknown creatures are discovered. So we can't be too quick to brush off these fanciful beasts as the product of overactive imaginations. It is true that often the only evidence we have of their existence is eyewitness testimony. But if these eyewitnesses are courageous enough to report their encounters, we believe they are telling the truth—or what they believe is the truth. That grey area between fact and fantasy is where you, the reader, have to make your own decision as to whether or not to believe. But after reading some of these tales, even the most diehard skeptics might find themselves thinking twice before entering the California wilderness alone on a dark night.

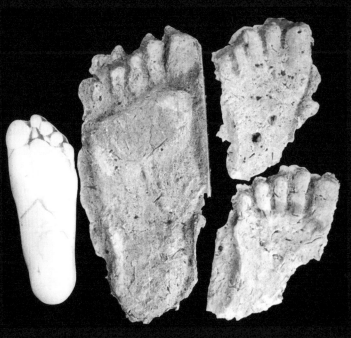

Bigfoots Don't Fear to Tread

Bluff Creek, a cliff-lined mountain stream that flows through the Six Rivers National Forest in the wild north of the state, is the center of Bigfoot country. By now, most Americans have heard of Bigfoot, the North American Abominable Snowman, usually from sleazy weekly tabloids or dubious TV documentaries. Still, a brief recap of the stories and legends is in order:

Bigfoot—a.k.a. Sasquatch, Skunk Ape, and so forth— is a wild, hairy, apelike creature who's been sighted sporadically in the forests and mountains of North America ever since Indian times. He's between seven and eleven feet tall and, judging by the deeply imprinted giant tracks that gave him his most famous moniker, weighs several hundred pounds. Bigfoot is often accompanied by an evil odor that resembles the stench of garbage or rotten eggs. Both male and female varieties of Bigfoot have been reported, and in 1924 a Canadian miner named Albert Ostman claimed to have been kidnapped for a week by a Bigfoot family.

Nobody quite agrees on just what the hairy beasts are. Some researchers think Bigfoot is a primitive hominid species that retreated into North America's forests and swamps when modern men began occupying the continent many thousands of years ago. Others believe it's a surviving relative of *Gigantopithecus,* an extinct giant ape. A third faction suspects that Bigfoot is a miragelike phantom formed by unknown geophysical forces. And of course, there are the skeptics and debunkers, who write off the whole phenomenon as a product of overactive imaginations and yellow journalism.

Indian tribes are usually the most reliable authorities on Bigfoot. Traditionally, they tend to regard the beasts as evil and avoid them. The creatures, in turn, generally avoid us. Unhappy with human incursions into their territories, Bigfoots have been known to vandalize backwoods construction sites and lob rocks at hunters who invade their domain.

These creatures have been spotted in every state of the United States save Hawaii, but California—our own fair state—has the highest number and concentration of sightings.

Bluff Creek, the "hot center" of Bigfoot Country in northern California, flows about twenty miles southward from the Siskiyou Mountains to the Klamath River. In the 1978 book *Sasquatch: The Apes Among Us,* veteran Bigfoot hunter John Green wrote that over sixty people had seen some seventy sets of tracks along the creek and had spotted the beasts eight times. This made the mountain stream the most active area for Bigfoot sightings in North America.

Though there had been rumors of mysterious giant footprints and "ape-men" in this land of steep, heavily forested coastal mountains all the way back to gold rush days, the real excitement began in 1958. That year a timber road linking the then primitive and uncrowded Highway 96 with Highway 199 was being carved out of the uninhabited wilderness along Bluff Creek. Around late August, work crews began noticing that something with sixteen-inch feet and a four-foot stride was leaving tracks around their camp at night.

A bulldozer operator named Jerry Crew became intrigued by the tracks and made a plaster cast of them. He took them to the *Humboldt Times,* told a reporter about the mystery animal, and had his picture taken with the huge footprints. The story soon got onto the AP wire and was reprinted all over the country. The press appropriately dubbed the beast "Bigfoot," and the name stuck.

For years afterward, road workers and loggers at Bluff Creek kept finding giant prints along the road and creek bed. Some of them reported that they'd seen huge, hairy, humanoid creatures loping around in the woods. At night, they raided human outposts and scared crewmen with their aggressiveness and strength. In the Laird Meadow region, a Bigfoot-like animal toppled loaded trailers, overturned 450-pound barrels, and threw a four-foot concrete culvert into a ditch.

Many expeditions to capture the beasts have been mounted, yet to this day none have definitely proved that the creatures exist. There are only plaster casts of footprints, eyewitness accounts, tapes of what purport to be a Bigfoot screaming eerily, a couple of blurry photos—and the Patterson film.

Bigfoot on Film?

The Patterson film is the most powerful evidence the Bigfoot supporters have. The thirty feet of 16-mm color film, which show a large apelike creature shambling away from the cameraman, have been shown countless times in movies, TV documentaries, and news programs. The film remains the best suggestion to date that huge hirsute monsters are wandering around northwestern California's wilderness. Not surprisingly, it was taken on Bluff Creek.

The late Bigfoot hunter Roger Patterson shot the film during a close encounter with one of the creatures in the early afternoon of October 20, 1967. He was out horseback riding at Bluff Creek with his friend Bob Gimlin. As they rounded a bend in the creek, the two men spotted a Bigfoot sitting calmly beside the water. Patterson's horse reared in fright, and he dismounted quickly, scrambling for the movie camera. Gimlin remained mounted, readying his rifle for action. Then Patterson quickly turned on his camera and ran about eighty feet toward the animal.

The camera caught a hairy biped with simian features, virtually no neck, and pendulous breasts. It stood still for a moment, looking back at the camera, then strode off into the brush, its long arms swinging at its sides. Right after this encounter, the men found fourteen-inch footprints where the beast had walked.

The Patterson film is highly controversial—dismissed as a clumsy fake by some and embraced as undeniable evidence by others. Most of the latter maintain that the creature in the film is female, because of its distinctive breasts. *Argosy* magazine, the first to publish the film stills, dubbed the beast the Adorable Woodswoman.

In the wake of the film's release, searchers have tried mightily to photograph, capture, or kill the hairy creatures—all to no avail. Bigfoot has eluded all captors, and though sightings in the area have become less frequent in recent years, it's likely that this most persistent and frustrating zoological mystery in the Western Hemisphere still roams free along the steep banks of Bluff Creek.

Roger Patterson with a Bigfoot track

The Big Hairy Man of Cherokee Road

Charles Jackson and his son Kevin got the shock of their lives on the afternoon of July 12, 1969. They were at their home on Cherokee Road in Oroville, well south of Bluff Creek, but not very far from the Plumas National Forest. Father and son were working peacefully in their backyard, burning rabbit entrails, when a huge apelike creature loped out of the woods and stopped to stare at them.

The beast was seven to eight feet tall, had large breasts, and was covered with three-inch-long grey hair except on its hands and face. The Jacksons, only fifteen feet away at the time, said that after it spotted them it walked up to the outhouse, looked around, and suddenly ran back into the woods.

Another Cherokee Road resident had a run-in with the "ape-man" around the same time as the Jackson incident. For weeks, Homer Stickley's farm had been haunted by something that screamed in the woods at night and stole apples from his trees. Then, one moonlit night, Stickley saw the culprit: a tall, hirsute, two-legged creature that walked through a nearby meadow, pausing to stand by a stump.

By September, at least a dozen people had reported giant ape-things running around Oroville, but the Cherokee Road sightings remained the most documented and credible of the lot. Six years later people were still seeing the beasts and finding their huge footprints in the area, but the creatures remained at large. By then, Oroville had established itself as another home of North America's most famous land monster, Bigfoot.

Gateway to Bigfoot Country

A mountain hamlet at the junction of Highways 96 and 299, Willow Creek is the gateway to Bigfoot Country. The townspeople know it, and they've put themselves on the map with what must be the strangest town-square statue in California.

Standing in front of the tourist bureau office is a life-size wooden sculpture of Bigfoot carved by a local man, Jim McClarin, in honor of the area's most famous resident. It's a traditional first and last stop for Bigfoot hunters, who usually console themselves after fruitless quests by shooting pictures of each other in front of the wooden replica.

Locals will tell visitors their favorite stories about the big brute; it seems that everyone in town has either seen it or knows someone who has. Store clerks, outfitters, gas station attendants, and Hoopa Indians recount tales of huge footprints left in front yards, eerie humanlike screams echoing through the wilderness, and hairy shambling animals caught in headlight beams at night.

A lot of the stories might just be made up for the benefit of tourists, but there are still probably more sincere Bigfoot-believers per capita here than anywhere else in the state. To Willow Creek residents, it is their neighbor and friend, albeit a shy, retiring one.

Wild Giants of Big Rock Canyon

This rugged canyon on the San Gabriel Mountains' northern side is a sort of Bluff Creek South. The area is believed to be the home base of southern California Sasquatches who have terrified hikers and homeowners in the San Gabriels and the Antelope Valley.

These creatures have been rumored to exist in the southern California backcountry for many years. During Spanish colonial times, Indians told Spanish padres of the hairy giants who supposedly live near certain dry arroyos. In 1876, white hunters spotted an apelike beast roaming the mountains near Warner's Ranch in San Diego County.

But southern California's real Sasquatch epidemic hit in the mid-1960s. In 1966, newspaper reports told of a girl pawed by a seven-foot-tall, slime-covered beast in the Lytle Creek wash north of Fontana. A few weeks earlier two boys hiking in the wash had seen "an ape in a tree" there. And in Quartz Hill, on the west end of the Antelope Valley, two young men told L.A. County sheriff's deputies that they had seen a dark, giant biped silhouetted against the sky on a hill.

Such reports tantalized and perplexed Sasquatch hunters. They had concentrated their search for the creature in the rugged wilderness of the northwest. It seemed incredible, and more than a little disturbing, that the big ape could be lurking on the outskirts of Los Angeles.

Hunters picked up the southern California Sasquatch trail in Big Rock Canyon in 1973, a year in which huge apelike creatures were spotted all over Antelope Valley. Frightened homeowners and frustrated lawmen were never able to capture any of the beasts, and believed that they hid out in the neighboring San Gabriel Mountains. Sasquatch expert Ken Coon hired a plane, flew over the mountains, saw forested, creek-fed Big Rock Canyon, and guessed that the wild mountain valley was probably the Sasquatches' Los Angeles County lair.

And sure enough, the beast turned up there. On April 22, 1973, three young men from the San Fernando Valley saw one near the Sycamore Flats campground. The three were riding in a pickup truck at about ten p.m. when an eleven-foot Sasquatch jumped out of the bushes and chased the truck for about twenty seconds, its long arms swinging in front of its chest.

The boys reported the incident to the sheriff's office in Lancaster and went straight back to Big Rock Canyon. There they located the spot where the big ape had appeared and were amazed to find hundreds of huge footprints along the road, some of which they later preserved in plaster of paris. These prints were especially odd in that they were three-toed. To date, all other Sasquatch tracks had been five-toed.

Soon hunters were scouring Big Rock Canyon for the three-toed Sasquatches, and more sightings and track casts rolled in. Something left twenty-one-inch tracks with a twelve-foot stride at South Fork Campground. Sasquatch hunter Margaret Bailey saw a "huge figure" in the moonlight at Sycamore Flats. Then, inevitably, reports tapered off. Once again, the hairy giants retreated from public view and headed back to whatever strange twilight world they inhabit.

They were seen around Big Rock campground, at the top of the canyon, one more time each—in 1974, 1975, and 1976. William Roemermann, who had become Big Rock Canyon's answer to Roger Patterson, made the last two sightings. *Weird California* was told that Sasquatch was last seen in the region at Devil's Punchbowl County Park a few years ago, when two girls and their horses were scared senseless by an apelike monster. Since Devil's Punchbowl is just west of Big Rock Canyon, it's possible that the creatures are still dwelling in the area and might make a comeback before too long.

The Santa Cruz Sea Serpent

One of the strangest creatures ever coughed up by the Pacific Ocean beached itself on a rocky shore two miles northwest of this coastal town back in 1925. At the time, conflicting reports were given on the size of the dead, foul-smelling beast. It was said to be anywhere from thirty to fifty feet long. Luckily, a photographer was on the site and took clear pictures for posterity. The photos show a creature with a duck-billed head, a long, slender neck, and a body trunk that tapers off into a finlike appendage. Close-ups reveal what looks like an elephant's leg on the animal's neck. One witness said that it had several pairs of these legs on its body, complete with ivory toenails! To the observer, the beast resembles nothing so much as a *plesiosaur*: a finned aquatic dinosaur that supposedly died out 65 million years ago.

And that's just what naturalist E. L. Wallace, who inspected the carcass, pronounced it to be. Wallace said the animal was toothless, weak-boned, and probably a vegetarian swamp dweller. He theorized that it had been preserved in glacial ice that drifted south and gradually melted. The carcass was cast adrift, and it eventually washed up on the outskirts of Santa Cruz. Finally, an "official" scientific examination was made. The verdict was that the monster wasn't a dinosaur, but a rare species of North Pacific beaked whale, *Berardius bairdi,* which was unknown outside British Columbian waters.

This didn't quite close the book on the case. Numerous witnesses still maintained that the beast wasn't a whale or even a known sea creature. To this day, the Santa Cruz Sea Monster remains a contentious issue among people fascinated by sea serpents and the possibility of surviving dinosaurs.

Tessie, the Monster of Lake Tahoe

The state's largest freshwater lake, Tahoe has long been rumored to be home to both an underwater Mob graveyard and a huge unknown creature.

A story often told around Tahoe is that a few years back, a fisherman trolling off the south shore got his hook caught on something in the deeps. When he finally freed his catch from whatever had ensnared it, he reeled it back to his boat and found a well-preserved human ear on the end of the line. (Another version of the tale has the fisherman snagging a three-fingered human hand.)

According to local legend, the nine-hundred-foot-deep waters off the south shore served as a dumping place for Mob victims from the 1920s to the 1950s. Hundreds of gangsters' corpses are suspended in the depths, they say, preserved from decay and prevented from gas-bloated surfacing by the near-freezing deep waters. So pervasive is this tale that many local fishermen refer to the area as the Graveyard, and a Tahoe-boat Mafia execution was featured in the climax of *The Godfather, Part II.*

Even stranger are the tales of Tessie. Locals maintain that a large, unidentified, serpentlike creature lives in the deepest parts of the lake and usually appears around June in even-numbered years. Dubbed Tessie in homage to Loch Ness's Nessie, the beast allegedly appears in Washoe Indian legend and may have been spotted by nineteenth-century settlers.

Tessie made headlines in the *San Francisco Chronicle* on July 12, 1984, when the paper reported that two women had seen the Lake Tahoe leviathan a month earlier. Tahoe City residents Patsy McKay and Diane Stavarakas were hiking above the west shore when they spotted the creature swimming in the lake.

McKay said the beast was about seventeen feet long. She watched it closely and saw it surface three times "like a little submarine." Her companion said that the creature had a humped back and seemed to surface in a whalelike, lethargic manner. She was also sure that it wasn't a diver, a log, or a large ripple.

Two years earlier a pair of off-duty Reno policemen had also taken a turn with Tessie. Officers Kris Beebe and Jerry Jones were water-skiing in the lake in June 1982 when an "unusually large" creature swam by them.

Another story about Tahoe asserts that there's an underground river system that links the lake with Pyramid Lake, fifty miles to the north in Nevada. Apparently, the bodies of people who have drowned in Tahoe have surfaced in Pyramid Lake. This phenomenon, however, might be due to the corpses' floating over the north Tahoe spillway onto the Truckee River and then downstream to Pyramid Lake.

The closest anyone ever came to figuring out Tahoe's mysteries was in the mid-1970s. Famed oceanographer Jacques Cousteau brought a minisubmarine to the lake and did several dives in search of the bottom, 1,600 feet below the surface. When he came back up, he is alleged to have said, "The world isn't ready for what is down there." To his death, Cousteau refused to release any pictures or data from the expedition.

What did the legendary diver find? Pinstripe suited, bullet-riddled corpses bobbing in the dark depths? A colony of living, amphibian dinosaurs? Or something even weirder?

The answers still lie in the chilly depths of blue Lake Tahoe.

Riverside Bridge Monster

Charles Wetzel was just trying to get home, and he never bargained for what happened to him on the night of November 8, 1958. As he neared the point where North Main Street crosses the Santa Ana in Riverside, he found that the river was overflowing the road and he slowed down. Suddenly, he noticed that his radio signal was being drowned out by static. Almost simultaneously, something leaped out of the underbrush and landed right in front of his car. "It had a round, scarecrowish head," he said, "like something out of Halloween. It wasn't human. It had longer arms than anything I'd ever seen. When it saw me in the car, it reached all the way back to the windshield and began clawing me. It didn't have any ears. The face was all round. The eyes were shining like something fluorescent, and it had a protuberant mouth." He later recalled that the thing's legs stuck out sideways from its body and the skin looked "scaly, like leaves."

As the lanky hoobajoob clawed at his windshield, Wetzel reached for a .22-caliber pistol he kept under the seat. Quickly changing his mind about opening the window or shooting through the one thing that separated him from the monster, he floored it. The creature tumbled off the hood to the ground. Not caring what the thing was or particularly concerned for its safety, Wetzel ran it over. He felt the scraping underneath and heard screaming and gurgling. He hightailed it to the nearest police station.

Officers noted scratches on the hood and windshield of his car, and smears along the oil-covered underside. However, when they returned to the scene with bloodhounds, they found nothing. The next night another spooked driver reported a similar experience. If anyone else saw the pumpkin-headed ghoul, they kept it to themselves, and the Santa Ana River basin has been quiet since then—except in the 1970s, when Bigfoot-like tracks were discovered nearby.

In his book *Mysterious America,* researcher Loren Coleman has pointed out the preponderance of weird things associated with place and personal names. Wetzel was high on the list, along with Fayette, Hobbs, and, of course, anything associated with the devil. Coleman also discovered that another Charles Wetzel, this one in Nebraska, had seen something that resembled a kangaroo hopping around his farm in July of the same year. Weird, huh?

"It had a round, scarecrowish head," he said,
"like something out of Halloween. It wasn't human.
It had longer arms than anything I'd ever seen."

Mutant Offspring of a Mad Farmer?

At the end of a twisting mountain road in Aliso Canyon, six miles west of Santa Paula, lies the lair of one of California's most grotesque and frightening creatures: the Billiwack Monster.

The beast takes its name from the abandoned Billiwack Dairy, built by August Rubel in 1925. Rubel sought to create a state-of-the-art, high-tech operation, but the Depression ruined his plans, and he barely managed to keep his business going through the 1930s. The dairy was finally abandoned in 1943, after Rubel was killed while driving a U.S. Army ambulance in North Africa.

Soon after his death, there came rumors of ghosts and monsters haunting the old dairy. People said that a huge humanlike creature lurked around the ruins at night. It was described as being muscular and powerful, with grey hair covering its body, long talons on its fingers, and a horned, ramlike head. One witness said that it had shining, feline yellow-green eyes. Its most dramatic appearance was back in 1964, when the beast terrified a group of boys hiking in the canyon. The incident made headlines all over California.

Through the years, the monster has made infrequent nocturnal appearances in Aliso Canyon, and there's been much local speculation about it. Though many dismiss it as the creation of overactive juvenile imaginations (many of its witnesses have been teenagers), others are convinced the beast is real. It's been variously called a deformed Bigfoot and a simple—if fantastic-appearing—ghost.

The latter explanation may be the most popular one. Recently, a local paper's poll asked Ventura residents who their favorite ghost was. Despite stiff competition from history-haunted central California's many phantoms, the Billiwack Monster was the hands-down winner.

Borrego Sandman

Old prospector stories are so unreliable that there is even an annual liar's contest held in Borrego Springs in honor of one Peg-Leg Smith, whose lost gold mine is still rumored to exist in the desolate mountains northeast of the desert town. There is, however, no good reason not to listen, and the many stories told about the Borrego Sandman beg for attention by any serious aficionado of the strange.

The Borrego area in California's desert south is crisscrossed by countless arroyos, crevasses, and canyons. The local Native American tribes tell stories of vast underground labyrinths hidden in the landscape, and the famous mud caves of Borrego are now visited by thousands every year. Perhaps these very real caves and crevasses, dark and forbidding, are the source of some of these tales.

The area is now part of the largest state park in California, but in the nineteenth and early twentieth century, various desert rats and seekers of fortune roamed the wilds here. One local man, who requested anonymity, was interviewed in the 1970s and reported that he was camped near the Borrego Sink in 1939 when he was accosted by a tribe of giant upright-walking apes covered with white fur. He said that the creatures' eyes glowed red. They were apparently frightened of his campfire and kept their distance.

A man named Victor Stoyanow was exploring the sink in 1964 when he came across fourteen-inch-long tracks in the sand dunes. Warren Smith's 1969 article, "America's Terrifying Woodland Monster-men," published in the real-man-adventure magazine *SAGA*, reported Stoyanow's description of his find. "The prints ran in pairs," he said, "generally parallel and averaged about 14 inches in length and nine wide at the instep." Stoyanow returned to the area several times to make plaster casts and take photos of the footprints, but the present whereabouts of these artifacts is unknown.

In the same *SAGA* article, Smith reports the odd experience of Harold Lancaster, who was prospecting in the area in 1968. Lancaster was making his breakfast when he saw a man walking in the desert. "The figure came closer. I thought it was another prospector," he recalled. "Then I picked up my binoculars and saw the strangest sight in my life. It was a real giant apeman." The prospector grabbed his .22 pistol and fired some shots into the air. The beast "jumped a good three feet off the ground," looked straight at Lancaster, and turned tail.

The Sandman of the Borrego Badlands has not been sighted since the late 1960s. Maybe the creature has become annoyed with hordes of off-roaders encroaching on the outskirts of his stomping grounds and has moved on to some other more forsaken wilderness.

Giant Rabbit of Tick Canyon

You may want to include the little-known cryptozoological story of the Giant Tick Canyon Rabbit in your book. I was the first to encounter the beast back in March 1969, while out at Tick Canyon mapping the rocks in the area as part of a UCLA geology field mapping course. Tick Canyon is located in northern L.A. County, about a mile west of Vasquez Rocks State Park and a half mile north of the Antelope Valley Freeway. The animal was 5.5 feet tall, weight about 150–175 pounds.

At first I thought it was a kangaroo; it was facing me, about 7 feet away so I couldn't see its tail. But there was no pouch. When it finally turned and hopped away I saw a white cottontail. This became a legend at the UCLA Geology Department, and in subsequent years, other students who had not heard my story also reported the giant rabbit in the Tick Canyon area.

Attached is a scan of an article that appeared about 12 years ago in the annual alumni magazine of the UCLA Geology Dept. Dean Hall's conclusion couldn't explain my encounter; the timing is 20 years off. The illustration of the wallaroo is somewhat similar to what I encountered, but the long tapering tail is all wrong; the ears on my animal were 2 or 3 times taller; the long feet are accurate but the legs were much more massive.

I received my PhD in 1974 (geology-paleontology) and am a fan of cryptozoology.

–Stephen P. Alpert, Los Angeles

Monkey-Men of Napa

A year ago I heard the local legend of the Rebobs in Napa County.

They are said to be monkey-men that stalk Partric Road in Napa. As the legend goes, two lovers were making out by the cemetery on Partric Road when they heard something on the roof of their car. They were scared so they didn't get out. When a driver drove by, he stopped and got out and took out a shotgun. Then the couple heard something jump off the roof of the car. In the headlights they saw what looked like half monkey, half man. It ran.*–Ethan Rogers*

Filling out the ranks of venerable yet vague beings such as Yeti, the Abominable Snowman, Bigfoot and the Loch Ness Monster, we now have...

The Tick Canyon Rabbit

a special report from our correspondent in the field, Dean Clarence Hall

During the early seventies, Stephen Alpert (UCLA Ph.D. 1974) first chronicled the Tick Canyon Rabbit. It was never quite clear if Stephen was serious or if he had hatched an Alpertian Loch Ness Monster that inhabited the region near Vasquez Rocks, about 45 miles from Los Angeles. A number of us went along with the "gag," an Instant Seminar was held on the subject, and every once in a while the story of the five-foot-tall Tick Canyon Rabbit was repeated during a lunchtime conversation with a new group of students. Thus, any sightings claimed by new students were suspect, even if the story had ostensibly not been related to them.

Curiously, the sighting of the Rabbit occurred relatively often, certainly once every two or three years. One smiled at the wily student and trudged on after a discussion of how tall the rabbit was. All sightings noted that the Rabbit was between three and five feet in height. For those who taught the Tick Canyon class, clearly Stephen Alpert was immortalized. This then is the background for what I believe will be the final chapter in the saga of the Tick Canyon Rabbit.

Unable to resist the lure of that locale, I have been making a relatively detailed geologic map of the region between the crystalline basement rocks to the north of the Tick Canyon
area mapped by UCLA students and the basement rocks bounding the southern flank of the Soledad basin along the Soledad fault. One hot spring day in 1991 I stumbled out of a tributary canyon to Tick Canyon, approximately two miles south of Davenport Road. I was startled, as I came into the Canyon, to see a large elephant being ridden by a bikini-clad young

woman. She and I exchanged pleasantries, or else I stammered something inane, the elephant started throwing sand over his back and over me, and I went away thinking that this was not a story that I could tell for fear of confirming my frailties to students and colleagues.

A few weeks later, now the early part of summer, I returned to the southern reaches of Tick Canyon to map and to secure permission to enter private property. On this outing I discovered the home of the elephant. In the Canyon a few miles south of
Davenport Road there is a wild animal farm: lions, monkeys, a camel, parrots an as an assortment of other animals which ma could make a cophony of wild noises as one approaches the owner's house.

Said owner, Brian, and I chatted about what it was that I was doing, and he gave me permission to enter his property, "as long as you don't get eaten." I recounted the Tick Canyon Rabbit legend, to give him a good chuckle, and told him I now had a story about the Tick Canyon Elephant that was going to be just as farfetched, which could cause some to question my sanity. Imagine my surprise when he indeed formed me that the students had just as I had seen an elephant. In fact, he said, the students had probably seen at least two Tick Canyon Rabbits.

So, I thought, here was the reincarnation of Stephen Alpert. But no, such was not the case. Brian informed me that several years ago two wallaroos (approximately three feet in height) had escaped from his animal compound, leading to those sightings of monstrous rabbits—the Tick Canyon Wallaroos! 🐾

The Blood Sucking Chupacabra

The Chupacabra is another legendary beast that is sometimes reportedly seen in California. The name is Spanish for "goat sucker." The reason the creature has a Spanish name is that it was first seen on the island of Puerto Rico. Sightings spread from there to Mexico and parts of Latin America. Unlike Bigfoot sightings, which date back for more than a hundred years, Chupacabra sightings, according to most authorities, began no earlier than the '60s or '50s. Because of this and because they were at first mostly limited to Latin American countries, it was assumed by many that the Chupacabra was no more than a superstitious regional legend and that supposed encounters in southern California were simply an extension of the Latino legends. But this does not explain reports of thousands of slaughtered livestock, particularly goats and chickens, all found with peculiar puncture wounds and their bodies drained of blood. Nor does it explain repeated sightings of an oddly shaped beast lurking around the areas where the dead animals are found.

A composite of alleged eye-witness accounts pictures the Chupacabra as about four feet tall, weighing up to seventy pounds, having grey skin with spikes or perhaps hair running down its spine, short arms with claws, and rear legs like those of a kangaroo.

The following abridged letter is presented here courtesy of Joyce Murphy, president and founder of the Beyond Boundaries UFO Research Organization.

Close Encounters of the Chupacabra Kind

We have lived in this current home in Phelan, near Hesperia for two and a half years and have had several interesting sightings. We have been seriously debating sending this to you, as we really didn't want to be seen as nuts. This is so unusual for us that at first when my family was seeing strange things, we all teased each other and thought we were seeing things.

The most recent problem we have noticed is a very rapid decrease in the coyote population. Until recently the coyotes were getting so bold they were eating dog food off our porch. Suddenly they are just all gone. We don't see them, we don't even hear them. We also aren't seeing any rabbits. This time last year they were everywhere, which I think is why the coyote population was so high. Just starvation would not account for this decrease. It would have taken much longer to reach this level of no coyotes.

Last month, my pig was going nuts outside. I looked out and didn't see anything but she was going crazy squealing. As a reenactment educator I am handy with a sword and so I went outside with it. I encountered something trying to get to my pig that was unbelievable. This creature stood on two legs and is a dark smoky grey. It seemed to be covered by a sort of peach type fuzz in the same grey color. The eyes are enormous and almond shaped and appeared to be black. The head was an oval shape that was much wider on the top. The arms had three digits that had very long claws on the ends. The arms themselves were very thin and gave the appearance of limited power, and yet I watched in fascination as it tore open the chain link of the pigpen almost effortlessly.

It resembled a mini person about three to four feet tall and approximately 75 to 80 pounds. It had these spiky things on its back like porcupine quills that seemed to move independently. When I got close they began to twitch and I was thoroughly convinced that this thing could launch them if he chose to.

My dogs were barking under my house and when they realized I was out there they came out and moved toward this thing. They seemed to be afraid of it until I was there to back them up. The thing looked at them and then at me and seemed to be afraid of the sword that I was carrying. I had the sword in a striking position; the dogs charged the creature, and it took off behind the house jumping our three-foot fence that sags in the middle. It then disappeared into the bushes. The dogs chased it to the fence, stopped, and came back. I think they were too afraid to go after it. Now I am getting a little worried for my dogs if this creature or creatures have exhausted the coyote population. We are very near the foothills with few neighbors.

We have also made two amazing discoveries in the past few days. First, after a party, as is our usual fashion, we give our pig the left over soda and beer from the cans. She really loves the beer. That night, this thing came after her, only when it got close it raised its head in the air, spun around and took off. It clearly didn't like the smell of the alcohol. We have been feeding the pig a beer a night since then, and it has been left alone.

The other discovery happened after a heavy freeze. We put out some rock salt to melt the ice and to prevent further icing. The next morning we found the three-clawed tracks of this thing all around the salt, but it never came inside the salt. We have also created a safety zone around the house in rock salt now as well. I can't tell you why these things worked, only that they do. I would highly recommend the techniques to others trying to protect their livestock.

—Name withheld by Beyond Boundaries

This creature stood on two legs and is a dark smoky grey. It seemed to be covered by a sort of peach type fuzz in the same grey color. The eyes are enormous and almond shaped and appeared to be black.

Campout with the El Chupacabra

I live in California now, but growing up in Texas, and having many Mexican friends, I had heard a lot throughout my life about the Chupacabra. It was supposedly a vicious killer, and would not hesitate to kill men. For my whole life, I dismissed it as a good story, but nothing else.

In the summer of 1999, I was camping on my friend's property. There were three of us out there that night. We had just graduated high school, were all going off to college in the fall, and spent as much time as we could hanging out, goofing off, and doing the sort of dumb things kids that age do. We often camped on Ray's property. We'd make a fire, drink some beers, smoke cigars, that sort of thing.

That particular night, Ray seemed out of sorts. He wouldn't tell us what his problem was for the longest time, but after a couple of brews he loosened up and started talking.

He was shaken, he had said, due to a strange discovery he had made on a road a few miles away from his property a few nights before. He was driving home when he noticed a dead deer laying in the brush. He walked over to it, like he was drawn to it. He was thoroughly creeped out to see that the deer was not road kill, as he presumed. Instead, it had three puncture marks around its head and neck. There was no blood around or any sign that the thing had struggled with a predator. It looked like something pounced on it and killed it effortlessly, with no struggle. Ray knew this area like the back of his hand and he'd never seen anything like it. He couldn't help but think of the story of the Chupacabra when he saw it. It really messed his head up. He told us how he couldn't rush fast enough to get back to his pick-up.

Now, Phil and I responded to this heartfelt confession just like a couple of high school kids would—we laughed and mocked Ray as mercilessly as we could for the next few hours before going to bed. I awoke a few hours later to Phil shaking me. Ray was already sitting up.

"I heard something," Phil said in a panic. I laughed again. The story had gotten to him.

"Shut up and let me sleep," I told him. He swore that he had heard something. After a couple minutes we all calmed down and laid back down in our sleeping bags. That's

> He was thoroughly creeped out to see that the deer was not road kill, as he presumed. Instead, it had three puncture marks around its head and neck. . . . It looked like something pounced on it and killed it effortlessly, with no struggle.

when I noticed something really foul—literally.

"Do you smell that?" I asked. Both guys told me that they did. There was an intense, bad odor infecting the tent, and it was getting worse and worse. It smelled like rotting flesh. We all were on the verge of vomiting. It was decided among us that we needed to get out of the tent and clear out whatever the hell was making that stink.

Standing outside, we saw nothing that could have possibly been producing the rancid odor. What we could perceive was that there was something severely off about the area. There wasn't a single sound. No rustling of animals, no birds . . . just silence. That is until we heard a screech come from the darkness.

Ray shined his flashlight in the direction of the sound just in time for us to see a small creature that looked kind of like a really muscular light green monkey with no tail rise up from behind a rock. The thing had bristly hair and big bug eyes. It very clearly had sharp teeth, as it was baring them at us, and claws. It took off out of the light. Ray tried to follow it but couldn't find it. We were all freaking out. We took off sprinting the considerable distance back to Ray's house, leaving the tent and all our stuff behind.

The next morning we made our way back to the campsite only to find that the tent had holes torn into it and our belongings were scattered about. We stopped camping out. I still see those guys whenever I visit my parents' house, and we still talk about our run-in with the infamous Chupacabra. That night made a believer out of me.—*Chris Pico*

Local Heroes and Villains

They walk among us, colorful characters and local loonies. Every town across America can claim at least one of its own. For some strange reason, though, California seems to have more than its fair share of kooks, crackpots, and visionaries. They might be locally famous, or even infamous, for what they are doing or for what they have done in the past. They might be historically significant or just someone who marches to the beat of a different drummer.

Since California is the entertainment capital of the world, it comes as no surprise that many of our local heroes are also nationally, and even internationally, renowned (and sometimes notorious) celebrities. Meanwhile, some of our local villains are so vile that their terrible misdeeds have become legendary not only here in their home state but around the world.

While many of these folks may have sought the limelight, others were thrust into it unwittingly, sometimes under the most bizarre circumstances. Some have even found more fame in death than they ever could have hoped to achieve in life.

So just who are the heroes and who are the villains? Often it's a little hard to say. But whether their acts were hilarious or heinous, the people featured in this chapter have done something unique to set themselves apart from the crowd. Because of this we feel they are worthy of attention. It is, after all, the people of California that make this state the truly weird place that it is.

The Emperor of San Francisco

Most Americans assume that the Declaration of Independence did away with the rule of kings on these shores. Perhaps so, but less than a century after the declaration was signed and the War of Independence won, an English emigrant named Joshua Abraham Norton declared himself the Emperor of the United States—and reigned in San Francisco for twenty-one years.

Born in England in the early 1800s, Joshua Norton moved to San Francisco in 1849, where he used a $30,000 fortune made in South Africa to supply provisions for San Francisco's growing population of gold miners. Within six years, he had become a highly respected businessman and landowner. It was then, in 1855, that he hatched a bold scheme to supply San Francisco's other large population—the Chinese. He quickly cornered the market on all the rice supplies in the Bay Area, and it looked as though Joshua was on his way to another fortune. But then two unexpected ships laden with rice steamed into the bay, and Norton was ruined. For the next three years, his fortune and holdings vanished in a series of court actions, and, by 1858, he was broke.

After his last court action, Norton disappeared for nine months. Then, in the summer of 1859, he strode into the offices of the *San Francisco Bulletin* and handed the editors a prepared statement. The newspaper dutifully ran the declaration on the next edition's front page:

At the peremptory request of a large majority of the citizens of these United States, I, Joshua Norton, formerly of Algoa Bay, Cape of Good Hope, and now for the past nine years and ten months of San Francisco, California, declare and proclaim myself Emperor of these U.S., and in virtue of the authority thereby in me vested do hereby order and direct the representa-

tives of the different States of the Union to assemble in Musical Hall of this city, on the 1st day of February next, then and there to make such alterations in the existing laws of the Union as may ameliorate the evils under which the country is laboring, and thereby cause confidence to exist, both at home and abroad, in our stability and integrity.

Norton I
Emperor of the United States
September 17, 1859

Thus began the reign of the first and only Emperor of the United States, Norton I. In the years that followed, he abolished Congress, dissolved the Republic, and declared himself the Protector of Mexico. He also called for a convention to purge the Bible of its "false lights" and promote a universal religion. And he banned the Bay Area's most offensive "F" word—Frisco—the use of which was named a High Misdemeanor, punishable by a $25 fine to be paid to the Imperial Treasury.

Although clearly off his rocker and initially given newspaper space only for a lark, Norton was treated with great respect by many in the city. A Sansome Street print shop issued treasury certificates in the emperor's name (secured by all property of the empire and decreed to be accepted everywhere as of the same value as gold coin), which many local merchants accepted. He dined well, and gratis, at the finest restaurants, which took to putting up plaques reading BY IMPERIAL APPOINTMENT.

However, like all empires, Norton's was not always peaceful. For a time, the Grand Hotel gave him lodging, though it eventually evicted him in a move he called rebellion. He decreed, "We, Norton I, do hereby command the Water Companies to close down on them, and the Gas Company to give them no light, so as to bring them to terms." Taking the joke just so far, the water and gas

Aside from dealing with the occasional mob, the royal duties were fairly straightforward. Norton performed daily inspections of San Francisco neighborhoods, dressed in a blue naval uniform with gold-plated epaulets, wearing a beaver hat decorated with a rosette and a peacock feather, often carrying a cane or umbrella. He would examine the condition of public property, sidewalks, and cable cars, inspect police officers, and philosophize at length to whoever would listen.

In 1880, Norton collapsed and died in the street on his way to a lecture. The following day, the newspapers ran front-page obituaries with headlines like LE ROI EST MORT (THE KING IS DEAD). A local businessmen's club bought him a handsome rosewood casket, and the city paid for him to be interred at the Masonic Cemetery. The funeral procession was two miles long, and as many as thirty thousand people paid their respects.

Joshua Norton's remains have now been moved to the Greenlawn Cemetery in Colma, but his impressive gravestone is not the only testament to this towering presence in the world of the weird. In the fourteenth year of his reign, he commanded the cities of San Francisco and Oakland to appropriate funds for a suspension bridge from Oakland Point via Goat Island to San Francisco. Although it opened sixty-four years after Norton's decree, the five-mile bridge stands today as a memorial to this true visionary. But how many of the 259,000 drivers that

companies failed to comply.

Embattled though he might be, the emperor looked out for his people. In the 1860s, during an ugly race riot against the Chinese population, Norton intervened directly and quieted a mob. He stood between the rioters and their intended victims and recited the Lord's Prayer until they quietly dispersed.

jaunt across the San Francisco Bay Bridge realize that they owe their commute to America's first and only emperor?
—Matt Lake

Satan's Spawn or Misunderstood Lounge Act?

Like any good satanist, Anton LaVey needed a place to worship and to discuss the daily rigors of evil curses, rites, and rituals in praise of the Unholy One. So in 1966 he opened the Church of Satan, known as the Black House, at 6114 California Street in San Francisco. With his clean-shaven head and diabolic black goatee, Anton LaVey was called the Black Pope by his followers. But was the author of *The Satanic Bible* really a practitioner of the black arts or merely the P. T. Barnum of the satanic set?

Most of LaVey's stories seem to be fabricated—from tales of an early career as a lion tamer to his friendship with Sammy Davis Jr. and his affairs with Marilyn Monroe and Jayne Mansfield. But the devil is not known for his truthful tongue, is he?

Even LaVey's real name seems to have been of his own invention. Though he says he was christened Anton Szandor LaVey, his 1930 birth certificate from Cook County, Illinois, states his given name as Howard Stanton Levey. And while LaVey claimed it was his Transylvanian Gypsy grandmother who introduced him to the Dark Side, his grandmother was actually Ukrainian and had no Gypsy blood.

To see two very different pictures of the man, just compare excerpts from his official bio offered by the Church of Satan to the personal remembrances of his daughter, Zeena.

According to the Church of Satan's literature, written by Magus Peter H. Gilmore: *LaVey worked for a while as a photographer for the Police Department.*

Zeena LaVey begs to differ: *San Francisco Police Department past employment records include no "Howard Levey" nor "Anton LaVey."*

Church of Satan: *LaVey was . . . attracted to the keyboards. . . . This talent would prove to be one of his main* sources of income for many years . . . in bars, lounges, and nightclubs.

Zeena LaVey: *According to LaVey's first wife, Carole, his only income of $29.91 a week was generated by his regular engagement at the "Lost Weekend" nightclub, where he was the house Wurlitzer organist.*

So how did this cocktail lounge organist come to be the high priest of satanists? The answer to this question too seems to be debatable.

Church of Satan: *Through his frequent public gigs as an organist . . . LaVey became a local celebrity and his holiday parties attracted many San Francisco notables. . . . From this crowd LaVey distilled what he called a "Magic Circle" of associates who shared his interest in the bizarre. When a member of his Magic Circle suggested that he had the basis for a new religion, LaVey agreed and decided to found the Church of Satan. And so, in 1966 on the night of May Eve—the traditional Witches' Sabbath—LaVey declared the founding of the Church of Satan.*

According to Zeena LaVey, his reasons were more monetary than philosophical: *In 1966 ASL supplemented his income by presenting lectures on exotic and occult topics . . . and he charged $2 a head. Publicist Edward Webber suggested . . . that he "would never make any money by lecturing . . . it would be better to form some sort of church and get a charter from the State of California. . . . In the summer of 1966 . . . a newspaper article about ASL's lectures offhandedly referred to him as "priest of the Devil's church."*

LaVey's media blitz began when Avon Books approached him to write *The Satanic Bible,* hoping to cash in on the satanism fad. LaVey borrowed passages from authors to meet Avon's deadline. In 1968, he released a record album, *The Satanic Mass.* LaVey emblazoned the symbols of pentagrams and goat heads on his book and record jackets. He followed *The Satanic Bible* with several more books.

Despite LaVey's claims that church membership was in the hundreds of thousands, it apparently never exceeded three hundred. But his seminars attracted '60s subculture types, including Manson family member Susan Atkins.

The Church of Satan was run out of LaVey's modest house in San Francisco's Richmond District. The church's black-and-purple façade stood out on the residential street. The interior was painted glossy red, black, and purple, and had secret passages and rooms. LaVey's grotesque paintings were hung in the entrance hall, and murals depicting the devil were displayed throughout the house. The fireplace had a trapdoor that led to the "Den of Iniquity," where the more bizarre activities of the church allegedly occurred. With its secret openings, chambers, and ritual rooms, LaVey had created the ultimate "nightmare of the psyche" dwelling.

So in what does a practicing satanist believe? Is the "religion" all about animal sacrifices and carnal orgies, as the low-budget cult films would have us believe? In 1967, Anton LaVey laid down eleven commandments for being a good satanist:

THE ELEVEN SATANIC RULES OF THE EARTH

1. Do not give opinions or advice unless you are asked.
2. Do not tell your troubles to others unless you are sure they want to hear them.
3. When in another's lair, show him respect or else do not go there.
4. If a guest in your lair annoys you, treat him cruelly and without mercy.
5. Do not make sexual advances unless you are given the mating signal.
6. Do not take that which does not belong to you unless it is a burden to the other person and he cries out to be relieved.
7. Acknowledge the power of magic if you have employed it successfully to obtain your desires. If you deny the power of magic after having called upon it with success, you will lose all you have obtained.
8. Do not complain about anything to which you need not subject yourself.
9. Do not harm little children.
10. Do not kill nonhuman animals unless you are attacked or for your food.
11. When walking in open territory, bother no one. If someone bothers you, ask him to stop. If he does not stop, destroy him.

There is evidence that LaVey himself might have had some difficulty practicing what he preached. His daughter Zeena stated that he routinely beat and abused the female disciples with whom he had sex, and his fits of rage and cruelty extended to animals.

In 1991, LaVey filed for bankruptcy. He lived the rest of his life subsidized by California state aid and handouts from friends and relatives. The Black Pope died on October 29, 1997, though the date was changed on his death certificate to Halloween. After his death, the church fell into disrepair, and the building was demolished in October 2001.

So was Anton Szandor LaVey the spokesman for the devil here on earth or simply a master showman? Perhaps he was a bit of both. The Church of Satan has the last word.

LaVey was a skilled showman. . . . However, the number of incidents detailed in his biographies via photographic and documentary evidence far outweigh the few items in dispute. . . . The Church has survived his death, and continues, through the medium of his writings, to continually attract new members who see themselves reflected in the philosophy he called Satanism.

The Spaced Brothers of Unarius

WELCOME SPACE BROTHERS reads a sign atop a hill on the outskirts of El Cajon in southern California. Whether you know it or not, the Space Brothers are destined to land on this ground owned by the Unarius (UNiversal ARticulate Interdimensional Understanding of Science) Academy sometime in the very near future.

On this acreage thirty miles east of San Diego the federation of thirty-three planets will arrive in jewel-bedecked spaceships carrying 30,000 space masters to teach us earthlings (who are the only ones not advanced enough to join the federation) our mistakes from our past lives on Earth, as well as indoctrinating us into the ways of the galaxies. The spacecraft will land on top of each other and interlock, forming the first intergalactic university on this planet. The Unarians guarantee everyone it will be the dawn of a new age.

These cosmic revelations and otherworldly wisdoms come from one of America's oldest and most successful alien-contactee groups, which was founded in 1954 by Ruth and Ernest Norman after they met at a lecture in Glendale. (Ernest was the lecturer, speaking on "Inner Contact from the Higher Beings.") Soon after, Ruth changed her name to Uriel (Universal Radiant Infinite Eternal Light), and they began to publish books about past lives, reincarnation, the glorious future, and the outer cosmos.

Unarian spokespeople Kevin and Tracey Kennedy are happy to explain the origins of the movement: "Ernest L. Norman was a tremendous visionary and psychic," Kevin told *Weird California*. "And he immediately knew that

Ruth was the woman that was incarnated at this time on this planet to help him bring this mission forward—to tell people about this better way of life. Shortly thereafter they got married, and they began putting books together and he began channeling the books. [By "channeling the books," Kevin means that Ernest was receiving the text directly from the aliens and dictating the messages to his wife.] She began the publication of the books, and then he made his transition in 1971."

By "transition," Kevin means that Ernest died. But, Kevin explains, "We do not die, just move on to another plane."

The Unarians believe Ernest has moved on to Mars, where he acts as the Moderator of the Universe for the Confederation of the 33 Planets. Meanwhile, Ruth continued her recently "transitioned" husband's great work in grand style, donning the regal robes of an interplanetary princess. Uriel's wardrobe might best be described as "Elvis meets Liberace in drag—on acid." Her over-the-top outfits consisted of flowing satin frocks laced with lamé and dripping with rhinestones. Her red, or sometimes blond, wigs were puffed into gravity-defying bouffants, topped with a dazzling tiara of celestial moons and stars. And, of course, she always carried her jewel-encrusted royal scepter in one hand and usually held a fresh-cut long-stemmed rose in the other.

But the Unarius Educational Foundation wasn't always so flamboyant. When Ernest and Ruth met, he was an unemployed electronics engineer. For years, membership in Unarius was thin, and there wasn't much to distinguish it from any of the other UFO groups of the day. The Unarians came to the spotlight after Ernest's transition, when Ruth took over the organization. Her charisma and charm attracted many who were seeking spiritual enlightenment. Ruth boasted of being the reincarnation of Confucius, Mona Lisa, Ben Franklin, Socrates, Queen Elizabeth, Tsar Peter the Great, and many other luminaries. The earthbound ate it up.

The Unarians often take offense at being called a religion and prefer to be called a scientific research organization. The basic principles of Unarian teachings are to research their own past lives through channeling, recognizing their bad karma and purging it all through study, practice, and understanding of one's own self.

When *Weird California* visited the international headquarters of Unarius in downtown El Cajon, we were a little surprised at what we found. From the outside, the academy doesn't look much different from any strip mall storefront. On the inside, however, the academy reveals its true interstellar splendor. The spacious interior of several thousand square feet is adorned with classical columns and gilded furnishings. Pastel fresco vistas, painted by students, adorn every wall, punctuated by numerous

portraits, busts, and statues of Ruth Norman—and one picture of Ernest. There is also a large-scale model of the future city the Space Brothers will construct once they touch down, adorned with multicolored glass jewels, mirrors, and semiprecious stones.

Of course our visit to the Unarian Academy would not have been complete without a trip out to the landing site where our Space Brothers will soon arrive to herald a new age of enlightenment. To our delight, Kevin and Tracey offered to drive us there in Ruth "Uriel" Norman's car. We expected that anything Uriel drove had to be a pretty stylish ride, but this car was out of this world! The 1968 Cadillac El Dorado was tripped out with spacey imagery and topped with an electrified flying saucer. The message airbrushed on the fenders proclaimed WELCOME YOUR SPACE BROTHERS; the license plates read UNARIUS, and the hood bore the name URIEL, in big bold letters.

Unfortunately, while the Uriel-mobile might *look* space-age, the thirty-seven-year-old Caddy engine is hardly in shape for any intergalactic (or even interstate) travel. It took several tries before the old girl turned over, and once started she bucked and stalled all the way out of town. Still, we couldn't help but feel like some sort of higher life-form while tooling around in this vintage luxury sedan with the flying saucer on the roof.

When we reached the predetermined landing site — which as luck would have it, the Unarians had been able to buy — we noticed a flying saucer–shaped metal sign mounted on a steel post sticking out of the ground. On it were the words WELCOME SPACE BROTHERS. Beneath those words were faint marks where the numbers 2002 had once been affixed and then were removed.

That was the year Uriel had said the aliens would be arriving. So, we wondered, what went wrong?

"Well," Kevin and Tracey told us, "after September 11, 2001, it must have been pretty obvious to the Space Brothers that we weren't quite ready as a planet to join their federation just yet." As for Archangel Ruth "Uriel" Norman, well, she had transitioned to another plane about eight years earlier, back in 1994. But before she went, she left her Unarian followers confident in the knowledge that "the future of the earth world is positive progressive, we promise you, we Brothers of the light and space promise you."

We just hope that when the Space Brothers do finally arrive, they save a seat for us on their cosmic bus.

Heaven's Gate Cult—Rancho Santa Fe

UFO contactees and their fans are not usually known for killing themselves en masse, but there are exceptions to all rules. The flying saucer "religion" founded by Bonnie Lu Nettles and Marshall Herff Applewhite survived for over twenty years in various guises until thirty-nine stragglers went out with a very loud whimper in northern San Diego County on March 26, 1997. It remains the biggest mass suicide in United States history.

Applewhite was the overachieving son of a Presbyterian minister. He had a magnetic personality and could make almost anyone accept his ideas. In his late thirties, he was dismissed from his teaching post at an Alabama university for having an affair with a male student. His marriage broke up soon afterward, and in 1972 he admitted himself to a psychiatric care facility in Houston. Convinced he was a sex addict and losing his mind, he believed that the hospital stay would cure him.

While in the hospital, he met Bonnie Lu Trousdale Nettles, whose marriage was also on the rocks. The two discovered a mutual interest in theosophy and soon left the institution to start their own study group and bookstore, which they dubbed the Christian Arts Center. Their philosophy borrowed heavily from the writings of theosophy founder Helena Blavatsky as well as the Bible, but also threw UFOs, astrology, and elements of science fiction into the brew.

This is where that troublesome book of Revelation enters the mix. Nettles and Applewhite believed that they were the incarnations of alien beings who were millions of years old and the embodiment of the "Two" from chapter 11 of Revelation, made manifest on earth to "harvest souls."

In 1973, Nettles abandoned her husband and four children, and she and Applewhite hit the road to start harvesting souls. They told prospective followers that they (Applewhite and Nettles) would be persecuted for their beliefs and murdered, but would rise after three days and be taken up on a UFO. The only way for people to guarantee salvation was to follow the Two and leave behind their dreary lives of work, families, and sex. This is sort of appealing, except for the sex part.

Eventually the group was rechristened Human Individual Metamorphosis (HIM), and recruiting stepped up to a fever pitch. The Two gained a national stage for their message. During one news broadcast, Applewhite summed up the ideas of HIM: "When a human has overcome his human-level activities, a chemical change takes place and he goes through a metamorphosis just exactly as a caterpillar does when he quits being a caterpillar and he goes off into a chrysalis and becomes a butterfly." (When they were found in 1997, the bodies of cult members were covered in a "chrysalis" of cloth.)

In 1975, Applewhite and

Nettles announced that a spaceship full of peaceful and beautiful aliens would be arriving soon to pick them up. HIM members waited all night with their leaders, and not surprisingly, nothing happened. While partly blaming the failure on the members for their lack of attention to their "personal growth," they invited anyone who wanted to leave to go. Many chose to stay in the comforting and increasingly insular womb of HIM.

After the UFO failure, the group wandered the southwestern United States, staying for months at a time in tents at camping sites until they were thrown out, or in hotels or apartments when wealthy new recruits gave up all earthly possessions to the collective. Adherents came and went, but the caravanning band managed to hold on to an average of about forty souls.

Throughout the 1970s and '80s, Nettles and Applewhite changed their earthbound space alien names whenever inspiration struck. The Two first became Guinea and Pig, then Bo and Peep, and finally Do and Ti (referring to notes on the musical scale). In 1985, Do

(Nettles) lost a bout with liver cancer, and Applewhite had to explain to the flock that Do had "gone on to the next level to prepare the way." Over the years, the group placed ads in newspapers and magazines announcing that time was running out for those who wished to take a magic saucer ride into immortality. Most observers interpreted the warning as simple "end of the world" drivel from another bunch of kooks. This would turn out to be a tragic mistake.

Through the contributions of its members, as well as a lucrative Web-design business, the foundation, then referring to itself as Heaven's Gate, rented a mansion in the secluded and exclusive Rancho Santa Fe area of San Diego County and waited.

In late 1996, the world was poised to witness one of the most spectacular celestial events of the late twentieth century. A comet, named after codiscoverers Alan Hale and Thomas Bopp, would become clearly visible in the Northern Hemisphere in the summer of the following year. Enter maverick (some say wacko) amateur astronomer Chuck Shramek, who appeared on the Art Bell radio program to announce that he had detected a "companion" object of massive size pacing Hale-Bopp as it made its approach to earth. Maverick (some might also say wacko) remote-viewer Courtney Brown and his assistant Prudence Calabrese confirmed that an "alien ship" was following the comet. (Bell denied any complicity in the subsequent events, saying he was not responsible for anything people chose to do with the information.)

Ti and his brood took notice of the news and posted a quotation-mark-littered announcement on their site:

Whether Hale-Bopp has a "companion" or not is irrelevant from our perspective. However, its arrival is joyously very significant to us at "Heaven's Gate." The joy is that our Older Member in the Evolutionary Level Above Human (the "Kingdom of Heaven") has made it clear to us that Hale-Bopp's approach is the "marker" we've been waiting for—the time for the arrival of the spacecraft from the Level Above Human to take us home to "Their World"—in the literal Heavens. Our 22 years of classroom here on planet Earth is finally coming to conclusion—"graduation" from the Human Evolutionary Level. We are happily prepared to leave "this world" and go with Ti's crew.

The group thought that Nettles was either riding the mystery object or at least had sent the comet as a sign to "just do it."

Applewhite urged members to videotape a few last statements, which were played back for weeks after the suicides. In their final moments, the shaved-headed followers smiled and even joked about what they were going to do. Years of mind control actually filled them with joy at the idea of doing away with their "earthly containers."

On March 21, the residents of 18241 Colina Norte Drive descended on the local Marie Callender's restaurant for a last supper of iced tea, turkey pot pie, and salad, followed by blueberry cheese-cake. Between March 22 and 24, thirty-nine people helped each other step into identical crisp new black jumpsuits emblazoned with colorful AWAY TEAM logo patches. Each then ate a bowl of phenobarbital-laced applesauce, chased with vodka

to control any side effects. It was the first alcohol to touch their lips in years. The dying was done in shifts over two days—Applewhite was the last to go, making sure that no one backed out at the last minute.

He had thoughtfully mailed two copies of the "last statements" video to former member and Los Angeles resident Richard Ford; they were delivered on March 25. Fearing the worst, Ford called his boss, Nick Matzorkis, and the two drove to San Diego. Ford, who had left the cult only five weeks before, entered the house to find eighteen women and twenty-one men lying on freshly laundered sheets in cheap bunk beds, covered with purple shrouds. In a move that took the shoe company months to live down, all were wearing brand-new black Nike track shoes. Everyone had a passport clutched in one hand and $5.75 cash in the other.

What in the heavens did they need with passports and money? One creepy and remarkable clue is found in a 1907 story entitled, "Extract from Captain Stormfield's Trip to Heaven," by none other than Mark Twain. In this tale, the protagonist leaves for "an extended excursion among the heavenly bodies" on the tail of a comet. Captain Stormfield takes along his passport and $5.75 in cash for the fare.

The Heaven's Gate mansion was eventually sold for less than half of its original value. The new owner changed the address, and the local authorities renamed the street to throw off necrotourists. The camouflaged address is 18239 Paseo Victoria. The house is, of course, closed to visitors. The Marie Callender's "last meal" restaurant is at 5980 Avenida Encinas, just off Highway 5 near Palomar Airport Road.

Now That's a Dysfunctional Family

The Manson Family murders were some of the most horrific and brutal in Los Angeles history, and laid bare the evil side of the Love Generation.

Charles Milles Manson spent most of his life in the pokey. Before the killings, his last stint had been at Terminal Island Federal Prison near Los Angeles. During his jail time, he had absorbed the teachings of Scientology and often used the terms and practices in later interactions with family members. While he was behind bars, Manson also learned to play guitar, a talent he used to bring himself to the attention of music producer Phil Kaufman, who was serving time at Terminal Island on a marijuana charge. Kaufman was so impressed that he gave Manson the names and numbers of music and film producers, an act that would come back to haunt him.

Manson walked out of jail a free man in March 1967, and with his parole officer's permission, he moved to San Francisco, just in time for the "summer of love." Thousands of seekers and outcasts were flooding the streets of the Haight, and Manson fit right in. Across the bay at U.C. Berkeley, Manson recruited his first acolyte, librarian Mary Brunner. Before long, he was sweeping lost female souls off their feet and into his bed at a furious rate.

The deflowering of the flower children was surprisingly easy for the prison-grown guru. The mystical mumbo jumbo he spouted was tailormade for creating the illusion of breaking down personal hang-ups, leaving Manson as the only answer to the void that was left.

With a gaggle of young women (and a couple of men) in tow, Manson decided to make the trek south and use the contacts that Kaufman had innocently provided. In the late 1960s, it seemed that anyone with a guitar had a good shot at a record deal, and Charlie wanted a piece of the action. He got hold of a broken-down school bus—which the group painted black, with the words Holywood Productions painted on the side. (The French girl who did the lettering misspelled Hollywood.) Inside, most of the seats were ripped out and the bus was transformed into a rolling pleasure palace.

Once in the sunny south, the family stayed for a while at a house at the foot of Topanga Canyon Boulevard owned by a middle-aged woman, known only as Gina, whom they had met in San Francisco. A winding stairway going up to the second story led some of the girls to quickly dub the place the Spiral Staircase. While living here, Manson picked up more pointers from all manner of self-styled gurus who wended their way through the house. In the swirl of activity, Manson met Robert K. Beausoleil, an aspiring musician and actor. Beausoleil was friends with Gary Hinman, a music teacher who lived on an isolated back road farther up the canyon.

One day, two of Manson's girls thumbed a ride from Beach Boys drummer Dennis Wilson, who took the girls home for an afternoon of fun and frolicking. The next dawn, when he got back to his house after a recording session, Wilson found that the whole family had moved in with him. After a while, Wilson got tired of the mess the group made and had his manager throw them out.

They quickly found another home, at an unused western movie set near Chatsworth, owned by an octogenarian named George Spahn. Manson got his girls to attend to Spahn, while he used this new base of operations to steal, buy, or rehab dune buggies and other equipment for a move to the desert.

Around this time (mid-1968), Manson began to think in apocalyptic terms, feeding his growing mania with quotes and ideas from the book of Revelation and other such "end-is-nigh" claptrap. After a botched drug deal, he shot a man named Bernard Crowe (who was black) in the stomach. His fear about the repercussions from this incident grew, and he imagined that the Black Panthers had put him on a death list. In Charlie's mind, the family was chosen to wait out the turbulent end of the world as we know it, hiding in an underground paradise he was sure was located near Death Valley.

Manson's paranoid view was that the world was headed for an Armageddon that would be started by a black revolution. When the blacks finally took over the country, they wouldn't know how to handle it, and the family would emerge to take charge.

In November 1968, the Beatles released the legendary "White Album." Even though Manson had been gleaning secret meanings from pop songs for a while, his heightened sense of fear made him certain that the song "Helter Skelter" prophesied the revolution that was soon to grip the world. He programmed these messages into the minds of his flock, all of whom were expected to become one with "Man's Son."

By the summer of 1969, Manson was tired of waiting for Helter Skelter and decided to give it a jump start. Dennis Wilson had earlier introduced him to a music producer named Terry Melcher, who, Manson thought, was renting a house in Beverly Hills at 10050 Cielo Drive. But unknown to Manson, Melcher had sublet the place to Polish film director Roman Polanski and his new wife, Sharon Tate. Manson decided, apparently on a whim, that Helter Skelter would begin there, on the night of August 9. Just two weeks earlier, Robert Beausoleil had tortured and killed his good friend Gary Hinman at his home at 964 Old Topanga Canyon Road, saying that he owed the Manson family money. Perhaps Bobby had unknowingly taken the lead.

After receiving directions from Manson, Susan Atkins, Patricia Krenwinkel, Linda Kasabian, and Charles "Tex" Watson drove to the gate of the Cielo Drive home at about twelve thirty a.m. The killing began with Stephen Parent, a friend of the property's caretaker, who was shot four times by Watson at the security gate. Then Watson, Atkins, and Krenwinkel went up the hill and broke into the house. Kasabian decided to wait outside, but was a witness to the bloody rampage that followed.

Sharon Tate was in a bedroom talking to her friend Jay Sebring, "hairdresser to the stars." Voytek Frykowski, one of Polanski's friends from Poland, was asleep on a couch in the living room, and Abigail Folger, heiress to the coffee fortune and Frykowski's current love interest, was reading in another bedroom.

All four people staying in the house were killed by the Manson family members, either stabbed or shot to death. Manson had told his followers to leave a sign, to give full

Susan Denise Atkins, Patricia Krenwinkel, and Leslie Van Houten laugh after receiving the death sentence for their part in the Tate-LaBianca murders.

Rosemary. The couple had just returned from a weekend at Lake Isabella and were relaxing on a quiet Sunday night. Manson told the others to wait in the car as he broke into the house. He tied up the couple and told them that they were not going to be harmed. Returning to the car, Manson told Watson, Krenwinkel, and Van Houten to go up to the house and kill the couple. Obedient followers, they obliged, stabbing both Rosemary LaBianca and her husband multiple times. Before leaving, the family members used blood from the killings to write "DEATH TO PIGS" and "RISE" on the walls, and, most significantly, "HEALTER SKELTER" [sic] on the door of the fridge.

spook value to their deed. Before they left, Atkins took a towel, dipped it in Tate's blood, and wrote "PIG" on the front door.

The next night, Manson piled the same group into the car with him, also asking Clem Grogan and Leslie Van Houten along. They drove aimlessly through Pasadena; then Charlie told Kasabian to point the car in the direction of the Los Feliz neighborhood. They stopped in front of a home they knew from LSD and peyote parties that the family had attended. "You're not going to do that house, are you?" someone asked. "No, the one next door," Manson said.

The one next door was 3301 Waverly Drive—the home of grocery store chain–owner Leno LaBianca and his wife,

In the last week of August, Manson, Clem Grogan, and Bruce Davis, along with the rest of the family tortured and killed Donald J. "Shorty" Shea, one of the employees at Spahn's ranch, whom they suspected of squealing to police about their illegal activities. Then, in early September, the family moved to Death Valley. One of his girls had told Charlie that her grandmother, Arlene Barker, owned property near Death Valley in the Goler Wash area, and that's where they headed.

No one knows how they managed to get the old school bus up the treacherous road to the Barker ranch, but it lies there still. Manson and the family occupied both the Barker ranch and the nearby Myers ranch. There they started a program of desert "maneuvers" with the family's tricked-out dune buggies, some of which had been fitted with scabbards for shotguns and rifles, and huge gas tanks that gave them a thousand-mile range. All of this was in preparation for the coming of Helter Skelter, when the family would wait for the revolution to die out, at which point they would reemerge, now numbering 144,000 (as foretold in the book of Revelation) and take over.

This grand plan was waylaid by a few stupid mistakes, not the least of which was Manson's decision to burn a National Park Service tractor that was ripping up "his" desert. This act brought the family to the attention of the authorities, who descended on the hippie compound in a series of late-night raids from October 10 to 12.

The Manson family was jailed in the small town of Independence, and the officers there were sorting out the myriad of petty and not-so-petty charges against them, when word arrived from Los Angeles that Susan Atkins, incarcerated for car theft in the Sybil Brand women's prison in L.A., had been bragging to other inmates about the Tate and LaBianca murders. The Inyo County authorities were stunned. They had no idea that their scummy bunch of hippies were probably responsible for the most brutal murders in California history.

Manson and others directly involved in the Tate and LaBianca slayings were put on trial, and almost all the defendants were eventually sentenced to death. They were given a reprieve when the Supreme Court decided that the death penalty constituted cruel and unusual punishment in certain cases. In 1972, their sentences were commuted to life with the possibility of parole, although it is nigh-impossible that any will ever be let out in their lifetimes. Manson currently resides at the California Correctional Facility at Corcoran.

Death Valley Diva

If art is the true mark of any civilization, then Death Valley Junction is way ahead of the cultural curve. Today the population of the town needs about seven more people to reach double digits, but eighty-two-year-old dancer-actress-musician-painter Marta Becket has conquered the naysayers and brought civilization to this very small desert-dwelling community.

As the legend goes, in the spring of 1967 Marta was an already seasoned performer who'd been dancing since she was three. Tired of the grind of Broadway, Radio City, and the entire New York scene, she and her husband at the time traveled out to California for a one-week camping vacation in the anti-Big Apple: Death Valley. On the morning their vacation was to come to an end, they awoke to find a flat tire on their rental car and were directed by the park ranger to the nearest gas station—thirty miles away. As the local mechanic took to repairing the problem, Marta used the opportunity to wander about.

Strolling around the lonely buildings, she was stunned by the tallest structure on the strip. It was a theater. She pulled on the front door, only to discover it was locked, so she ran to the back and was able to peek inside.

It was obvious the stage hadn't been used for years. The floorboards were warped, the once colorful playhouse curtains had faded, and debris spotted the entire room. In that instant, Marta Becket understood her fate.

"Peering through the tiny hole," she said later, "I had the distinct feeling that I was looking at the other half of myself. The building seemed to be saying, 'Take me . . . do something with me. . . . I offer you life.'"

Immediately the city dancer located the town

manager and negotiated a $45-a-month rental contract, with the stipulation that she also assume responsibility for the repairs.

Marta not only restored the dilapidated old theater, she ensured a sold-out show every night by taking the next six years to completely cover the bare walls and ceiling with a mural of an audience straight out of the sixteenth century. Upon her fortifications, kings and queens sit pleasantly beside hookers and gypsies. Toreadors dance with the bulls, and decorated mystics from the Orient amuse and delight nearby monks and nuns. The paintings themselves are truly impressive, reason enough to visit the Amargosa Opera House. And then there's Marta, Renaissance woman. Whether the crowd is human or gouache, Marta Becket still feels the magnetic pull of the spotlight and has kept to her twice a week performance schedule religiously since the curtain first came up almost four decades ago.

She creates her own costumes, choreographs her own dance moves, has designed all of her own stage props, and written her own plays.

Now in the twilight of her years, Marta still moves with the grace of a woman who was born to walk the boards. At a recent function in her honor, the ever spry performer mused, "I'm so grateful that after thirty-five years I don't have to worry about a full house: It's just there. I only wish I were twenty years old again."

The Amargosa Opera House is located somewhere in Death Valley Junction. You can't miss it. It's the tallest structure on the strip.

The Outlaw Who Wouldn't Give Up

Imagine this: 1973, Steve Austin, astronaut— a man only kind of alive. 1911, Elmer J. McCurdy, an outlaw—very, very dead! Who would have thought that these two show biz personalities would ever meet up?

Lee Majors played the role of astronaut Steve Austin on television's *Six Million Dollar Man* from the years 1973 to 1978. But it was in the year 1976 that the mummified body of outlaw Elmer McCurdy was discovered hanging around with the film crew of the *Six Million Dollar Man* as they began setting up for the day's shoot.

The crew was filming in Long Beach, at a funhouse called Laugh in the Dark. The place contained the regular spook show decor, including wax figures, ghosts, and fake skeletons. While setting up at the location, the producer noticed a Day-Glo orange wax figure hanging from a makeshift gallows and asked one of the crew to take it down, as he didn't like the way it looked in the scene.

The stagehand grabbed at the wax dummy's left arm, only to have it come off in his hand, revealing a human bone sticking out from its shoulder. The crew immediately called in medical examiners and forensic investigators,

Gather 'round my children, and I'll tell a tale of woe
About a famous cowboy outlaw who lived a hundred years ago. . . .
A hundred years have come and gone since he spoke his final words.
I'm not afraid to die and leave behind this rotten world.
So go and pull the lever hangman, now my race on Earth is run.
And he thought his life was ended but it had only just begun.
— Brian Dewan, "The Cowboy Outlaw"

who took the wax figure and determined that it was a mummified human body. It had been shot by a .32-caliber bullet, determined to have been manufactured between 1830 and 1920. Upon further examination, the mouth of the mummy was found to hold a 1924 penny and a ticket from the Museum of Crime in Los Angeles. The discovery of that ticket led police to help identify the body of outlaw Elmer McCurdy, and the many roads he had taken, both alive and dead, that led him to that Long Beach funhouse.

McCurdy decided on a life of crime after being told that the woman he thought was his aunt was really his mother. This apparently annoyed him no end. He joined up with a few outlaw gangs, killed a few people, then planned on robbing a Missouri Pacific train that

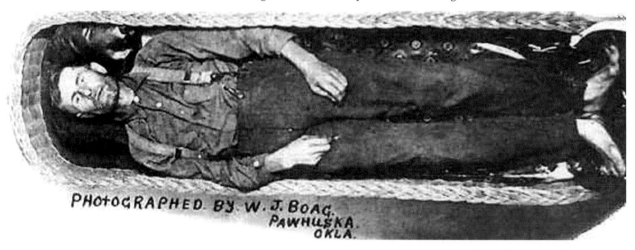

PHOTOGRAPHED BY W. J. BOAG.
PAWHUSKA.
OKLA.

supposedly was transporting over $1,000.

On October 6, 1911, McCurdy pulled off the robbery of the train in Oklahoma, but when he opened the safe, he discovered he had robbed the wrong train. Only $46 was inside. However, he did manage to find a sizable shipment of whiskey instead.

Heading into the Oklahoma farmlands a few days later, drunk and tired, McCurdy stopped at a farmhouse and fell asleep in the hayloft. A three-man posse that was tracking the outlaw trapped him in the barn and began firing. After an hour, a farmhand was asked to go into the barn and tell McCurdy to surrender. He refused, saying, "They can go to the devil." The barn was shot up, and McCurdy was discovered dead soon afterward.

The body was brought to a funeral home in Pawhuska, Oklahoma, but McCurdy was never identified, and no one came to claim the corpse. The undertaker embalmed him with arsenic (with seven hundred times the dose used in Egyptian mummies) and came up with a very entrepreneurial idea. Since the body looked very well preserved and was all dressed up in his last gunfightin' suit, he named the corpse the Bandit That Wouldn't Give Up, and for a nickel he would let the citizens of Pawhuska view it. The nickels were dropped into the mummy's mouth, later to be retrieved by the undertaker.

The mummy was on view for over five years, and the undertaker refused many offers from carnivals and sideshows for his bandit corpse. The nickel-swallowing mummy became a regular attraction for the funeral home in Pawhuska, so hey, why give up a good thing?

One day two men showed up at the funeral home claiming to be cousins of the mummy, and the undertaker

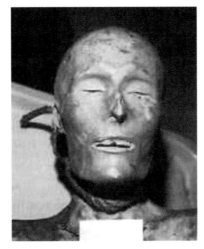

had no choice but to give up the stiff to its next of kin. The two men turned out to be sideshow promoters themselves and had bamboozled the undertaker into handing over the corpse, supposedly for a proper burial. Instead, they took old Elmer along with them throughout Texas with the same billing: the Bandit That Wouldn't Give Up.

After Texas, McCurdy traveled around the country, often showing up at amusement parks, lying around in an open coffin in an L.A. wax museum, and believe it or not, was used as a prop in a few low-budget films. He was known sometimes as the Thousand Year Old Man. After a while, his body was coated with wax to help preserve it during his many road trips. His greatest tour was in the 1930s with Louis Sonney, a sheriff who acquired McCurdy for his traveling Wild West show.

Eventually Elmer faded into obscurity. No one knows exactly how he ended up at the defunct Laugh in the Dark funhouse in Long Beach, but when the *Six Million Dollar Man* crew found him, his final journey to the grave was almost over. Medical examiners identified him with a little-known method called "medical superimposition." Known photos of McCurdy were overlaid with X rays of the mummy's face, and a positive ID was made.

McCurdy was given a proper funeral in Summit View Cemetery in Guthrie, Oklahoma. The town residents gave old Elmer the full treatment: a parade ride to the cemetery in all his Wild West finery. To be certain that show biz days were behind him, the Oklahoma state coroner ordered that two cubic yards of cement be poured into McCurdy's grave. Elmer will never again be thrust into the limelight against his will.

Patty "Tania" Hearst: Heroine or Villain?

Newspaper heiress Patricia Hearst had been missing for two months when police noticed something strange in surveillance pictures of a recent holdup at the Hibernia Bank in San Francisco. The victim of their number one kidnapping case was standing near a wall brandishing a military-issue rifle as three other women and a man cleaned the bank out of $10,000. When the pictures hit the papers, the whole nation was stunned. Had this child of privilege suddenly taken up with a gang of anarchist hoods?

Some may say that the kidnapping of Hearst from her expensive apartment on February 14, 1974, was a kind of karmic retribution for the yellow journalism churned out by Patty's grandfather William Randolph. The self-styled Symbionese Liberation Army (SLA) certainly saw it that way. To them, Patricia Hearst was the perfect target. And their plan succeeded beyond their wildest dreams when she apparently became a willing participant in their revolution. She was nineteen years old.

The SLA was founded by mostly middle-class whites in the Berkeley area in 1971. Then Donald DeFreeze escaped from Vacaville State Prison in 1973 and forcibly took over the organization. DeFreeze pushed the SLA into a violent phase: The Hearst kidnapping was one step in a string of destabilizing acts that he planned to carry out.

DeFreeze (who had taken the revolutionary name Cinque Mtume) made a decision to bring down Patty's father, whom he regarded as the "Man," using one of his own innocent daughters. They hustled Patty into a nondescript apartment in San Francisco and locked her in a tiny hallway closet for two months. While in captivity, she was subjected to continual abuse, attacks, and a lack of privacy even in the bathroom. All the while, DeFreeze and others "reprogrammed" her with the philosophy of the SLA.

When she had been sufficiently trained, her captors decided to test her loyalty with the bank job. She not only cooperated, she was even observed to smile at DeFreeze as they left the scene. Hearst later claimed that the others were pointing their guns at her during the job.

While on the lam, Hearst made periodic statements denouncing the establishment and her parents, and declaring herself "a soldier of the people's army." She now called herself Tania, after Che Guevara's girlfriend.

SLA house

A four-hour siege ensued, during which several other non-SLA members emerged from the house, safe, but just barely. When it was over, the residence was in flames, burning in a fire started by the tear gas, and six SLA members were dead. DeFreeze was later found to have shot himself. Amazingly, no spectators or other neighborhood residents were killed or even hurt.

Millions watched the drama live on television, including the last three SLA "soldiers" in Los Angeles: Hearst, and husband and wife Emily and Bill Harris. Hearst and the Harrises released a recorded statement condemning the police and went back to San Francisco, where they robbed another bank in April. An elderly woman depositing church funds was killed in the holdup. Emily Harris later said, "It doesn't really matter, she was a bourgeois pig anyway." All of the gang, including Hearst, were caught and arrested the next month. At the booking, when asked her occupation, she replied, "Urban guerrilla."

The Hearst family hired flamboyant attorney F. Lee Bailey to defend their daughter, but Bailey submitted a weak defense which the jury didn't buy, despite expert witnesses who testified that Patricia Hearst was the victim of skillful brainwashing. In March 1976 she was sentenced to seven years in jail, but President Jimmy Carter commuted the term barely two years later. Under further pressure from Carter, Hearst was issued a full presidential pardon by Bill Clinton in January 2001. After marrying her bodyguard and settling down to raise a family in Connecticut, she appeared in five of John Waters's films and used the publicity and experience to begin a new life as an actress.

Only in America. . .

Only a month after the robbery, on May 16, Hearst was in Los Angeles sitting in a getaway van while two other SLA members shoplifted items from Mel's Sporting Goods Store in Inglewood. When they were observed and ran out of the building, Hearst fired several warning shots that barely missed the store owner and several bystanders. Ditching the van and stealing several cars, the three fugitives hightailed it to a hotel near Disneyland.

Meanwhile, back at the safe house, the other SLA members heard about the botched shoplifting and hastily moved out. They drove around awhile and finally took over another house simply because it was the only one with lights on at four a.m. On an anonymous tip, four hundred police officers and SWAT team members converged on the residence the next afternoon.

"Occupants of 1466 East 54th Street, this is the Los Angeles Police Department speaking. Come out with your hands up!" they bellowed through a bullhorn. A child and an older man walked out. After more attempts to get the occupants to leave, tear gas canisters were thrown in. Gunshots erupted from within, and the cops returned fire.

Personalized Properties

"I never did anything artistic my whole life—I'm a tree trimmer by trade. Then one day about four years ago I painted my door purple, and once I got started I couldn't stop."

—Richard Margolin, creator of Encinitas's Rock 'n' Roll Tribute House

California has always had more than its fair share of eccentric folks. Would you really expect them to live out their lives in cookie-cutter suburban houses? Not likely! For our state's individualists, their homes are more than just a place to find shelter from the outside world. The space they inhabit is a canvas on which to express their innermost personality to the outside world.

This sort of thing, call it habitational expressionism, can seem pretty strange at times. That is until you take a closer look and really see what these wonderfully unique homeowners are saying as they use their living space as the medium to get their message to the masses. These statements can be glimpses into the souls of the people who made them. Or they could just be the result of some weird homeowner wanting to create an idealized environment, customized by his own off-kilter imagination.

Either way, all of the people you will read about here have at least one thing in common: They have boldly reinvented their surroundings to better suit their needs and aesthetic sensibilities. And, in so doing, they have created some truly amazing environments.

Salvation Mountain—Niland

Imagine if you will, '60s pop artist Peter Max erecting a mountainload of the Lord's word in the middle of the southern California desert, and you'll have an idea of what Leonard Knight's Salvation Mountain looks like. Over three stories tall and spanning more than one hundred feet (and expanding daily) this man-made Technicolor homage to the Old and New Testaments is an impressive sight regardless of your religious beliefs.

Leonard Knight is a soft-spoken, wiry framed man in his seventies, with more energy than most people half his age. His skin has been weathered and tanned from years of living under the stars in this otherwise barren wilderness, and he possesses a peaceful smile that suggests he honestly believes he has spoken to God, and vice versa.

In 1971, handyman Leonard saw a hot air balloon fly over his Vermont home. It didn't say GOD IS LOVE on it, but he wished it did.

Years later in Nebraska, Leonard built his own balloon with that message emblazoned upon it. The balloon never actually ascended to the heavens, and eventually it rotted out, but Leonard remained undaunted in his mission to have his simple statement of divine love noticed.

"My God, it's amazing what happened to me," Leonard told us on a recent visit up the mountain. "Back about 1967, in Lemon Grove, California, I start saying, 'Jesus, I'm a sinner. Please come into my heart.' And I said, 'God, I don't know what I'm doing.' And God, I started crying like a baby, and Jesus, he really came into my heart."

"I got out here about twenty years ago to let people know that God and Jesus love everybody they ever created."

In 1984, Leonard Knight made his pilgrimage to Niland, an arid small town that at the time had little to offer visually other than trailer homes and power lines. About three miles off Main Street he began his Noahesque project, cubit by cubit if you will. He's been working on it daily ever since.

The people of Niland have taken to Leonard. When the heat gets too much for him, he is more than welcome to sit for hours in the little restaurant up the street. He has been the King of the Tomato Festival Parade, and even art

historians have noticed his work. At one point, there was talk of demolishing the mountain. The government claimed that Mr. Knight was a squatter and that the paint was lead-based and therefore toxic. While it seems Uncle Sam was correct on both counts, Leonard is still here, and his mountain is in no danger of going anywhere either.

"I got out here about twenty years ago to let people know that God and Jesus love everybody they ever created. I only really wanted to stay a week and make something about eight feet tall, but twenty years and

Leonard lives in his truck year-round in a town where temperatures can soar as high as 120 degrees in the summer months.

100,000 gallons of paint later I'm still here." Leonard beams as he tells the story of his mountain, but his pride is not one of ownership or even craftsmanship. He is proud to spread what he considers to be the reason he was put on this earth. "I just want to prove to the people that God is love. It says so in the Bible. . . . And if the holy Bible says something, I believe it."

It also says so on Salvation Mountain. The giant mound is constructed of adobe, and Leonard guesses there must be one thousand bales of hay and tons of mud in it. Peppered in for good measure are the occasional sticks and car tires. It appears like a multihued mirage out of the dry desert dirt. Flowers and waterfalls, American flags and hearts are artistically married to passages from the Bible and simple messages of joy, peace, and goodness. It's nearly impossible to suppress the childlike urge to climb to the top the minute you see it.

Leonard is well aware that some people will miss the spiritual significance he intended, but he is happy to have visitors enjoy his mountain any way they can. He does pass out postcards with his Sinner's Prayer on it, though.

JESUS, I'M A SINNER, PLEASE COME INTO MY HEART, it reads. "I like to give postcards," he says, "but I don't want to insult anybody. If I insult anybody, it's when I'm shaving in the morning."

Leonard lives in his truck year-round in a town where temperatures can soar as high as 120 degrees in the summer months. His home is a beat-up 1940s cab, with a wooden shack reminiscent of the Little Rascals clubhouse built atop. Naturally, the truck, as well as every other car and bus that Leonard owns, is painted to match the mountain.

About the only thing that isn't painted on this government-owned property that Leonard took over years ago is his dog, Boy.

"I suppose I'll leave him just as God created him," said Leonard, and chuckled.

If you decide to visit Salvation Mountain, feel free to bring old cans of paint, but cash is appreciated too. "I've got lots of paint sittin' round," Leonard told us, "but I can't eat paint."

Grandma Prisbrey's Bottle Village

Tressa "Grandma" Prisbrey was known, by her own insistence, to take "nothin' from nobody," and this held true in all aspects of her life. That's not to say that when it came to her art and her many collections she was above scouring the town dump.

Prisbrey was a self-sufficient, independent-minded woman who depended mainly on herself and her own ingenuity throughout her long life. She was born in Minnesota, lived in North Dakota and the Pacific Northwest, and by the time she married her second husband she was tired of moving around. So after they purchased their one third of an acre in Simi Valley she unhitched the wheels of their trailer home and began building more permanent structures around her. She was nearly sixty years old by then, but the environment she so single-mindedly created—which became known as Bottle Village—would become one of the local delights. In all likelihood, it also provided a sense of stability for a tough old woman who outlived six of her seven children.

Grandma Prisbrey's motivation for building her first bottle building, in 1956, was weird in and of itself. She needed a place to house her collection of thousands of pencils. Building a structure with concrete blocks was too expensive, so instead she used mortar and old glass bottles to make walls and a roof for her Pencil House. She collected the bottles at the nearby dump, which provided further inspiration. From the discarded goods there she salvaged over five hundred dolls and piles of other flotsam and jetsam, including old headlights, television sets, fluorescent tubes, shot glasses, and much more. Over time, as you might imagine, she needed more than a Pencil House to shelter her new collections.

By 1960, sixteen buildings fashioned from bottles and various other materials had been completed. Among the odd things Grandma built were a Rumpus Room for her grandchildren to play in, a School House, and a Shell House, meant to be a home for a son dying from cancer. Not forgetting her Maker, Grandma also built various shrines. One of these, the Shrine for All Religions—created primarily from blue milk of magnesia bottles—celebrated the diversity of visitors to the village with a Madonna, a Star of David, and religious statues from different

faiths. A cement wall made of bottles and found objects enclosed the compound, where for twenty-five cents Prisbrey would entertain visitors with her keen sense of humor during guided tours. She continued to work on her buildings for nearly twenty years, saying that it was something to keep her busy in her old age.

By 1972, Grandma Prisbrey's husband had died and she was too frail to continue to live in her village on her own. She was invited by one subsequent owner to stay on as a caretaker, but when the land changed hands again the new owner, a developer, evicted her. Finally, in 1986, Bottle Village was purchased by a group, Preserve Bottle Village (PBV), intent on saving it.

Grandma Prisbrey died in 1988 in a nursing home, and the 1994 Northridge earthquake severely damaged Bottle Village. However, PBV raised money to repair the damage and pay back property taxes and interest fees. Such charity might have made Grandma Prisbrey balk, but it saved her weird and strangely beautiful creation. PBV is now striving to preserve, promote, and eventually reopen the site to the public — ensuring that Grandma Prisbrey's fiery spirit of independence will live on.

Calico's Bottle House: Don't Throw Stones!

One room fixer-upper, situated in the middle of abandoned spooky ghost town. Organic (dirt) floors. One-story building approximately 12 x 12, made almost entirely of glass bottles. Big six-point star on side of house.

A tough sell nowadays, but apparently bottle houses weren't that unusual an abode for hopeful prospectors trying to cash in on the silver rush during the late 1800s in the Calico Mining District outside Yermo.

Between 1881 and 1907, the boomtown produced $86 million in silver and $45 million in borax. The settlement of Calico officially collapsed in 1929, but during its heyday the tiny hamlet had a population of over 1,200 and maintained over twenty taverns and one whorehouse.

Today the Calico Ghost Town is little more than a roadside attraction right off I-15 in the desert of San Bernardino County, which draws occasional coastal southern Californians on their way to Las Vegas. Bought in 1951 by Walter Knott (of Buena Park's Knott's Berry Farm fame), the town was restored from turn-of-the-century photographs, although there were apparently no pictures of a bottle house on the premises. However, in many such towns it was common for the workers to either live in a boarding home or cobble makeshift habitats. It would have been an incredible expense for indigent miners, who most likely had no intention of living in town long enough to invest in a proper home, to buy lumber at a premium price and transport it to Calico. A typical home of the day was made with whatever was durable and available. It is easy to imagine bottles would have been plentiful in a town with lots of saloons and no recycling station in sight.

Bottle Tree Ranch

This surrealist bull's-eye sits fifteen feet in the air at Elmer Long's Bottle Tree Ranch, just outside Helendale on the Old National Trails Highway, also known as Route 66. Long has built over two hundred "trees" on his property, using scrap metal, antique bottles, and telephone-pole insulators, and topping them off with such found objects as an Underwood typewriter, a Radio Flyer wagon, half a surfboard, a Lionel train, an alto saxophone, and a 1922 Smith & Wesson (shown here, aiming at a wagon-wheel target).

As a child, Elmer Long took many trips with his father out to the desert, combing the dunes and brush for the refuse of bygone days. The elder Long kept extensive diaries of their findings, logging descriptions of bottles and their locations. Elmer has turned those childhood adventures into a magnificent obsession, decorating his acreage with bizarrely fascinating sculptures welded together out of scrap iron. Long's storage sheds and lawn hold thousands of insulators, lengths of rebar and pipe, cement fixings, and doodads awaiting his next wave of inspiration. He gives a simple justification for the clutter hanging around his property: "My mother never told me to clean my room."

One particular tree is topped by over two hundred glass bottles. Another is surmounted with a cage holding a couple dozen green plastic soda bottles. A toaster, a truck spring, a pitchfork with phone insulators on each tine, a 9/11 tribute painted on an I beam—these are among the hundreds of unusual findings that Long has mounted on his tall, glistening trees.

While most of the tree-toppers are things he just happened to pick up, a few have more personal significance. One tree bears the Lionel locomotive that Long received when he was four years old. When his son gave up his musical pursuits to study computer science, up went his saxophone onto a tree. Hundreds of visitors have stopped in to see Long's handiwork since his first tree went up in 2000, and he's had many postcards and return visits from fans around the world.—*Todd S. Jenkins*

The Unintentional Flamingo House

He's not really much of a flamingo guy, but you'd be hard-pressed to guess that if you drive by John Currens's Pescadero Creek Road home in Loma Mar.

Originally Currens placed a few of the pink plastic birds outside his home simply to announce his presence. That house had been abandoned for a number of years before he bought it, and it had become something of a beer-drinking hangout for local kids.

"I just wanted to send a message that someone was moving in, and so I put up a few flamingos that my sister gave me as a gag gift," says Currens, who in his other life is a data processing consultant.

The young drinkers took the hint, but somehow the flamingos started to multiply. "I haven't actually bought too many of these things myself," Currens maintains.

"Friends bring them by, strangers leave them at my front door. One guy gave me a whole truckload of them once."

Currens estimates there are now over five hundred of the gaudy pink ornaments loitering on his property. They perch on his lush, green, ferny front yard. They have made themselves comfortable in his backyard. They patrol his driveway and sit on his front porch and atop his house. There are flamingo wind chimes, flamingo reflectors, and flamingo flags. That's a lot of flamingos for even a bona fide flamingo aficionado, which Currens certainly is not.

Neither is at least one of his neighbors. "One person had a problem with them. So I pointed all the birds towards her house," he chuckles, "and it worked. She moved out."

Everyone else, it turns out, loves the collection, especially elderly women and children. "I definitely get more compliments from old ladies and little kids than anyone else," Currens says, "but everybody I talk to seems to like them."

If you are a legitimate admirer of plastic pink flamingos and would like to own a set of five hundred for yourself, now is the time to act. Currens has put his handsome three-acre home up for sale, and he's not taking the flamingos with him. Chance of a lifetime!

Life in a Fishbowl

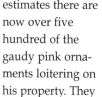

Dear Purveyors of Weird;

This is the "Fish House" located on Mathews Street in Berkeley. Hope you like it. The architect built it for his parents who live there. The neighbors hate it because people always come to gawk and take pictures.

—Your fan Tessie Wilson

Forestiere Underground Gardens

Hidden under a busy commercial strip in suburban Fresno is an intricate underground labyrinth. No, it's not a subway system or natural caverns—it's the residence and gardens of the late Baldasare Forestiere.

Forestiere, a Sicilian immigrant who came to the San Joaquin Valley in 1905, envisioned developing citrus groves in the fertile valley. But after he purchased his property, he became concerned that the intense heat would be hostile to his venture. Being a creative thinker, Forestiere came up with a novel idea: He would take his dream underground. That way he could control the climate and, he hoped, his trees would flourish.

Chiseling through hardpan rock with simple hand tools, Forestiere eventually carved out an enormous subterranean

compound. He planted his citrus grove, and over the course of forty years, he also developed an intricate series of passageways, patios, courtyards, and rooms — a true architectural wonder.

Forestiere designed the passageways' width and curvature specifically to modulate the air flowing through them, which created an innovative underground ventilation system. He lit his underground world by skylights that allowed the trees to catch some rainwater. Excess water dripped from sloped passageway floors into sand "sump pits," so flooding was never a problem. The gardens were laid out in a series of corridors lined with peepholes and alcoves, and grapevines and trees heavy with fruit flourished during the growing season. Protected from both heat and frost, a variety of trees abound — from jujube, pomegranate, mulberry, date, and palm to all manner of citrus — and through grafting, Forestiere created single trees that bear a variety of fruit.

So pleased was Forestiere with his underground groves that he built his home there — complete with a kitchen, a library, two bedrooms, a living room, a bathroom, a fishpond, and an aquarium. In all, he built almost one hundred rooms. Hailed as a visionary engineer and architect as well as a skilled horticulturist, for decades Forestiere resided full-time in his underground home. He died in 1946, and the gardens were named a registered historic landmark in 1979. Today the gardens are open to the public, maintained as a museum by Lorraine, Ricardo, and Andre Forestiere — Baldasare's niece, nephew, and great-nephew.

Litto's Hubcap Ranch

Hubcaps hang from the trees, like so much metallic fruit. They sprout off telephone poles and fences buried halfway in the ground. They spell out the name Litto fifteen feet high on the roof of the old barn. A handwritten sign just to the right of the long and sparkling driveway alerts you to the fact that you are entering a special place. The sign announces, and there is no sense in disputing it, that you are in the domain of the POPE VALLEY HUBCAP KING.

Visitors to the kingdom must travel up the dirt driveway, which is surrounded on either side by the often dented silvery shields. Two old-fashioned wood toolsheds are bejeweled with license plates from across the country, as well as pie trays, metallic children's toys, and of course, dozens and dozens of hubcaps.

There is also a more official commemorative inscription. It reads LITTO'S HUBCAP RANCH. THIS IS ONE OF CALIFORNIA'S EXCEPTIONAL TWENTIETH-CENTURY FOLK ART ENVIRONMENTS. The plaque goes on to say that for over thirty years Emanuelle "Litto" Damonte (1892–1985) collected the more than two thousand hubcaps that adorn the large rural property. The truth is, there are probably closer to four thousand, since Litto added more before passing on to the great automotive store in the sky.

As with so many homegrown personalized properties, Damonte's masterwork came about by lucky accident. The road that stretched in front of his home was full of potholes and cracks, and travelers would constantly lose their hubcaps on the twisty and rutted terrain. Damonte would gather the discarded wheel coverings and hang them along his fence so the unfortunate motorists might claim their belongings. As it turns out, passersby were not inclined to reclaim the caps, so they just became decorations. Soon people were coming to the elderly Damonte with hubcaps they had found and asking if he'd be so kind as to display them on his property as well. And so the shiny museum to dented auto parts began.

Twenty years after Damonte's demise, his grandson works the ranch, and he is happy to give the hubcaps, which he sometimes finds by the garbagebagful, a place at his grandfather's estate. If flashy automobile parts are your thing, you'll find Litto's Hubcap Ranch at 6654 Pope Valley Road, in Pope Valley.

Cranky Old Man's Cement Garden

Ask the locals in rural Willits how to get to the Tin and Cement Garden, and they will look at you like you have a hole in the middle of your forehead. But if you can describe the place, they will tell you exactly how to get there. They just never knew it had a name.

Not much is known about the creation of this particular group of folk art, but people seem to remember its always being there. Perhaps a good reason the place is shrouded in mystery is that the owner of the property, "Old Man Sully," has a less than neighborly reputation when it comes to outsiders inquiring about the strange objects that adorn his yard. He is even less inclined to be reasonable to an intruding writer with a camera out for a story.

Upon being warned about Sully's famous temperament at a local diner by a truck driver who lives in town, I had one important question. Was Sully just a crotchety old man or was he a crotchety old man with a gun? My new friend looked up from his huge plate of eggs and pancakes, smiled, and chuckled. "Probably better if you expect the second one."

Keeping this in mind, your intrepid reporter drove to Sully's place anyway and decided to chase the story. As it turned out, the story chased me.

Finding Sully's wasn't that hard at all. Driving up to his house on the dirt road while trying to be undetected was a bit rougher. As I was snapping pictures at Sully's dwelling (one object was a decomposing skeleton . . . probably a dog, but who knows?), I was startled to see an older man walk out and then head briskly back into his house. Keeping in mind the advice I'd gotten at the diner, I didn't stick around to find out if he was going to come back

with a lemonade or with a shotgun and see if he could be the one to place that hole in the middle of my forehead.

Faster than Bo and Luke Duke's lesser known and much more cowardly brother, Fraidy, I hightailed it out of those woods quicker than you can say Babe the Blue Ox (I'm pretty sure that's what one of the sculptures was supposed to be).

From the pictures I took it seems that some of the statues were made out of cement and some of the other images that adorned the house were created from tin. This would explain the reason that my kindly (and safe from harm's way) editors told me this place was called the Tin and Cement Garden, even though no one else in the small town had ever heard it referred to as such. I also know that I am made of flesh and blood, and so at one time was the skeleton of whatever it was I jumped over to get back in my rental car and out of bullet range. If you're ever in Willits, you should check out the Tin and Cement Garden. You can see it pretty clearly for a second or two if you drive a steady 65 mph.—*Joe O.*

Romano Gabriel's Wooden Garden

For almost thirty years, Italian immigrant Romano Gabriel devoted nearly all his free time to carving and painting the vibrant wooden flowers, trees, carousels, and characters that filled up the front yard of his humble one-bedroom Eureka home.

A carpenter and gardener by trade, Gabriel was able to incorporate both of his professions into a singular passion. "Eureka is a bad place to grow flowers," he was once quoted as saying, so until about 1967 Gabriel created, from discarded fruit crates, the Italian flora he remembered so fondly from his youth. (After that, the boxes were no longer made of wood.)

Hundreds of individual carvings festooned and dwarfed his house and modest thirty- by thirty-six-foot property. Many of the figures were based on political or religious people of the time, and it is said that the introverted Gabriel enjoyed hiding among his creations to watch the reactions of his visitors. By controlling a series of ropes and motors, he would make his handiwork move just to see the surprise and wonderment on the faces of those who walked by.

Romano Gabriel passed away in 1977, but Harvard and M.I.T. have since studied his masterpiece, and it's also been featured in such notable magazines as *Architecture Plus* and *Art News.* The colorful decorations are no longer in front of the home Gabriel once dwelled in, but every piece has been taken down and carefully preserved by the Eureka Heritage Society. They are now on display at 315 Second Street in Old Town Eureka.

The Desert Museum looks at first as if it were individual clubhouses built by industrious street urchins from a Hal Roach movie.

Noah Purifoy's Outdoor Desert Museum

Way off the beaten track in the town of Joshua Tree sits Noah Purifoy's Outdoor Desert Art Museum, two and a half acres of pure folk art or, as Noah preferred, "assemblage sculptures."

Bowling balls, folding chairs, computer terminals, bicycle parts, the bottom half of a mannequin, and Astroturf all integrate agreeably in Noah's garden. With many of the pieces held down against the harsh winds with chicken wire, cables, and cement, the Desert Museum looks at first as if it were individual clubhouses built by industrious street urchins from a Hal Roach movie, but upon closer inspection you can see the sly political and social commentary. A four-page brochure at the edge of the property encourages the visitor to browse the grounds and informs of the artists' motives and muses.

Check out the fanciful locomotive made of discarded old parts and captured in motion on a makeshift railroad track. According to the brochure, "The railroad of long ago stood as a symbol of hope and progress for the well-to-do, built by the poor who saw their creation more emblematic of lost property and lost dreams." Not far away is a "room" that gives the impression of a postapocalypse office complete with electrical wires, cubicles, and keyboards strewn about. One building looks like a fortress—intimidating and dangerous—and yet many of the other pieces give off the feel of a playground or a carnival. There's *Carousel,* for example. It's a brightly painted circular structure that was created for a seven-year-old girl and "one of my favorite artists in the community," Noah was quoted as saying.

Noah Purifoy was the founder of the Watts Towers Art Center, where he taught art during the Watts Riots of 1965. An educated man, he held three separate degrees: one in social science, one in social service, and the third in art form. Quite an accomplishment for anyone, but especially impressive when considered that Noah Purifoy is a black man born in 1917 in Alabama.

On the way out of the museum stands a drinking fountain with a sign above that reads WHITE. Three feet to the left is a yellowed toilet bowl. Its sign reads COLORED. It is said that Noah encouraged his audience to "see the world as it truly is, not with anger but with understanding." It's a fair commentary.

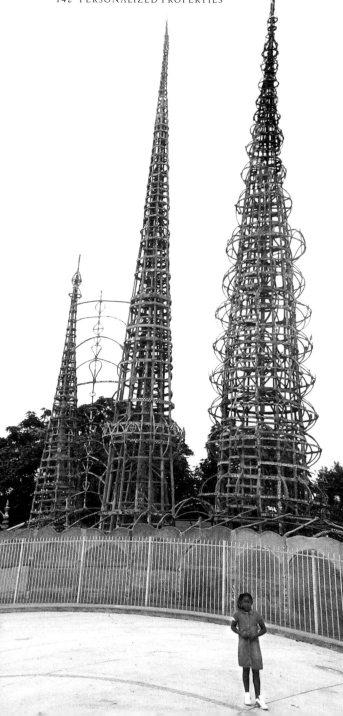

Watts Towers

They are at once menacing and childlike. Barbed and threatening, colorful and imaginative, they are as intimidating as a fortress—yet as entertaining as a playground. It's not hard to believe that these are perhaps the ancient remains of the great civilization of Atlantis itself. Steel skeletal cathedrals bedecked in multihued bits of pottery, ceramic tile, abalone shells, and glass. Or maybe a once mighty fantastical sailing ship, traveling from adventure to adventure, always outracing the sea serpents, always discovering the treasure, now landlocked and pillaged.

Visiting the Watts Towers can be a daunting proposition. The parking lot has at least one armed guard on duty at all times, and the neighborhood is scarred by years of urban blight. Watts was the scene of the eponymous and infamous Watts Riots in 1965, a large-scale "civil disorder" between the Los Angeles police and the mostly African American populace of the neighborhood. The riots lasted six days, claimed thirty-four lives, and resulted in an estimated $100 million dollars in damage. Watts itself is still economically depressed and has earned a reputation for gangs and violent crimes.

There was a time, however, when Watts was just another rural town in southern California, and it was during this time that Italian-born Sabato "Simon" Rodia decided to "do something big."

Simon Rodia was a small man who stood just under five feet in height. A logger/coal miner/construction worker by trade, he purchased a home on a triangular plot of land near the railroad tracks in 1921 and began his life's work, Nuestro Pueblo, as he called it: "Our Town."

Over a period of thirty years, Simon Rodia built three separate spires around his house, as well as a patio, a gazebo with a circular bench, three birdbaths, and a number of other functional artistic creations. Impressively, he built it all without the benefit of machine equipment, bolts, scaffolds, ladders, or even a blueprint.

This tiny but powerful man would gather his supplies wherever he could find them. Neighborhood children were paid pennies for fetching bottles, metal, wire, plates, and various other materials, but Rodia constructed the entire edifice himself, single-handedly. No fitted pipe was taller than ten feet long, and all were bent and forged by Rodia against the tracks of the railroad. The primary pipes were buried in the ground, secured by cement. The subsequent smaller pipes were held together using cement and wire, and by jamming nails into the grooves. Rodia would climb the structures using only a window washer's belt and buckle, carrying a bucket of wet cement or mosaic tile or whatever was needed at the time.

The tallest of the steeples is ninety-nine and a half feet above the ground and contains the longest slender reinforced concrete column in the world. Rodia's work is physically connected to itself as if it were one giant cement-and-steel spiderweb.

Legend has it that Rodia sold the property to a friend for only a dollar in 1955 (when he was seventy-five) so he could move closer to his family. The house caught on fire the following year, but his masterpiece spires still stood tall. At one point, the city fathers, in their wisdom, ordered the property demolished. But the Committee for Simon Rodia's Towers in Watts devised an engineering test more stringent than building codes required and proved that the structures were sound. The city reversed itself and decided against razing the beloved spires. Today the Watts Towers are listed on the National Register of Historic Places. The irony is that Watts will probably always be remembered more for destruction than for creation.

La Casa Formica

Sabers and chandeliers, golden warriors, and emerald mermaids . . . oh, yeah . . . and a lion. A real, live lion. This is La Casa Formica, in El Cerrito.

Joseph Formica is the kindly old sovereign of La Casa Formica, and the full-grown lion no longer roams Mr. Formica's backyard, which is probably somewhat of a relief to the neighbors.

Large predatory carnivorous mammals aside, there is nothing threatening about Joseph Formica or his house. He is a smallish, gentle man just over five feet tall, with a twinkle in his eyes and a lot of pep.

There are tens of thousands of bric-a-brac and collectibles all around his home and in his yard. He has entire rooms devoted to model sailboats and empty liquor bottles in the shape of Revolutionary War heroes. Another room looks like a captain's chamber on a good-guy pirate ship, complete with circular port windows and a bust of Napoleon.

His home is a pastiche of disparate found elements that wouldn't work together in a junkyard, yet come together quite nicely despite what believers in feng shui would have you believe.

Ornately stitched pillows sit on a thronelike chair, behind which stands a life-size black-and-white cutout of Marilyn Monroe in a one-piece tassel dress and fishnet stockings. Glow-in-the-dark stars adorn the ceiling, and the entire collection of *All in the Family* on VHS sits atop his vintage television set. Joseph Formica has no idea what his collection of unconventional possessions is worth, nor does he care. Each one is a memory, and his memories are not for sale.

Nitt Witt Ridge

He was known as Captain Nitt Witt. He was also known as Der Tinkerpaw. To the residents of the coastal community of Cambria, however, he was probably best known as that crazy old guy who lives in that weird three-story house that he carved in the side of a hill using little more than hand tools, all the while stealing pieces of plumbing and lumber and Lord knows what else from Hearst Castle, as well as neighborhood junkyards.

His actual name was Art Beal. Art Beal—artist, hermit—whose impressively offbeat residence is called Nitt Witt Ridge.

Legend has it that Beal started constructing his home, which has been called the poor man's Hearst Castle, in 1928, and worked on it consistently for the next fifty-one years. A jack-of-all-trades, Beal used a pick and shovel and his own extraordinary ingenuity to dig out the face of the hill, which he used as the foundation for his house.

Beal worked for a time as a laborer at the Hearst Castle in nearby San Simeon. This job provided him the opportunity to "borrow" certain materials. But while much of Nitt Witt Ridge was constructed from ill-gotten gains, a good deal of it was made from indigenous materials, such as driftwood, large rocks, and abalone shells. The remainder was assembled using neighbors' refuse, which Beal would bring home from his job as a garbage collector. Old stoves, car tires, and empty Busch beer

cans are employed not only aesthetically but also structurally.

If all this whackjob ever did was dig a huge hole in some hillside near the beach, that would be impressive enough, but with no formal training Art Beal is the architect of the state of California's Historical Landmark Number 939.

Nitt Witt Ridge is located at 881 Hillcrest Drive and is now owned and operated by Michael and Stacey O'Malley. Michael conducts several informative and entertaining tours a day.

Casa de Tortuga

It hit us the second we walked into the place: turtle smell.

Remember those smells from when you were young? Lunch ladies had their own identifiable odor, the weird kid who wore his wool army jacket well into June had his particular funk, and turtles had a smell.

Now multiply that by two hundred, and that's the aroma that greeted our unsuspecting nostrils when we met Mr. Walter Allen, the Turtle Man of Casa de Tortuga.

Not that it's a foul scent, and don't get us wrong, Mr. Allen is a fine housekeeper, but we'll be damned if we could get the odor of turtles (and tortoises) out of our noses for the next few days.

Mr. Allen is the owner of Casa de Tortuga (House of the Turtle). He is a man obsessed with the creatures and has been for about forty years now. "I've always liked 'em," says Mr. Allen. "I suppose I fell in love with them and have been taking care of them ever since."

Taking care includes converting two backyards and an entire home into a turtle-tortoise sanctuary. (Mr. Allen lives in a separate house right next door.) We were hard-pressed to find a space on his walls or shelves that was not turtle or tortoise related. There are turtle-tortoise posters, T-shirts, cartoons, faxes, ceramics, mugs, and refrigerator magnets plastered all over this guy's place, not to mention rooms full of stacked aquarium tanks which house . . . well, you probably guessed it. Up until recently, Mr. Allen gave tours, ran a turtle-tortoise adoption program, sold turtle supplies, and cared for as many as eight hundred turtles and tortoises of approximately one hundred different species. You didn't know there were that many species? Neither did we. We

didn't even know the difference between turtles and tortoises, until Mr. Allen educated us.

"Put simply, a tortoise lives on land and eats on land, a turtle lives in water and eats in water." And then he pointed to the turtles, which were eating in the studio apartment–size turtle pond he had created for his beloved unhurried friends. There they were, eating in water, doing turtle things, while just a few feet away a couple of giant Galapagos Island tortoises were enjoying a feast of lettuce and carrots, and for dessert, hibiscus flowers.

When asked why he was giving up the turtle-tortoise game, Mr. Allen replied, "I'm getting too old to do the tours anymore."

We also learned that turtles and tortoises can live to be over two hundred years old, and so, on behalf of the turtle-tortoise population of southern California, we'll wish Mr. Walter Allen, the Turtle Man of Casa de Tortuga, many, many happy returns.

Old Trapper's Lodge Statues

When frontiersman John Ehn gave up the trapper's life in Michigan for sunnier skies in southern California, he didn't abandon his pioneer spirit. When he opened the Old Trapper's Lodge motel in Woodland Hills in 1941, he commissioned a giant trapper sculpture for the motel grounds to serve as an advertisement.

"This looks easy!" is what Ehn must have thought while watching the sculptor at work, because after the trapper was installed, Ehn decided he could create his own statue, but he didn't stop at just one. From the mid-1950s until he died in 1981, Ehn fashioned cowboys, Indians, dance hall girls, and gold rush miners—complete with their own boot hill graveyard—out of concrete. The statues tell a story of how the West was won—from one man's perspective. Nevertheless, they were considered visionary folk art and declared a California state cultural landmark in 1984. Despite landmark status, the lodge was destroyed to make way for new construction. But the statues were spared and relocated to a back corner of the campus of nearby Pierce College, where they reside today.

Prayer Tower Totem Pole

Ron Henggler moved to San Francisco in 1974 while in his twenties, and by California standards that makes him a native.

Henggler and four other artist friends wisely moved from a tepee in Arkansas, where they grew their own crops and fetched their own water (a quarter-mile away) to a twenty-five-room Queen Anne mansion on Fulton Street. These days Henggler makes his living as a waiter in one of the city's more tony Nob Hill restaurants. He may have shaved off the bushy beard, and he wears a more conservative haircut now, but that hasn't stopped his bohemian way of thinking. And if he chose, his artwork could probably more than pay the bills. The problem is, he's never tried to sell his creations.

His most famous piece will likely not be on the market anytime soon either. Constructed in 1993 with discarded steel from torn-down freeways, this "constant work in progress" stands forty-five feet tall, is decorated with found objects from the city he loves so much, and sits in his front yard. Henggler calls it his Prayer Tower Totem Pole, and he can tell you exactly where he found each decoration that hangs from the tower. "The brass pipes are from Pier 39, the gears are from the Embarcadero, the glass lampshades came from some little café in North Beach.

"It's really an homage to Saint Francis of Assisi, the patron saint of this city," he explains, "and Mozart's *The Magic Flute*. There's kind of an opera motif in there, with the cherubs, and the forest and the bells, and when the wind blows, it's really like a giant wind chime symphony."

There's also a six-foot peace sign which alone holds over 2,700 tiny ornament lights, and while Henggler won't commit to how much the monthly electric bill is for the mansion and its lighted tower, he does say, "It's way too much."

Way too much is never enough for Henggler when it comes to anything regarding the Golden Gate city. A history buff and pack rat by nature, he also owns over 10,000 hardbound books, many on the history of San Francisco, with 3,000 tomes devoted to the gold rush alone. In his attic, he has hundreds of mason jars of San Francisco-centric stuff. Contained in the jars are pieces of several different shipwrecks, rubble from the 1906 earthquake, bones from the 1700s Spanish presidio, chips of brick from the old Ferry Building, pieces of the Collis Huntington mansion's retaining wall up on Nob Hill. There are tufts of fur from the buffalo in Golden Gate Park, vines that climbed up the Embarcadero freeway before it was torn down, rusted iron bolts from Meigg's Wharf (the site of today's Fisherman's Wharf), and candles from the Grace Cathedral memorial service that was held the day after the Twin Towers came down on 9/11.

When asked if he ever plans on selling any of his art, Henggler sounds a touch unsure. "I don't know if I'll ever do that, but I've had a lot of offers from people who want to buy my stuff."

One thing seems certain. If Henggler ever decides to sell his artwork, it looks as if, just like his day job, the patrons of his favorite city will eat it up.

Madonna Inn—San Luis Obispo

Men, here's one for you: Located downstairs near the wine cellar of the Madonna Inn in San Luis Obispo is a world-famous gentleman's privy. It has become a tradition to have a picture taken at the waterfall urinal—for both men and women. Many an embarrassed customer has unzipped, only to hear feminine giggling and see camera flashes coming from the doorway.

The contraption is activated by an electric eye that triggers an eight-foot-high cleansing cascade whenever someone or something interrupts the waist-high beam. Kitschy comfort is further assured at the washbasin, where the spigots are solid brass and the sinks are made of giant clamshells.

This precious landmark of our cultural heritage was the brainchild of eccentric philanthropist Alex Madonna (his real name), who made his fortune in ranching and road building, then decided to build a hotel on the central coast. It opened for business in 1958. Of the 109 rooms at the Madonna Inn, each has a unique theme: the Caveman Room features rock walls and zebra skin–print sheets on the bed, while the Pick & Shovel Room has tractor seats for barstools, a thirty-one-foot leather couch, and sleeps nine. Madonna and his wife never tired of coming up with gimmicks, such as the hotel restaurant, called the Copper Café. Visitors eat off shiny copper tables, and to sweeten the coffee there is sugar that has been colored a vivid blue.

The visionary who bequeathed this wonder to the world died in 2004. His daughter now manages the property and continues in her father's independent spirit. A few years ago she proposed the construction of a topless-optional swimming pool on the grounds.

The Exotic World of Dixie Lee Evans

What was once racy and forbidden has become an almost PG-rated attraction in the high-desert town of Helendale. Here the hallowed, and until recently lost, art of striptease has found a home in the sprawling domain of retired exotic dancer Dixie Lee (a.k.a. Evans), once billed as the Marilyn Monroe of Burlesque. Exotic World, located appropriately enough on Wild Road, is the only place on earth dedicated to preserving the art and paraphernalia of the golden age of strippers.

After retiring, "Bazoom Girl" Jenny Lee (not to be confused with Dixie) owned the Sassy Lady nightclub in San Pedro. In the 1960s, she bucked convention and decided to put memorabilia from her past on display at the club, and the seed of Exotic World was planted. Later Lee decided to buy an old goat farm in Helendale. On her death in 1990, she bequeathed her still growing collection of stripper mementos to her friend Dixie, who quit her job and moved to the property.

With loving care and not a little elbow grease, the collection began to grow as fans and former dancers from all over the world began to send in their own artifacts. The walls of the museum fairly sag with thousands of posters, feathered boas, signed publicity photos, pasties, and elaborate jewel-encrusted costumes. Stage props and personal effects of such storied temptresses as Blaze Starr (Louisiana governor Earl Long's paramour), Lili St. Cyr (underwear magnate after she retired), and Chesty Morgan (star of *Chesty Morgan's Deadly Weapons,* wherein the starlet concealed a couple of .45-caliber roscoes in her bra) are all here. One 8 x 10 shows a busty, flat-bellied dancer who apparently billed herself as the Whip Cream and Cherry Bandit.

Dixie Evans reveals the stories behind it all. She begins with the biblical story of Salome and continues with a detailed history of vaudeville, comedians, and finally burlesque, giving it all a wholesome favor as she describes the girls baring their all for the working class. Old-line burlesque performers consistently mined their acts for laughs, she tells us, but the art died away in the late 1950s, killed off by *Playboy* magazine and other pretenders.

Exotic World is entered on a dusty road through an elaborate filigreed gate guarded by two white plaster lions. Small monuments line the long entrance, each crowned with the names of strippers long gone. Some have plastic flowers or small, faux-Greek statues underneath. A sign in the parking lot advises visitors to HONK TWICE, presumably to give Dixie a couple of minutes to prepare her stage.

Each year Exotic World hosts a burlesque convention called Miss Exotic World. Retro performers from all over the globe vie for the title. The dancers are under strict orders to peel down only to their G-strings and pasties, and alcohol and profanity are forbidden. Evans reminds the camera-toting revelers that burlesque excites the imagination "with what is concealed, rather than what is revealed," and the contestants are judged as much on their coquettish creativity as their looks.

Thankfully, Exotic World survives to remind generations X, Y, and soon Z, how titillation was once an art form, and strip clubs had their own stars instead of borrowing headliners from the latest XXX video.

Roadside Distractions

The saying "It's not the destination, but the journey that counts" has always been our credo when traveling around this great state of California. Fleeting glimpses of things truly unique that you see along our highways, byways, and back roads can sometimes make you shake your head in disbelief. They may be beautiful or ugly, graceful or bizarre—but they are like nothing you'll see anywhere else.

As Californians, we are fortunate to be living amid such perfect examples of quirky and imaginative roadside oddities. Architecturally strange, eccentrically innovative, and sometimes downright beguiling, our state's roadside landscape has developed an identity all its own. The peculiar objects we find along our roadways not only speak volumes about who we are as a culture in twenty-first-century California, they also make traveling a whole lot more fun.

In this chapter, we will take you on a journey that is just a bit different from your ordinary tourist excursion— a sort of asphalt vision quest. Of course, since we live in an age when the car is king, our journeys of profound discovery must be conveniently located near a major travel artery. Hey, this is California we're talking about, after all. While previous generations of explorers may have had to scale steep Tibetan mountain ranges or bravely traverse angry seas in their quest for enlightenment, all that we modern-day adventurers need do to satisfy our wanderlust is jump into our car and drive. So gas up the tank, throw your maps in the glove compartment, and let's hit the open road.

Size Matters!

How do you make a common everyday object seem more impressive and important? Supersize it! Even the most diminutive and mundane items can seem more noteworthy if blown up to colossal proportions. The weird thing about this is how making something ordinary into something extraordinary really forces us to see objects we thought we knew well as if for the first time.

Hot Dog! Tail o' the Pup

In ultrachic Los Angeles, where expensive trends start and end in the same twenty-four hours, it is hard to think of anything less high-brow than a hot dog stand, unless it's a hot dog stand in the shape of a giant hot dog.

Constructed in 1945 and relocated in the late '80s a block away from where it originally stood, the Tail o' the Pup has served its simple high-cholesterol menu for sixty years, which translates into well over five million franks. Hollywood legend Orson Welles is said to have had his limo driver pull up to the oversized frankfurter and place his order while he remained in the back seat. The wall of celebrities tells the story of other show-biz stars who have enjoyed wolfing down the occasional lunchtime sandwich at this architectural landmark. Jay Leno, Pamela Anderson, Barbra Streisand, Magic Johnson, and Whoopi Goldberg have all partaken of the stand's beefy plumpness.

The Tail o' the Pup has also made cameos in many movies, including Brian De Palma's *Body Double* and Steve Martin's *L.A. Story.* The moral of the story seems to be, It doesn't matter who you are in this town, from the toppest top banana to the smallest small fry, it is impossible to resist the allure of a giant wienie. You can find the Tail o' the Pup at 329 North San Vincente Boulevard, Los Angeles, walking distance from the stylish Beverly Center Mall.

Mmm . . . Really Big Doughnut

Just a few miles up the 405 freeway, north of LAX airport, stands possibly the most famous doughnut shop in the world. Built in 1952, Randy's Donuts in Inglewood has become almost moviemaker shorthand for "this story takes place in Los Angeles." In much the same way a glimpse of the Eiffel Tower suggests the elegance of Paris or the Coliseum cues the viewer to the antiquity of Rome, the twenty-three-foot-diameter cement pastry that sits upon the roof of the donuttery implies all that is kitschy about the City of Angels.

Movies that have used this storefront of sugar-coated cakes as a backdrop include *Earth Girls Are Easy*, *Stripped to Kill*, and *Problem Child 2*. While the aforementioned films may be less than pieces of cinematographic genius, the doughnuts themselves are pretty tasty. Randy's Donuts is on 805 West Manchester Avenue. Do yourself a favor and grab a bear claw, or perhaps a honey-glazed. If nothing else, it'll be more palatable than *Problem Child 2*.

Tess, the Fifty-Foot-Tall Woman

If you're the type who has an inquiring scientific mind AND a fetish for eviscerated giantesses, then the California Science Center in Los Angeles is the place for you. Sure, it's a proper science center, with informative and interactive exhibits. There's the Amazing Living Head, a fun and educational, custom-made illusion by comic magicians Penn and Teller. The 3-D IMAX movie, hosted by Tom Hanks and entitled *Magnificent Desolation: Walking on the Moon,* is visually spectacular, not to mention instructive. But the BIG draw here is, without question, Tess.

Tess is billed as the Fifty-foot-tall Woman with Visible Organs, and there is no room to dispute that claim. Of course, room is always an issue when you're sharing a space with an animatronic woman of that size. You can only imagine how big her shoe closet must be. Tess, however, doesn't wear shoes; she's naked . . . well, not so much naked, as sliced open to reveal the inner workings of the human anatomy.

Upon walking into the exhibit, you may feel as if you are viewing an enormous autopsy, like something you'd see on *CSI,* but the advantage here is that the organs can still move. Viewers find out the importance of such body functions as sweat and how the heart pumps faster when under physical and emotional duress. Want to know how homeostasis works? It could be explained very simply, but it's way cooler if you see it for yourself, complete with huge blinking, light-up pulmonary veins and Tron-ish special effects.

Tess and her cartoon pal, Walt, perform their edutainment in twenty-minute shows several times a day. The California Science Center is just a stone's throw from the L.A. Convention Center, assuming you're fifty feet tall and don't throw like a girl.

World's Largest Rubber Band Ball

Tourists in San Francisco will undoubtedly know enough to grab some crab at Fisherman's Wharf or take a stroll through Chinatown after eating an egg roll. Many sightseers are inclined to pay a visit to Alcatraz, just to see where the Birdman spent all those hellish years. But somewhere above the blue and windy sea, and beyond the average visitor's travel plans, is the Mission District.

The Mission District is the oldest neighborhood in San Francisco, but it just doesn't get the out-of-towner's dollar. That is, until now. Forget the seafood; forget the storied history; put the sports teams out of your mind. The new and only reason to swing by the City by the Bay is rubber.

The largest rubber band ball in the entire world is located at 3398 East 22nd Street in a narrow convenience store named Pride Superette. Brothers Samir and Nabil Keishk are the proprietors of the shop and, more importantly, the owners of the oversized orb of elasticity in question. The two siblings started working on the four-foot-tall bouncy ball in 1999. It has been guesstimated to weigh over 2,850 pounds at present.

According to Nabil, there was another contender for the crown, but that rubber band ball was tossed out of a helicopter in a stunt to see how high it would rebound off the ground, and while Nabil didn't know the heights attained, he did cackle with unbridled glee, "That ball is f*#$%d up now!"

Should you decide to stop by the Mission District and check out San Francisco's greatest hidden treasure, beware. The ball is half covered in a garishly colored beach blanket and atop sits a sign that ominously reads DO NOT TOUCH and NO PHOTOS.

The brothers are very protective of their construction, and depending on which Keishk you talk to and what mood they are in, the family members can be either overly forthcoming about the creation or downright surly. It is, however, wise to remember that heavy is the burden of shouldering such an undertaking. Heck, even Atlas shrugged, and he didn't have the tourist trade to worry about.

The Dentist's Big Statues

The art of dentistry is a skillful craft that takes years of training and a steady hand. However, for Dr. Kenneth Fox of Auburn, the beautiful smiles he creates as a dentist take a definite backseat to his real art—the giant statues that populate the town with colorful characters. These humungous concrete folk range in size from thirty to forty feet tall, the largest weighing more than one hundred and fifty tons.

A self-taught artist, Fox began creating the statues in the 1960s, pouring concrete over massive steel frames. At first, Auburn citizens were outraged. They felt the statues were eyesores—especially the naked ones (yes, there are some naked ones)—and they even changed the school bus route so children would not be exposed to the very large figures outside Fox's office, where the statues originally resided. However, over time, the townspeople began to embrace Fox and his colossal constructions, eventually going so far as to commission him to create the statue of the gold miner who perpetually pans for gold in the center of Old Town Auburn. (The miner is Claude Chana, a Frenchman who, in 1848, was the first to discover gold in Auburn.)

Some of the statues (an archer woman raising her bow skyward, a naked man struggling to be free of chains à la Prometheus, and an Amazon woman holding a spear) are still located behind Fox's office on Auburn Ravine Road. Others are scattered around town—among them a Chinese transcontinental railroad worker pushing a wheelbarrow, who stands next to the chamber of commerce on Lincoln Way.

Fry's Electronics—Burbank

Nothing inspires consumer confidence like a giant angry interplanetary octopus with yellow daggers for teeth and a deadly hypnotic stare that suggests—for all brave enough to look back into the beast's eyes—that we humans are all mere appetizers in the galactic smorgasbord for a terrorizing colossal overlord. Nothing except, perhaps, giant nuclear-mutated ants dangling ominously ten feet above the Maytag washers and the Amana ranges. Or maybe a dozen menacing little green men in foil spacesuits who hide high in the ink cartridge aisle, spying on patrons like snipers from another planet.

Oh, mere mortals, don't fight it. We have no chance; we have no choice. Get on your collective knees and bow to the superiority of our new master, the electronic superstore known as Fry's.

For those who don't know, Fry's Electronics is a chain of retail mega-markets located up and down the

West Coast and stretching east into Texas. It caters to high-tech professionals, as well as your average PC user. Each store has its own weird theme, but Burbank's B-movie retro-space motif seems to garner the most attention.

Possibly that's because you can't help but wonder what the marketing gurus were thinking when they came up with this brainchild. "I've got it. . . . We'll decorate the entire store in things that look like they'll kill you if you wander too close to the commodities!"

"Genius idea, Witherspoon! I can see it now: fangs, claws, tentacles, ray guns, machine guns. It will be impossible to keep our wares in stock!"

Because of, or in spite of, the marketing decisions at the Burbank store, customers are never in short supply, and thanks to its close proximity to Hollywood,

celebrities have even been known to pick up the occasional USB cable or stack of blank CDs.

You can imagine movie stars such as Ed Begley Jr. (pictured here) or Ed Begley Sr. (had he not died fifteen years prior to the launch of the first Fry's in Sunnyvale) shopping in the warehouselike store, unbothered by the awkward gaze of the public. Who's going to look twice at Ed Begley, senior or junior, when an extraterrestrial spacecraft has crashed and burned into the façade of the structure?

What does all this have to do with quality merchandise at low, low prices? Do not try to figure it out, humans. Our brains are too tiny to comprehend the brilliance of the ultimate plan anyway. Just spend your hard-earned earthling dollars at Fry's and pray . . . pray very hard that you don't become a mere morsel for the Monsters of Mars! (Insert sinister laugh here.)

Cabazon Dinosaurs

The yellowed newspaper clipping in the belly of a brontosaurus tells the tale of a man named Claude K. Bell and his lifelong fascination with the massive reptiles of the Mesozoic Age.

In 1964, Bell, then sixty-seven years old, started erecting the one-hundred-fifty-ton concrete Dinney the Dinosaur on his property in Cabazon "without the help of a construction company or investors," says the clipping. Eleven years and nearly a quarter of a million dollars later, Mr. Bell's vision wasn't even halfway finished. Next was the *Tyrannosaurus Rex*, the undisputed king of the concrete colossals. The huge *T. rex*, complete with a sliding board for kids down its tail, was finished shortly after Bell's death in 1987. Remaining on the drawing board were concept sketches and models of a huge woolly mammoth and a saber-toothed tiger or two.

During the '80s, people across the nation were introduced to Dinney and Rex by their cameos in commercials, music videos, and most notably the movie *Pee-wee's Big Adventure*. But hard times hit the massive beasts in the '90s. Claude Bell's property went up for sale shortly after his death, and for a time it looked like his museum/gift shop/enormous kitschy homage to the prehistoric creatures might be bulldozed to accommodate a bigger, more ferocious modern-day monster—the strip mall. But intelligent minds prevailed, sort of. The dinosaurs are still in place. They now, however, have been forced to coexist with a Burger King and a Denny's restaurant.

Dinney and Rex also have had a recent touch-up. For the total sum of one dollar and a case of Dr Pepper, a painting contractor applied a more realistic coat of paint down Rex's back and altered Dinney from cartoony green to a more authentic grey. There are plans to have an electrical engineer install lighting so it will appear that the eyes are glowing fire red at night. These cosmetic modifications sound fairly modest in comparison to some of the work done on the local wealthy narcissists in nearby Palm Springs.

World's Largest Thermometer

Every town needs something to put it on the map. Los Angeles is the movie capital of the world. San Diego is America's Finest City. The tiny burg of Baker located near Nevada on Interstate 15 is not only the Gateway to Death Valley but also home to the World's Largest Thermometer.

The thermometer there is huge, to be sure, only seventeen feet shorter than the Statue of Liberty. Local businessman Willis Herron put up the $70,000 needed to build the tacky tower about twenty years after he first envisioned the thing that would put Baker on the map. In 1991, the thermometer was finished and started drawing Vegas-bound travelers who heretofore had only a couple of gas stations and a few restaurants to give them an excuse for a pit stop. The fact that the Bun Boy Café and hotel are located at the base of the thermometer has excited the imaginations and funny bones of many a smart aleck as well.

Herron made his fortune on the restaurant, which opened for business in 1926. "Aww, I know it's tacky," he told the *Los Angeles Times,* "but I also know people won't be able to pass it more than four or five times without saying, 'What is that?'" His statement was prophetic.

Soon after the thermometer was completed, a high desert windstorm broke off the top, which smashed a gift shop still under construction as well as a parked truck. Undaunted, Herron rallied his troops and rebuilt with reinforced concrete. Topped with a pink light and sporting 4,900 light bulbs, it can display temperatures in excess of 130 degrees, which is no blarney. Death Valley recorded 134 in 1913, which still stands as the U.S. record and is also, appropriately, the height of the Baker thermometer measured in feet.

In late 1999, the aging Herron sold the complex to a man named Steve Carter, who knows that you don't fix it if it ain't broken. Co-owner Larry Dabour pays out $5,000 a month in electric bills, even after he doused the bulbs between the numerical markers.

Embracing the strange, Baker is also home to the Alien Fresh Jerky store, with a ubiquitous bug-eyed head staring down at potential customers from the parking lot and a vast selection of spicy dried beef, as well as a decent collection of UFO-themed knickknacks for sale. (We researched it . . . there's not a trace of actual alien in any of their so-called Alien Jerky.)

Artists create their work to evoke an aesthetic reaction from the viewer on an emotional level. But such reactions are not experienced exclusively in museums and art galleries. There are visionary ideas and offbeat artistic statements to be seen all around us. But who created them and why are often a mystery. Roadside artists seldom work in the traditional mediums of paint, bronze, or marble, which are preferred by their more mainstream counterparts. They usually opt for unconventional materials, like bubble gum or old mufflers, to express their artistic soul. So is it art or is it something else? We leave that up to you to decide. Either way, it is definitely weird and worth a second look.

Muffler Family

Surrounded by the picturesque Ortega Mountains in Riverside County, southeast of Los Angeles, Lake Elsinore is home to California's largest natural lake, a single A-baseball team, and of course the Muffler Family.

Gary Koppenhaver owns and operates G&R Mufflers and is the creator of the many muffler-made citizens that inhabit his establishment. Call him a folk artist, though, and he's likely to choke on the suggestion. A mechanic by trade, Koppenhaver fashioned his first muffler man in 1973 while working for someone else. "My boss told me it was junk and made me throw it out," Koppenhaver laughingly recalls. "I just do this because it's fun. I don't really think of it as art."

Now that he owns his own muffler shop, his "junk" has been critiqued and enjoyed by U.C.L.A. art classes and PBS television.

Bubblegum Alley

A person would be inclined to think that a city as chic and seemingly immaculate as San Luis Obispo would not put up with littering of any kind. But on the same street where a cup of coffee will set you back $7 and the purchase of a genuine porcelain Dalmatian is a cool ten grand, Bubblegum Alley is not only unhygienic, it's celebrated.

Legend has it that students of nearby Cal Poly San Luis Obispo started decorating Bubblegum Alley in various gums as early as 1960, and now the forty-foot lane is completely covered on both sides and up to twenty feet high with Wrigley's, Bazooka, Juicy Fruit, and for the trained eye, the occasional splotch of Freshen-up. (It was the original gum that went squirt.)

Of course, for some it is not enough to simply chew and stick. Many of the wall's contributors have spelled out declarations of love in this viscous substance. If a gentleman can't capture his lady's soul with a well-formed and pre-chewed heart with their initials inside, he ought to take the hint and realize this love was never meant to be.

Others have taken the opportunity to use the well-traveled walkway as advertising for their trade. Who among us would not want their carpet steamed and cleaned by the guy who affixes his business card in an alley with a few strategically placed pieces of Dentyne? Four out of five dentists recommend him . . . why not you?

No matter the temptation, please refrain from peeling the gum from the wall and chewing it yourself. Even in this well-heeled area, gum is still available at a reasonable price. So should you ever find yourself on Higuera Street just north of Broad, chew some gum and walk down the passageway at the same time. It's Bubblicious.

A Mural of Defenestration

We don't know if any living person has been thrown out of the old graffitied and abandoned three-story building on Howard and Sixth in the city of San Francisco, but now it appears that the furniture is being thrown out . . . literally. It's actually a sculptural mural called *Defenestration,* and was conceived and created by California artist Brian Goggin and one hundred volunteers.

The word "defenestration" means "to throw someone or something out of a window," and it's impossible to deny the incredible visual impact this piece has on the unsuspecting onlooker. The furniture (over thirty pieces in all, including coffee tables, sofas, lamps, and even a piano) has an almost animated way about it. It is not being thrown out, but rather, deciding whether or not to make the escape.

The legs of an armchair take on a spiderlike quality as they appear to crawl around the building. A bed, which is hanging precariously out of a window by three of its four legs, seems to be contemplating suicide by plummeting to the street below, and the kindly old grandfather clock has decided to stick his head out of his dwelling to see if it looks like rain. If Disney ever decides to add an Urban Blight Land section to their amusement park, they would do well to study this building.

It's not much of a jump to see that the artist is making sly social commentary with this form of street art. The impetus may have been to point out how a city can turn its back on a neighborhood, but the result is how one can make wonderment from refuse.

Only in San Francisco.

Railroad Bed Art—Near Vidal

The big attraction on this lonely stretch of desert road used to be a big tamarisk tree covered with hundreds of shoes. Someone burned it down in 2001, so another was started, but that was repeatedly cleaned up by some do-gooder and eventually people gave up trying. The same road beautifier also cleaned up the underwear tree nearby. Other shoe trees have been reported at various places in the Mojave Desert, continuing a worldwide tradition that stretches back for centuries. In fact, "rag trees" still exist in Africa and Asia, usually containing prayers written on pieces of cloth.

So what do you do when you want to make a lasting impression, but you know a shoe tree is not long for this world? The nearby railroad tracks, which parallel the blacktop, have already mucked up the desert, and rocks don't burn, so the only thing left for the creative desert rat is available in abundance on the bed of the tracks.

Heading west from Vidal on Highway 62, the railroad crosses the road diagonally and veers off to the right.

Within a few hundred feet, hundreds of messages appear in the rubble hill supporting the tracks. Some of the rocks are simply distinguished by their lighter shade, and others have been painted to make them stand out. Amazingly, almost none of the words are composed of four letters. Most spell out maudlin pledges of love, names, or simple "I was here!"–type exclamations. The "Cool Kids" stopped to turn a few stones over, and families have immortalized Mom, Dad, and the kids—at least until some railroad purist arrives to clean all of this up too.

It's always fun to piss off self-righteous cranks, so while you're there, do us a favor and start another shoe (or underwear) tree.

Desert View Tower

It was conceived as an homage to pre-asphalt nineteenth-century pioneers who attempted, and sometimes failed, to make the thirty-day trek across the unforgiving desert from Yuma, Arizona, to the beaches of San Diego. The Desert View Tower pops right out of the arid region along Interstate 8 in Jacumba; it stands seventy feet tall, and its stone walls are four feet thick.

It is interesting to climb the winding stairs that lead to the top of the tower. The "museum" inside the tower is little more than some old newspaper clippings, a bad oil painting of an Indian in a canoe shooting arrows at nondescript gigantic birds, a five-foot-long stuffed desert turtle, and photos that look like they were torn from a book on astronauts and later framed—poorly.

At the top of the conical tower are windows pointing in every direction. For instance, to the north the viewer can plainly see rock, sand, and desert, while at the south end of the tower the vista is more of a desert, sand, rock kind of thing. The eastern window displayed some rock, some sand, lots of desert, and some guy's dog. (The dog is not always part of the easterly view.)

Not to say this isn't fun, because strangely enough it is. You do get a sense of the early American "Go west, young man" spirit, but the real fun lies right behind the tower, at the Boulder Park Caves.

Having lost his engineering job due to the Depression, W. T. Radcliffe took one look at the quartz granite boulders that sit behind the tower and started to hand carve alligators, giant skulls, Indian chiefs, and beasts of pure fancy. No one seems to know why, but hey, it was the Depression, and while some people were busy jumping out of tall buildings or waiting in lines for a bowl of soup, Radcliffe did something productive. He carved things out of rock. There is no denying these carvings bring out the kid in most anyone who sees the sculptures.

Children and adults alike can be seen scaling the steep slopes that lead to the rocky maze where many of the stone creatures are found. Be careful of low-ceilinged passageways: Many a noggin has been bruised in these cartoonish caves.

The Desert View Tower and Boulder Park are official California Historical Landmarks and well worth stopping by to see if you ever find yourself in the rocky-sandy-deserty neighborhood.

Religion can be a very touchy subject for some people—especially when they see their faith included in a book called *Weird California!* So, before any of you readers get the idea that we are poking fun at your particular belief, we'd like you to know that this is not the case at all. Here at *Weird California* we find all religions equally weird and truly admire the unusual roadside monuments that some folks have created to express their devotion for all the world to see.

Desert Christ Park—Yucca Valley

Here on a sweltering rocky hillside in the high desert, Jesus is missing his hands and some of his disciples are missing their heads. The tragedy at this monument to one man's artistic and spiritual vision is the result of earthly spite and neglect, and at least one act of God, or Gaia, as the case may be.

Desert Christ Park was the realized dream of artist and former aircraft worker Frank Antone Martin. Born in 1887, Martin was orphaned early and ran away from his foster parents at the age of twelve. After life on the road, where he met his wife and married her in an Arizona mining camp, he finally settled in Los Angeles, finding work at the Douglas Aircraft Company during World War II.

Upon retirement in 1951, Martin fashioned a three-ton concrete statue of Our Savior in his Inglewood driveway. He was using his home as a staging area: The gargantuan figure with outstretched arms was meant to be installed at the rim of the Grand Canyon. Permit and permission problems ensued, so he dropped some of his expectations, packed up his family, and settled a mere one hundred miles away in Yucca Valley. If the great state of Arizona and the National Park Service wouldn't listen to him, Martin

would take his creation someplace else. And he would expand it to be something even the state and federal government didn't have: the New Testament in concrete. On Easter Sunday of 1951, the twelve-foot Jesus was installed on a hill overlooking the town and a ten-year labor was begun.

Martin started working on the rest of his project in earnest, mixing and hauling the concrete by himself. He was told repeatedly that sculpting in concrete was impossible, but he built armatures of steel rebar to support his structures, then finished them off with a mixture of plaster and white paint. Before he was finished, the owner of the land where he was working announced that he wanted to charge admission to the attraction. Martin didn't. In a fit of pique, he barged through his creations, smashing noses off the Apostles, Mary, and the Almighty himself. This wasn't a blind rage; Martin left Judas untouched, as a comment on the injustice he was suffering. The appendages were replaced, apparently when the property's owner backed off.

The back- and heartbreaking work took its toll, but Martin was able to realize his dream by the time he died, two days shy of Christmas in 1961, at the age of seventy-four. By then, the Scrooge-like owner of the property

seems to have faded from the picture, and Martin's statues passed to the Yucca Valley parks and recreation division. His legacy remains in ten biblical scenes scattered over three acres, between stands of Joshua trees and creosote bushes, and ever widening rivulets carved into the sandy soil by infrequent rains.

The largest group of statues depicts the Sermon on the Mount. The care that Martin invested in his creations is evident in the emotions sculpted into the figures. Some are obviously moved by the sermon, while others wear doubting or even hostile expressions. Closer inspection reveals the detail the artist put into his work: Hands are creased, waves of hair and cloth are sculpted to an astonishing degree.

The 1992 Landers earthquake was violent enough to destroy the west wall of the nearby Yucca Valley bowling alley and severely damage some of the statues at the park. Almost thirty years of vandals' work on the place combined with the harsh environment put Desert Christ Park in danger of closing for good. In a stunning case of pettiness, the ACLU brought suit in 1987 against San Bernardino County's use of public funds to maintain a religious landmark, which it had done to the tune of a paltry $4,000 a year since Martin's death. Concerned citizens formed the Desert Christ Foundation to look after the statues, but lacking significant contributions, Martin's legacy will, for the present, be left in a state of arrested decay.

From Interstate 10 take Highway 62 east to Yucca Valley. In Yucca Valley, turn left on Mohawk Trail and then right on Sunnyslope Drive. The park is on the left.

Palin' Around with My Buddy Jesus at Desert Christ Park

It's hard to tell if Desert Christ Park was intended to be a place of religious reflection, or campy Jesus kitsch. Every piece of evidence seemed to suggest that sculptor Antone Martin planned on constructing a place dedicated to, as the brochure reads, peace, tolerance, and love. But there's an eerie feel about the park that even the most reverential could not deny.

The creepiness may have to do in part with the fact that a 7.3 earthquake rattled the valley in 1992, causing a good bit of devastation. Heads and hands were violently shaken off the biblical figurines, exposing the rebar and steel skeletal remains.

The reinforced cement statues themselves are larger than life-size. (I'm making a guess here, although there is no historical evidence that suggests that Christ was taller than ten feet and weighed between 3 and 16 tons.) A few of the depictions of the New Testament represented are Jesus with outstretched arms, teaching his disciples during His Sermon on the Mount. The praying, pensive Jesus, in the Garden of Gethsemane, is particularly striking, complete with sleeping apostle statues a few feet away. But the pièce de resistance in this whole place is no doubt the Last Supper.

One hundred and twenty-five tons of concrete bas-relief, 20 feet tall and 30 feet wide, it's an interactive replica of da Vinci's *Last Supper,* with a square window cut out above the dinner table for the sole purpose of allowing tourists to pose with the giant alabaster Christ. It seems incredibly blasphemous at first, but it's impossible to resist the temptation to sling your arm around the Savior's shoulder and feel like the 13th apostle. Perhaps you'll playfully give Him the devil horns behind his head with your forefinger and pinky. Offer to pick up the check . . . don't worry, the waiter never appears, and that kind of stuff builds up heaven points. Your best bet to a spot inside the Pearly Gates might be tipping Jesus off to Judas's plans. "There he is, Lord. . . . There's the guy who's gonna rat You out to the Romans."

If you feel the slightest bit guilty or sacrilegious after spending your time in Desert Christ Park doing any of these things, don't worry. . . . He'll forgive you. It's what He does.
—Joe O.

Buddhist Disneyland

Hsi Lai Temple (Hsi Lai means "coming to the West") was completed in 1988 at a cost of $10 million. From the looks of the place, the Buddhists got every penny's worth. The area around the temple now commands exorbitant real estate prices, as living nearby is considered fantastically lucky. It is the largest Buddhist temple in the West and is the U.S. headquarters for the Taiwanese Fo Guang Shan sect. The complex stretches over fifteen acres and has more than 100,000 square feet of floor space, much of it covered in gold leaf. The Fo Guang Shan Buddha would most definitely approve; the Zen Buddha might not.

Neither would even want to know what happened during the 1996 presidential campaign. On April 29, during a swing through the city of Hacienda Heights to court the Chinese American vote, Al Gore met with the Venerable Master Hsing Yun, then head abbot of Hsi Lai. During the meeting, a group of monks and nuns, supposedly each making individual donations of their own money, gave what

amounted to $50,000 to the Democratic party.

A scandal erupted when the temple secretly reimbursed the acolytes, not only breaking the law but giving money to temple initiates who had taken vows of poverty. The funds had actually come, for the most part, from wealthier members of the congregation. Gore claimed to know nothing of these shenanigans, saying he had to visit the little boy's room and missed the dirty stuff. His chief fund-raiser, Maria Hsia, was later indicted on five counts of "conspiring to defraud the United States and causing the submission of false statements to the Federal Election Commission." Hsi Lai has, not surprisingly, taken on a less political face since then, or at least a lower profile.

The front entrance is surprisingly austere compared to the rest of the buildings. The paint on an elaborately carved gate has faded to muted colors, and the first temple building, called the Bodhisattva Hall, is large but only about thirty feet deep. A quick trip through the rear door leads to the central plaza, dominated by the main temple, which contains massive golden statues of three figures who achieved Buddhahood: the historical (Saykamuni), the Limitless Light (Amitabha), and the Healing (Bhaisajyaguru) Buddhas. Don't try to rub their bellies for good luck. Helpful "guides" will appear out of nowhere and take you to Buddha jail, or may just ask you to leave.

The rest of the grounds are covered with ornamentation; it appears that every available inch of space is used. Painted stone animals are scattered through the undergrowth, and seemingly hundreds of statues of some form of Buddha or priests or Bodhisattvas line the halls. Message boards announce Buddha Scouts outings and song competitions. There is an exhibit hall on the east side of the plaza that plays host to rotating art installations and a permanent collection of historical Buddhist artifacts.

It's the sort of ostentatious place your Granny would love. Take her to the gift shop for tea and the chance to buy a $500 statue of Kwan Yin. The Hsi Lai Temple is located at 3456 South Glenmark Drive in Hacienda Heights.

Don't Blame Us

We didn't make up the stuff that follows. But in traveling around our state, we couldn't help but notice that there are some rather randy things happening along our roadways, and we would be shirking our responsibility to report the weird and nothing but the weird if we didn't include them here. And to be honest, most of us harbor a juvenile sense of humor and prurient interest about such things, whether we admit it or not. Whether these roadside oddities make you blush or giggle, they are presented here in just good clean fun.

What the Train Saw

Laguna Niguel may be a part of ultraconservative Orange County, but at least once a year the citizens of this cautiously moderate town let their hair down. Or at least their pants.

It all started in 1979. K. T. Smith was celebrating his thirtieth birthday at the friendly local watering hole, Mugs Away Saloon. Mr. Smith, after a good deal of imbibing, encouraged his friends to walk the forty-some yards across the road and moon the passing Amtrak trains. Everyone who took Mr. Smith up on his offer was rewarded with free drinks for the rest of the night.

The following year more than fifty patrons decided to cheekily display their wares. Today, on the second Saturday of July, you can find more than three thousand people pressing their backsides against the chain-link fence that separates the railroad tracks from the street.

From infants to octogenarians, the fat and the thin, surfers and lawyers, all come to bare their butts during the annual good-natured tradition. CNN and the Travel Channel have covered the event, and the atmosphere of "Moon-Fest" has taken on almost Super Bowl–like proportions. Live bands play inside the bar, while outside, vendors are happy to sell you T-shirts commemorating the occasion or paint a little message on your bum to give the Amtrak passengers something to read during their commute.

Ordinarily, this type of behavior would not be tolerated in a town where $3 million will get you a modest-sized home with very little yard, but apparently both the sheriff's department and Amtrak are happy to turn the other cheek for the day.

Hanging the Amtrak Moon

If any of you have traveled by public transport recently, you'll probably have some understanding of at least one of the following two points:

a) A train or a bus that arrives on time is about as common as a five legged Panda-Dodo hybrid.

b) Many public transportation employees have something of the Dahmer (Jeffrey) about them.

The issue with public transportation is that it has a public image problem. In a nation obsessed with cars and air travel, it's hard to put faith in a service which many deem to be old fashioned, and inconvenient. But as transportation chiefs attempt to woo the public back onto buses and trains, things such as this probably won't help them earn the respect of the general public.

Every year people flock to Laguna Niguel in Orange County to participate in the Annual Mooning of Amtrak event. On the second Saturday of each July, an eager crowd of mooners synchronize belts and zippers and release their cheeks as Amtrak trains roar by.

After 8 pm you can witness another giant leap for mankind, when the "night mooning" session begins. People are encouraged to bring lanterns for the evening session, so that the bevy of backsides can be bathed in soft, warm light. Men and women are all welcome, and if you should fall asleep—don't worry. There's a good chance you'll wake up at the crack of Dawn.–*Dr. Wei, Ph.D.*

Baby Jane's Collectibles

Emilio Estevez does, but apparently Charlie Sheen does not. Gene Autry is a yes, while John Wayne is a no. Sean Connery has it, while successors Roger Moore, Timothy Dalton, and Pierce Brosnan do not. The elusive "it" in question is gay cachet, and not every Tinseltown leading man has "it."

What makes some heterosexual celebrities gay icons, while others are just ho-hum hunks? No one knows the answer to that, but the owners of Baby Jane's Collectibles certainly can tell you which beefcake photos sell like hotcakes and which sit on the shelf collecting dust. If you want a pinup shot of almost any male celebrity from Buster Crabbe to Tom Cruise, it's a good bet this place has it. If they don't, it doesn't exist.

From the obvious naked celeb shots (Burt Reynolds in *Cosmopolitan*) to the confusing (a scantily clad fat-ass senior citizen Marlon Brando), Baby Jane will no doubt be able to fulfill your particular, and perhaps peculiar, peccadillo.

Of course, they don't cater only to gay men. There are many snapshots of Hollywood's leading women. Agnes Moorehead, Jodi Foster, Joan Crawford, Liza Min-. . . who are we kidding? This place is pretty gay. Not that there's anything wrong with that.

But there are straight items on sale. Film buffs will find rare original movie posters and costumes, wigs, and accoutrements worn by some of the silver screen's biggest stars. (They have sold the original cowl worn by Michael Keaton in the movie *Batman,* as well as Arnold Schwarzenegger's jockstrap from the film *Running Man.*) This place is very well known in celebrity circles, and it's not surprising to see icons of yesteryear (Julie Newmar) or even today's headline grabbers (Courtney Love) browsing in the boutique. One customer confided in me that he was shopping when Jean Claude Van Damme came in, curious to see if his photographs sold well. They apparently did not. We are not sure what conclusion to draw from that.

Gay or straight, man or woman, if you're a sucker for genuine movie and/or television memorabilia, you can't go wrong by coming out to Baby Jane's, on 7985 Santa Monica Boulevard in West Hollywood. It's simply fabulous.

This One's for the Girls

Not many of the town's 15,000 residents are aware of its existence, but Ukiah boasts a commemorative memorial to the city's streetwalkers of the past.

The Prostitute Plaque is located on the corner of West Church and South State streets in front of what was a thriving brothel from 1890 till 1915. The venture did so well, in fact, that when the entire block of businesses was burned down in 1899, the first building to be reconstructed was the local cathouse.

Sometime in the late 1970s, Ted Feibush, a prominent town contractor, bought the property (the actual house having been long ago torn down) and subsequently learned the history of the place. In a tongue-in-cheek acknowledgment to the previous endeavor, Feibush had a plaque made and installed, without bothering to mention it to the Ukiah Chamber of Commerce. The plaque poetically reads TO THE LADIES OF THE NIGHT WHO PLIED THEIR TRADE UPON THIS SITE.

The Fountain of What?

I thought you might appreciate this photo of the new fountain at the Marriott/Heavenly Valley Gondola in South Lake Tahoe. You know, 2000 years from now some archaeologist will dig this up and tell the world it was a fertility rite statue. People will visit from all over the world to see it and wonder à la Stonehenge. It needs to go in the What The Hell Were You Thinking? File.

I spent the summer having fun, being juvenile, and trying to name it — here are a few examples:

Inspiration Point
Fountain o' Freud
The Mountin' Fountain

And my personal favorite:
The Wonderous Water Wang
of the Woods

I know there have to be more easy shots at this, but to quote Mark Twain "I shall draw the curtain of charity over this scene!" *—Cheers, Barbara Bastrup*

What the Heck Is THAT ?

Some things we see along the road just seem to shout questions at us, like "why?" and "what?" As in "WHY is that thing there?" and "WHAT was that person thinking?" These are the places that we refer to as head-scratchers. Sometimes the reasons such sites exist turn out to actually be quite logical or even mundane upon closer examination. But at first glance, these roadside oddities will no doubt cause you to raise an eyebrow and ask, "What the heck is THAT?"

Shoe Tree in the Park

Rumor has it that the first pair of shoes were tossed up into the branches during the celebration of a hole in one that decided a particularly close match of Frisbee golf. Little by little, other shoes started appearing on the lifeless limbs of a dead tree on Morley Field Disc Golf Course. In the mid-'80s, the city of San Diego decided to chop down the tree, but the course pro had taken a special liking to it because he considered it crucial to the design of hole number two.

Convincing a number of friends to decorate it with their old tennies and cleats, he then phoned the local newspaper, telling the reporter that the city was going to do away with the "world famous Shoe Tree." The story, along with photographs of the tree—now blooming with old shoes—ran the following day. For some reason, the city was deluged with pleading phone calls and letters to save the tree.

Regardless of how the sneakers first found their way up there, the Shoe Tree in Balboa Park is now legitimately famous and the home of hundreds of pairs of active footwear from all over the world. As we said, we don't make this stuff up.

Skeletons in the Closet

You're heading to Los Angeles on a business trip. Your wife may ask you to grab a little memento of your sojourn from one of the ritzy high-priced jewelry stores along Rodeo Drive. Your kids may beg you to bring them some mouse ears from the Magic Kingdom. Friends may ask for Angelina Jolie's phone number. But you're hanging with a distinctively different crowd if anyone requests a DOA toe-tag key chain from the L.A. coroner's office.

Fear not, because if that appeal is made, it—and many more ghoulish requests—can be granted.

It started as an office gag, and if one works in a coroner's office, office gags will have a decided flavor of gallows humor. Secretary Marilyn Lewis presented a T-shirt of a police chalk body outline, which read L.A. CORONER'S OFFICE, to

one of the doctors. The shirt was such a hit with the staff that it was suggested they print up some shirts, do up a few coffee mugs for good measure, and send the proceeds along to programs like Scared Straight to help the youth of Los Angeles stay out of trouble. That was 1992, and today, undoubtedly with the help of the Internet and high-profile celebrity homicide trials, the L.A. Coroner's Gift Shop brings in close to $300,000 annually.

So forget expensive jewelry, or the tchotchkes and knickknacks at big-name amusement parks. Give them something they'll never forget: merchandised death.

Whether you're in the market for beach towels, videos of gruesome local murders, body bag luggage, or the new one hundred percent cotton ladies V neck complete with embroidered L.A. coroner's seal, this is the one-stop shopping place for all your loved ones.

The L.A. Coroner's Gift Shop, a.k.a. Skeletons In The Closet, is located inside the coroner's building, 1104 North Mission Road. Hours are 8:30–4:30 weekdays, or you can purchase goods online at www.lacoroner.com/signpost.htm. Shop 'til you drop (dead).

Toad Hollow

It's not hard to see why the rest of the country takes the occasional potshot at the Golden State. The former mayor of Davis, Julie Partansky, is remembered as one of the state's more colorful elected officials. One of her soundest ideas was using taxpayer dollars to plant fruit trees on public property so "the homeless can graze on them." She once refused to fill in a severe pothole, because it had been there for such a long time. She suggested it be declared a historic landmark.

But the controversial artist-politician will not be best remembered for any of those proposals, memorable though they may be. Her legacy will undoubtedly be Toad Hollow.

Located just to the highway side of the town's post office, Toad Hollow is a $30,000 miniature toad city, complete with small buildings, a tiny toad outhouse, and cute little *Wind in the Willows*–style paintings of cartoon toads waving through their petite cartoon windows. A sign that reads TOAD HOLLOW clearly lets the affable amphibians know that they are close to the government-financed toad tunnel, specially designed to allow them safe passage under the busy thoroughfare.

Apparently, the one issue Mayor Partansky failed to factor in was that toads don't read English. There is still no shortage of splattered toad guts on the road in Davis.

One can't help but wonder: If Partansky were still in office, would she have championed some sort of toad literacy campaign to prevent such senseless tragedies? Fortunately for northern Californians, hope springs eternal for just that kind of forward-leaping thought.

Roads Less Traveled

No *matter what part* of our state you call home, there always seem to be certain roads that are not quite right. These strange byways possess a special kind of aura that sets them apart from other, ordinary, streets. Throughout California, we find supposedly cursed thoroughfares, mysterious bridges in the middle of nowhere, and inclined grades where the laws of gravity just don't apply. Over the generations, tales of the strange things that happen on these bizarre byways have become part of our state's local lore.

The mind can play tricks, though, and it may be that there is nothing scary to be found on these roads at all. It could be that they merely serve as a conduit, a pathway to our own innermost demons. It's undeniable that many of the tales told about these places reflect archetypal nightmare imagery such as ghosts, wild and ferocious animals, and evil cultists huddled around sacrificial bonfires. These nameless creatures may be the product of our own subconscious. If that is so, then a trip down one of these fabled paths may be for some a journey of profound self-discovery.

Of course, there is a case to be made for traveling such roads purely for the thrill of scaring the wits out of yourself and your friends. Who among us can say that at some time, perhaps in our teenage years, we didn't pile into an overcrowded car and set off to some allegedly haunted nightspot? Jaunts such as these usually build to a fever pitch before the intended destination is even reached, and that overanticipation alone might cause them to see apparitions.

Whether these roads are actually the epicenter of hyper-mystical activities, merely favorite destinations for rowdy nocturnal joyriders, or perhaps a little of both is open for debate. Whatever they are, one fact is indisputable. Winding through our state are many lonely roads that possess some kind of indefinable yet undeniable power.

Weird Encounters on Black Star Canyon Road—Irvine

It seems that the very moniker Black Star long ago destined this place to inspire unease. The name was derived innocently enough from the Black Star Mining Company, which started operations here when a coal deposit was discovered in the canyon in 1878. Elsewhere in the area are the remains of an Indian settlement with ancient metate grinding holes and fire rings.

Black Star Canyon is listed as a nice day hike in the Orange County register of parks, but of course the recreation department doesn't readily admit to the strange goings-on in this tree- and brush-choked canyon. Sometime in the last few decades, squatters moved in, and the authorities seemed content to let them stay. Today, however, reports from hikers and mountain bikers sound like something out of *Deliverance*. A toothless, bearded character called Black Star Bill accosts "trespassers" on the fire road and chases them away, and assorted crazies roam the area with shotguns and a mean look in their eyes. One mountain biker warned visitors not to park at the fire road gate, lest they return to slashed tires and smashed windows.

Robert Lawrence went hunting in Black Star when he was a teenager in 1995 and provided this chilling account:

We got very scared and headed for the car. Before we got there, we looked up at an exposed area on the side of the canyon, and both of us saw a sight I will never forget.

We both saw the same thing: a group of some kind of creatures walking together. They were all black, and seemed almost to walk in formation. We both were reminded of penguins by the way they walked. One peculiar thing was that the whole group moved in perfect unison. They headed down the hillside a ways, and stopped. After a brief interval, they all headed down the hill and stopped again.

I estimate the height of these things to have been about two feet tall, with an outline that suggested an upright creature, like a penguin or something. I know it sounds bizarre, but that is what they looked like. We were stupefied. After watching these things a while, one of us finally said that they were after us and that we had to get out of there. We then ran to the car, fearing for our lives.

But the game was not up when we got to the car. When my friend tried to start it, nothing happened. He turned the key a few times, but nothing. Finally, it turned over once or twice, and a loud popping noise came from the engine compartment, followed by black smoke that drifted up from under the hood. At this point, we were almost beside ourselves with fear. We opened the hood and looked at the engine, but there was no fire, and nothing looked amiss. We then tried it again, and it started.

Black Star Squatters Don't Like Company

From the gate, ride about one mile on semi-paved road. You will come to a fork, marked by a septic tank. Stop here, rest, drop off the kids, whatever. The important thing is that the next stretch is a sprint. Head right, sprint past the house on the right! These are squatters; they DO NOT LIKE VISITORS! Most times they have a roadblock set up. Just get past them before they come out and throw things at you.—*Anonymous*

Release the Hounds!

I would be careful, because when we got to the house on the right, they let these dogs go and they chased us all the way back to our cars.—*Britney*

The Vanishing Car of Black Star

Me and my friends went up to Black Star to see if all the scary stories were true. We arrived at the trail at eight at night. All fearing the worst, none of us wanted to get out of the car. After a couple of trips back, we saw something weird. As we were driving to the RV area, a car stopped a couple yards behind us. Feeling that something strange was going on, we turned back. Coming back, the car continued its route as soon as it saw our headlights. Wanting to know where this strange car was going, we did a U-turn and followed it. We must have been no more than six yards behind it when all of a sudden it vanished and tire marks were apparent on the road. Scared, we turned back and went home.—*Tescano*

Beware the Black Star Toothless

I have run into different guys that had guns and thought it would be fun to shoot off a few over our heads. This happened only once, but don't go alone. Watch out for the Toothless. . . . Park outside the gates, never inside if they are open. Head up past the house on the right fast and silently. They're not squatters, but have lived there for a long time and are armed with shotguns!!! Beware.—*Madjax*

Witchcraft and Worse, Under the Stars

There are stories of weird things that happen on the Black Star Canyon Road in Tustin—stories of witchcraft under the stars and KKK rituals. I went there on my prom night and was scared out of my mind. It was pitch-black there. I couldn't see a thing. I saw a tree off the road, painted half black and the other half white, as well as a halfway underground church.

My friend and his buddy went there another time. There is an opening in the fence, somewhere off the road, that reveals a trail. The trail leads to an abandoned campfire where the suspected rituals take place. When I went, there was still smoke coming from the fire. I had seven friends with me. We got scared and ran back to the car. When my friend went, he claimed that he was chased by a gang of guys on motorcycles. They found a cave and hid from the gang. He still says it really happened. My friend is the kind of person that would admit a joke after a few minutes. It's been three years and he still sticks to his story.—*Alex*

Animals Act Human in Black Star Canyon

There is a story about the Indians who used to live in the back hills of Orange. They say the Indians were all massacred late in the night by Spanish soldiers. Now people say that there are angry spirits and when you walk along Black Star Canyon Road you feel as if someone is watching you.

One day after eating dinner with some friends, we were talking about Black Star, so we all drove out to the canyon. We parked our cars on the side of the road because the entrance to the canyon is blocked so you have to walk to get in. We were there for no more than 30 minutes, and it started to feel as if we were being watched, so we made it to the beginning of this small hill and then we heard this noise. It sounded like heavy thumping in the ground like someone was bouncing a basketball on a sidewalk. Then up this hill we saw this dark figure making its way down to us. We all freaked out and ran out of there as fast as we could. On the way out in our car, we felt like something was watching us leave the canyon. It was very creepy.

People have said that the animals act as if they are humans, making odd noises. They act like they are immortal—nothing hurts some of them. The crows will follow you. Local legend also says that there are devil worshippers who roam in the canyon road and there are homemade NO TRESPASSING signs at the beginning of some trails.—*Pamela S. Richardson*

Night Ride on Black Star Road

This story is about Black Star Canyon Road in southern California. In order to get there, you would have to keep driving down Chapman until you pass the redneck houses, then drive for miles until you reach a barren area at the foot of the hills. At that point, the road will have slimmed down to barely a two-way street.

One late night, a carload of us went driving down there because we had heard about Black Star from so many people. It wasn't the driver's first time, so he knew his way around. So we kept driving and driving, anticipating any weird things we might come across. The headlights were the only source of light for miles. The closer to the mountains we got, the more visible a large white cross embossed on the mountain became. Supposedly, that's a mark of the KKK Klansmen, who have their headquarters there.

Not really paying attention to which way we were going, we ended up going down a street that led farther into the canyon. Because we were on edge, we couldn't help but pay attention to the small details of our surroundings. I noticed that the trees were moving a LOT more than they should be. There was no wind that chilly summer night. It was as if people were running alongside us to catch up with us and as an effect, the branches close to eye level were shaking really violently. My cousin floored it and we couldn't make a U-turn anywhere. We kept going and going and in some parts of the woods, it was really terrifying. We reached the end of the road and there was enough dirt at the shoulders to make a U-turn, finally.

Mid-U-turn, we acknowledged that there was a noose hanging above the ground and it looked like it had been there for a while. It wasn't over a platform or anything. We lowered our tinted windows to get a better look and noticed a very strong burning smell, like something was on fire. None of us could identify the smell. We pulled out of there so fast and didn't even slow down for the little rabbits that would dart across the road every other mile or so.

In order to get back to the actual Black Star Road, we had to cross over a small, feeble bridge that rested over the dead and shallow canyon. Just after we crossed, my cousin saw a big black coal rock next to the damaged BLACK STAR street sign. It was so out of place and stood out so my cousin made my sister get out of the car and pick it up because he wanted to take it home. He asked me first but I couldn't even move because I was so scared. There was no way I was getting out.

After that, he had the worst luck. He lost his apartment, his girlfriend dumped him, and big problems surfaced at his work. Plus, his mom got really sick, all within a week. After he took the rock back to where he found it, everything seemed to go back to normal.—*Beebee Agache*

The Batty Bridge

Most folks think bat colonies reside in dank caves far from civilization, but the furry flying mammals often make do with anything that looks promising. Up Santiago Canyon Road toward Black Star Canyon, an unused concrete bridge spans the blacktop just after the exit for Irvine Lake. Built as a temporary thoroughfare for construction, the bridge was on the brink of destruction when it was discovered that a colony of Mexican free-tailed bats had made their summer home and nursery beneath the span. A stay of demolition was issued in April 2004, and four months later Orange County supervisor Bill Campbell moved to have the structure set aside as a permanent bat roost and part of a backcountry trail system.

The bridge is the only one over the road and is easy to spot. Some 1,500 bats make their home here from spring through late fall, when they migrate south. It's hard to believe the cute little critters can get a good day's sleep with choppers and diesel trucks roaring past every few minutes, but they seem content to chitter and chirp away in the crevices running under the bridge. Look for two wide lines of guano marking the road and watch out, lest you get hit with bat pee. Black Star Canyon Road is reached by exiting the Costa Mesa Toll Road (Highway 55) at Santiago Canyon Road. Turn left at Silverado Canyon Road.

The Curse of Pacheco Pass

Take extreme care when seeing this Santa Clara County mountain pass by car. It's one of the deadliest stretches of highway in California. Drivers usually blame the hazards on the winding, hill-shadowed road that links Highways 5 and 101 and bottlenecks the traffic going either way. But there may be a spookier explanation for the road's numerous accidents and near misses.

Long before road rage became a pervasive syndrome of our auto-based society, Pacheco Pass had a reputation for provoking unexplained paranoia and violence from drivers. Highway patrolmen who cruised the pass had broken up many bumper-tagging wars and roadside fist-fights, and ticketed countless kamikaze-like drivers who tore through heavy traffic at suicidal speeds. It seemed as if people were afraid of the pass and wanted to get out of it as quickly as possible, back to the safety of the big interstates.

Writing about Pacheco Pass in *Haunted Houses of California,* Antoinette May said that she and other "sensitives" had experienced intense feelings of panic, menace, and dread there. They also had visions of marauding Indians and bloody battles between Hispanic and American settlers.

Ms. May wrote that after she had a particularly traumatic experience in the pass, she looked into the area's history. Throughout most of the nineteenth century, Pacheco Pass was the scene of tremendous violence among those who wanted to claim the territory as their own. Highway robberies and public hangings were also rife there in the old days. The turbulent region might have absorbed what ghost hunters call an "energy implant," a sort of negative emotional and spiritual residue left over from the bloodshed and tragedy that racked the land.

Whether caused by ghosts, a curse, an energy implant, or just the linking of two huge freeways with a narrow passage, the wild ride through Pacheco Pass is a grim reminder of the violent, dangerous emotions that can break out even in our laid-back state.

Phantom Indians Still Battle on Whitney Portal Road

Here, in the shadow of Mount Whitney in Lone Pine, lie the Alabama Hills, a range of red sandstone cliffs and crags often used as the backdrop for western movies. The setting is highly appropriate for Hollywood's frontier epics. In the late 1860s, the region was torn apart by battles between white settlers and Paiute Indians. The army was called in and its camp in the Alabama Hills, at what is now Whitney Portal Road, was attacked several times by the infuriated Native Americans.

In the 1960s, a woman living on the road, who had never heard of the region's bloody history, was preparing dinner one evening when she heard gunfire coming from a nearby creek. Looking out the kitchen window, she saw a black man dressed as an Indian warrior. He glanced back at her for a moment, then shouldered his rifle and

looked forward. Several Indian companions near him, crouching behind a fallen tree, fired their rifles and fell back to reload.

The battle raged on for about fifteen minutes, yet not one bullet hit the woman's house. Then, all of a sudden, the Indians disappeared and the air was silent. The woman rushed to her neighbors' house with the story. They believed her, having heard similar stories about phantom skirmishes along the road.

Records show that the spot where the Indians stood had witnessed countless ambushes and firefights between natives and the U.S. Army. As for the spectral black Indian, he was probably one of the many ex-slaves who had joined the native tribes, preferring their way of life to that of the "civilized" whites.

Bridge to Nowhere

Rising out of nothingness in the great voids of the Azusa Canyons is a weird structure that has come to be called the Bridge to Nowhere. An account of the oddball history behind this strange bridge can be found posted on the Internet by Christopher Earls Brennen at www.dankat.com/mstory/wild.htm. It reads:

The Bridge to Nowhere is one of the most bizarre artifacts to be found in the San Gabriel Mountains. Back in the 1920s, Los Angeles County planned to build a highway all the way up the East Fork canyon to the Mine Gulch Junction. From there the road would climb over Blue Ridge and drop down into Wrightwood. It would be among the most scenic roads in America. Construction began in 1929, most of the work being done by County prison work crews. By the mid-1930s the highway had reached The Narrows (2800 ft) where the East Fork flows through a very deep gorge, the deepest in Southern California. There it was necessary to construct a concrete bridge high above the waters of the gorge. A tunnel was also chiselled out of sheer rock. However, the winter after this difficult construction task had been completed, an unprecedented storm arrived on March 1–2, 1938, depositing many inches of rain on the San Gabriel Mountains. The result was a tremendous flood that roared down the East Fork, obliterating everything in its path including more than five miles of the painstakingly constructed highway. Only the bridge was high enough above the waters to be virtually untouched. The futility of the project having been so emphatically demonstrated, the County abandoned their plans leaving a brand new concrete road bridge standing alone in the middle of the wilderness more than five miles from the nearest highway. It became a popular destination for hikers who dubbed it the "Bridge to Nowhere."

Going Nowhere on the Bridge to Nowhere

In Azusa Canyons, famous for dead body Mafia drop-offs, cults— you name it—lies the Bridge to Nowhere. It's located by a four to six hour hike up a river after the end of the East Fork Road cul-de-sac. The bridge is a full-on cement monster with two supposed tunnels on opposing sides that conjoin two hillsides. How far the tunnels go into the hillside I cannot say. What is known is that for the amount it cost to build the monster it seems weird that there are no roads leading to or from it. Many roads travel through the canyon, but little by little they are being shut down to cars. Hikes and bikes are still allowed for those who are daring enough.

There is a road that was closed off very early due to rains and rockslides that are common in this canyon. This road, called Shoemaker, might have been the road that led to the Bridge to Nowhere. Other roads, like Azusa itself, hold greater mystery. A boulder trashed Azusa Canyon road at its highest point, and it has been swallowed into the road, creating a blocked single lane nightmare. Many of the roads in this canyon are open only seasonally because of rockslides, and many people die here each year. The canyon is vast enough that the bodies can never be found. The whole area is laced with secrets and unexplained mysteries.

We departed East Fork cul-de-sac at 10:48 for our rough trip to the Bridge to Nowhere. Both my friend the Pharmer and I knew we were in for a little bit of a hike as we traveled over a river, rocks large and small, trails, and steep cliffs. The bridge itself is five miles into the canyon; however, the many obstacles that lie in your way make this trip a treacherous seven miles over severe terrain. It was much longer and more exhausting than either of us would have thought, and with just two beers, a bag of pretzels, and one canteen of water, the sun was wasting us. The longer we traveled the more our thirst grew. You don't just go to the Bridge to Nowhere and take pictures of yourself next to it to look cool. You're beaten to a pulp upon arrival, and the return trip is twice as exhausting if you go back the same way you came.

One of the things about this exhausting trip is once you are on the bridge all your problems—everything that you struggle with in your life—seem small, and anything seems possible. This feeling of accomplishment is difficult to describe.

This edge goes on for about another 400 feet on a narrow path to a severe steep gorge. Standing on the bridge it's about a three, maybe four-hundred-foot drop. The gorge is narrow and the only way to continue on the road would be to tunnel.

This image is just an example of the terrain on the way to the bridge. It severely differs from paths, to depleted road segments, to large rounded rocks, to small paths, to strong current rivers.—*Paintchips*

Gravity Hills

Debate rages among believers and skeptics about the phenomenon of "gravity hills"—where cars placed in neutral seemingly roll up the slope. Scores of these roadbed oddities are located in California; one is probably near you. Locals and visitors pepper the locations with stories of tragedy that just ratchet the weirdness up a few notches.

Among the numerous mystery hills that dot this great land is the Santa Cruz Mystery Spot, located on a steep hillside in the mountains east of this beachside town. Former FBI special agent Walter Bosley says that the place was a favorite with the Russian agents and mafiosos he was assigned to follow. We didn't see anyone with Russian accents at the gravity hills we tested, but perhaps it's just a matter of time before secret meetings and deals are consecrated in cars slowly rolling up hills in remote locales. One of the most persistent legends associated with many of the hills is the "school bus tragedy." "Katie" relates the typical story on the message board of the Web site www.thelighthouseonline.com:

> I live in Southern California and there is a "Gravity Hill" in Moorpark. The story goes that a group of kids were on a school bus going on a field trip when the bus suddenly broke down. Some of the kids decided to get out and push the bus up the hill but when they did it rolled back and crushed them killing them instantly. Now when you park your car there supposedly the kids push you up the hill.

On the same Web page, "Darryl" posted a different version of the school bus tale, centered on another gravity hill near Livermore:

> Not so long ago, there was a bus filled with 5th graders on the way down Patterson Pass to drop off a child at his house down the road. Their bus got stuck going up the hill, so the kids got out to push. The gravity forced the bus backwards, and before the kids knew it, they were crushed. There is a road farther down named after the children, the road name is "Don't Forget Us." You can check that out, too.

A fun way to test the theory of the helpful children has been making the rounds for years. Dust the rear, or front—depending on the direction of roll—of the car with baby powder or flour before the emergency brake is released. The legend says that fingerprints will show up. These are supposed to be the prints left by children from beyond who are trying to save you from a fiery fate. (We tried this and found only our own prints on the car. But maybe we just don't have the right mojo.)

Party poopers have an explanation for the antigravity hills. A few have actually examined the mounds with carpenters' levels, topographical maps, and even laser beams. They contend that the effect is an illusion caused by the lack of visual cues, or the presence of erroneous ones, that usually tell us when we are going up or down. "Gravitational anomalies," they say, "are almost always located in areas where the horizon is obscured, and trees or other objects in the area are not exactly vertical." This seemingly reassuring explanation does nothing to prepare one for the real experience.

Southern California's gravity hills are many, and *Weird California* has tested three that seem to work. Remember to try this early in the morning or very late at night when traffic is light and you may be less likely to encounter other drivers—or the police, who apparently frown on this sort of recreation for some reason, but that's their job.

San Diego: Sorrento Drive exit from Interstate 5 south. Stop at the light. Your car will move backward up the hill.

La Jolla: West Muirlands Drive between Nautilus Street and Fay Street. The best effect was found when traveling west from Nautilus to Fay. Once you are on Muirlands, there is a sharp curve to the left. Shortly after this, stop and line up your right-rear tire with the telephone pole on the side of the street (the pole with three yellow reflective strips). Car rolls uphill. This street is quite busy during the day; be extra cautious.

Altadena: Exit Lake Avenue north from Route 134. Right at East Altadena Drive, left on Porter, then uphill to East Loma Alta Drive and go left again. After a couple of dips, the road curves to the right and a flood-control spillway appears on the left. Stop in front of the first house at the right. Car rolls backward uphill. (The same effect can be observed on the other side of the street, but it is not as pronounced. The strange thing about this is that there are not nearly as many visual clues in this direction!)

Los Angeles Gravity Road

I live in LA, and I just went to a gravity hill we have around here a couple nights ago. It's near Moorpark Community College. The story goes that in the 1940s a school bus was taking some kids to school when the bus broke down. The 6th grade kids were waiting behind the bus in the shade for someone to come to fix it or tow it or something like that. Apparently, one of the farmers who lived around there came driving down the road in his truck not paying any attention at all, and ended up running into the kids so that they were pinned between his truck and the bus. Now, when you go to the bottom of the hill in the road and put your car in neutral, you'll be pushed forward uphill. Legend is that it's the kids pushing you out of the way before the farmer can run you over.—*Christine*

San Diego's Gravity Road

A group of friends and I went to an off ramp on Sorrento Rd. Drive South. We stopped at the streetlight at the bottom and we tried the stalled car trick. We had heard all the different legends about the place so we tried it. The weird thing was it really worked. We started to move back up the road! —*Jennifer*

Gravity Hill Is All an Illusion

San Diego's Gravity Road is actually in Spring Valley, about 20 miles east of San Diego. You can't notice the illusion any longer since homes were built, but I live there and checked it out many times. Very cool, as long as you looked toward the hill. If you looked backwards you knew it was just an illusion. The name of the street is La Presa, on the SE side of Dictionary Hill.—*John W. Cavoulas*

Handprints in the Baby Powder

There is a Gravity Point in San Bernardino County. I have friends who have tried it and they say it works. The story is the same premise as the bus and the farmer who hit it, but it is railroad tracks, and supposedly when you put baby powder or dust on your rear bumper, you will see little handprints in it after being "pushed" onto the tracks.—*Jennifer McClure*

Mr. Toad's Wild Ride on Gravity Hill

Gravity Hill is located in Altadena, tucked away in the hills that are the entrance to a winding drive that us kids used to call Mr. Toad's Wild Ride. The twists and sharp turns made Mr. Toad's a great place for those of us with fresh drivers' licenses to haul ass through with reckless abandon. Gravity Hill is the area just before a rickety bridge that makes a great setting for an urban legend. On the hill before the bridge, you put your car in neutral and the car will mysteriously travel backwards up the hill at about two miles an hour. This is great fun when showing out-of-towners around the Pasadena/Altadena area. Of course with anything as amazing as our Gravity Hill, which is known mostly to local youngsters, there is a legend associated with it.

This road was used back in the day by people who'd travel in their horse-drawn carriages and such. An old Indian man was crossing the bridge and cornered too fast causing him to crash into the side of the bridge and plummet to his death in the shallow riverbed below. Legend has it that his restless spirit remains, to prevent such an untimely death from happening to anyone else who crosses this bridge. His spirit pulls you back up the hill to prevent you from going too fast around the curve and crashing to your death.

Well, as with any legend, there are many inconsistencies to this story, and to be completely honest, that last sentence I made up because the details on the last part were extremely fuzzy.

The entrance to Mr. Toad's is off of Loma Alta Drive, the 1200 East Block, between the Rubio Crest Drive and Sunny Oak Circle. Twilight at Gravity Hill is wonderfully eerie and creepy. Especially the area over the bridge where the Indian man supposedly died.—*Theodora Kelly*

More Push-Me-Pull-You Places to Check Out

Just to drive home the point of how widespread and pervasive gravity roads are throughout the state, here are just a few letters that we've received from readers telling us about their favorite antigravity locales:

Antioch

Cars are pushed uphill while sitting near a spot on Empire Mine Road. Supposedly, a school bus crashed here, and the ghosts of the children who died in the accident are responsible for the gravity defiance.—*Erika S.*

Corona

A broken-hearted girl was driving on Lichau Road just after being dumped by her boyfriend. In her rage she drove recklessly, hit a bump, followed by a tree, and died. Now those who place their cars in neutral on this bump are pushed away from the tree by her ghost. Look for the sign marked SANTIAGO as your starting point.—*Rachel T.*

Devore

One hundred yards beyond a set of train tracks on Glen Helen Road is a STOP sign. Cars on the hill leading up to this STOP sign roll uphill instead of down. This is the work of the ghosts of six children who died on the road.—*Kevin McCauley*

Jamul

In the San Diego suburb of Jamul, where I come from, there is a story that a school bus full of children was struck by a train sometime in the 1950s. Now, when one parks their car on the tracks, childish screams and laughter can be heard. Oftentimes, people say that they have been pushed backwards off the tracks by some unseen force.—*Jose Z.*

Moreno Valley

Motorists taking the Nason Street overpass south find that they are mysteriously pushed up the overpass when in neutral. This is said to be caused by the ghosts of children who were hit by a large truck there. Also in Moreno Valley is Priest Hill. It's said that on a lonely, dark night a priest broke down here and was struck and killed by a passing car. Now he pushes cars up the hill where he died—sometimes they'll even find his handprints on their car afterwards.—*Shaun B.*

San Bernardino

Motorists who take Old Waterman Canyon Road off of Route 18, also known as Rim of the World Drive, have experienced a gravity-defying phenomenon. Putting a car in neutral on the first small bridge will cause the car to roll backwards uphill. Me and my friends have tried it ourselves on many occasions and it really works!—*Jared R.*

Whittier

Turnbull Canyon Road is the supposed home of Satanic cults as well as a hotspot for UFO sightings. Motorists sometimes hear strange knocking sounds around their cars. Even more common are reports that placing your car in neutral on a certain hill on the road will cause your car to roll backwards uphill.
—*Samantha Quinn*

Twisting and Turning on Snake Road

The helpful Sanger police officer set us straight right off: "It's called Snake Road because of the twists and turns. It's actually named Channel Road." When asked about the haunting we'd heard of, he claimed to know nothing about it, but added that this didn't stop those pesky kids from racing up and down at all hours of the night and generally causing a ruckus and headaches for the cops. He gave exact directions to the area and wished us luck. He didn't know if anyone had been killed in a wreck there.

If the officer had checked the records, he might have encountered the story of a woman who somehow lost control of her car and plunged into the Kings River sometime in the not too distant past. The woman drowned, and her two daughters, riding in the back seat, were swept farther downstream in the car by the raging currents and also perished. Now she is said to wander the road at night, moaning and calling for her lost children. La Llorona, the old Hispanic tale of the crying woman who haunts the banks of creeks and rivers, is given a new twist.

Channel Road is not easy to find, even with directions. This country lane begins innocently enough among swaying eucalyptus trees and neatly planted orange groves at the intersection with Annadale Avenue, but soon devolves into a nightmare of hairpin turns that would tax the most sober of drivers.

The most confusing aspect about the drowned woman story is that the Kings River is not exactly next to Channel Road. There are vast sewage treatment ponds and marshes along its lower reaches, and the channel that gives the road its name appears to have been long ago hidden behind long, chain-link fences. About two miles farther east from the Channel intersection, Annadale Avenue does indeed cross the river, and perhaps the ghostly wanderer is looking in an area where her daughters may have been washed ashore downstream.

Although the road is not especially ominous during daylight hours, we did spot something bizarre and disturbing near the southern end of the street. Someone had killed two huge crows and tied them to a fence at eye level, with their wings spread and heads twisted. Whether this was part of some elaborate ritual, a warning to other crows, or a macabre teenage prank was not clear, but the creep-out factor was suddenly palpable. Across the street was a house with old cars on the lawn and scores of cheap plastic toys strewed about the yard—not really a place to arrive unannounced to ask about ghastly crow mutilations.

Saved by the Spirit of Snake Road

My ghostly encounter happened last year. One day my cousins told me about a road that was believed to be haunted. It was located in Sanger.

I'll admit I was a little intrigued but also very skeptical. After much pleading and begging by my cousins, my friend and I said we would drive them down it. We set off about 9:00 p.m. After about an hour of driving, low on gas, and frustrated about not being able to find the road, we decided to head home. It was at that point that I realized I had no idea where I was. I figured that since I lived south of Sanger I would take a road that went in that direction. I turned onto the first street that I came upon.

We were on the road for approximately two minutes when my cousin, who had fallen asleep in the back, suddenly woke up. She started whimpering at first, saying she was scared and wanted to go home. A few moments later she began yelling and screaming for us to hurry up and get out of where we were. I assured her that's what we were trying to do, but there was no calming her down. I sped up and was going probably about 65 mph on this dark country road. Up ahead about fifty yards in front of us I saw this small patch of fog. I say fog; my friend says it was an apparition. I slowed down as I came closer to it, but as I got closer, it began to evaporate. By the time I came up on it I was probably going about 15 mph. By the time I reached it, it had gone. I was about to speed up when I noticed a faded sign that said DANGEROUS CURVES AHEAD, a sign that I probably would not have seen if I had continued at the rate of speed I was going. In the back of my mind I thought, Could this be Snake Road? But quickly dismissed the thought because the road so far had been pretty straight. But the sign didn't lie. About 1/4 mile up ahead I suddenly came upon a series of sharp, twisting turns. This went on for about three miles when the road finally straightened out.

I drove about another two miles, then noticed some blinking red lights up ahead. I told my friend to look and see if the street name was visible and maybe we could have some idea where we were. I'll never forget the look on her face when we got close enough for her to see the sign. All the color seemed to have drained from her face. She said . . . you guessed it . . . the road was Channel Road.

I am skeptical no more. I do believe wholeheartedly that the apparition we saw was that of the young mother. And I do not believe she was there to scare us but quite the contrary. I do believe she saved our lives. Because had she not appeared before us I would not have slowed down but would have continued at the high rate of speed that I was going. I would have missed the faded sign and would have come upon the dangerous curves at breakneck speed. And may have suffered the same fate as this young woman and her two daughters.—*Tara Fletcher*

alifornia is so rich in history, legend, and lore, it seems only natural that all sorts of ghosts, spooks, specters, and unknown entities have chosen to make their presence felt here. Across the state, we hear tales of haunted houses, roads, cemeteries, and other dark places where the not quite departed are said to gather. Some of these apparitions have become so familiar that the ghosts have been given recognizable names. Other ghosts, though, shun notoriety and choose to make their presence known only to the owner of the house in which they dwell.

Golden State Ghosts

There are many theories about these manifestations. Some say that ghosts are victims of woe-filled lives or untimely deaths, and are eternally trapped. They cling to the here and now—perhaps trying to right old wrongs—and resist an afterlife they are not ready to embrace. Others say that ghosts don't know they have passed on. They may endlessly repeat a single action or movement, as if they were caught in a tape loop. They may appear for brief flashes, maybe passing between dimensions on their journey. In this state, they may be able to affect material objects. This is when the poltergeist, or noisy spirit, may make its presence known to us in all manner of terrifying ways.

In this chapter, we will visit some hot spots of ghostly activity around the Golden State and hear tales from its darker corners. Whether you're a believer or a skeptic, you may find yourself sleeping with the lights on tonight. So curl up, get settled in, and

The House That Fear Built

Sitting squat in the center of Silicon Valley, sprawling across nine acres of some of the most desirable real estate in San Jose, is an immense edifice that's a monument to those quintessentially Californian traits of nouveau-riche excess, brazen eccentricity, and occult-inspired paranoia—the Winchester Mystery House. This hundred-sixty-room Victorian behemoth was constructed for one purpose only, to house an army of ghosts.

The mansion was the creation of Sarah Winchester, wife of Connecticut firearms magnate William Wirt Winchester. Wealthy, attractive, and talented, Sarah was one of the bright lights of New Haven society—until both her husband and her only child went to early graves.

Half-crazed with grief, Sarah sought comfort from a spiritualist. He told her that her loved ones' lives had been taken by the restless spirits of the many men killed by the Winchester repeating rifle, the Gun That Won the West. The spirits would turn on her as well, he said, unless she moved west and built a home big enough to house all of them. He also told Sarah that she must never stop building and expanding the house. If work stopped, she would die.

Sarah took the medium's counsel literally and to epic extremes. Migrating to California in 1884, she bought an eight-room farmhouse on what was then the outskirts of San Jose. There she dedicated her $21 million inheritance and rifle royalty payments to granting the spirits' wishes. For the next thirty-eight years, she and an army of artisans expanded, rebuilt, and remodeled the house to hold the ghosts of Winchester rifle victims. The hammering and sawing never stopped at chez Winchester; Sarah's immense wealth and total obsession made sure that her well-paid workmen were busy twenty-four hours a day, three hundred and sixty-five days a year.

Sitting in a secret, blue-walled séance room deep in the house's interior, Mrs. Winchester held nightly court with the spirits, whose constant demands for more room guaranteed an ever changing floor plan. Balconies, fireplaces, rooms, and whole wings sprouted up from nowhere like fungi. The house grew to immense proportions. At the end of the four-decade construction binge, it contained forty-seven fireplaces, nine kitchens, ten thousand windows, and two thousand doors.

Sarah designed most of the features herself, and many of the additions and improvements reflected her own bizarre superstitions and fears, as well as the chaotic randomness of the building project. Doors opened onto dead-end hallways, blank walls, or three-story drops. Corridors tapered from normal width down to inches-wide crawl spaces. Stairways led nowhere, undulated like roller coasters, or compressed forty-two steps into a nine-foot climb with two-inch-high rises. It was said that she installed these strange features to confuse and thwart the many evil spirits who were constantly arriving at the house, courtesy of the Winchester '73 rifle.

Sarah never slept in the same bedroom of the mansion more than one night in a row. After the 1906 earthquake

struck San Jose, it took servants almost an hour to find her in the house's recesses, trapped in a room by a blocked door. Terrified by the quake (she thought it was caused by the spirits), she moved temporarily onto a houseboat, but soon returned to her monstrous mansion. There she remained until her death in 1922 at the age of eighty-five.

The house is a natural magnet for psychic investigators, and such famed occult detectives as magician Harry Houdini have visited it. Many séances have been held in the mansion's strange "blue room." Mediums have seen unearthly lights bobbing along the endless halls and have felt the presence of Mrs. Winchester's long-dead servants and workmen. Even Sarah herself has appeared posthumously in the earthquake-devastated Daisy bedroom and the ornate music room.

But one final, supreme irony hangs over the spirit-ridden house. Neither the psychics nor the countless tourists who tramp through the house every year have yet reported hearing, seeing, or sensing the ghost of anyone felled by a Winchester rifle.

No Photos Please

I finally fulfilled a lifelong dream during my last CA trip; my best friend Liz and I got to explore the twisting halls of the amazing, perplexing structure known as the Winchester Mystery House, which I have longed to visit since first hearing its story when I was a very young child. I was awestricken at the sight of the house the second it came into view—the sheer, massive size of it was UNBELIEVABLE. And, the weirdness started almost immediately. . . .

As we waited for our Mansion Tour to begin, I decided to shoot a few pics of the place. I used my LCD screen to line up the shot, but the second I aimed the camera at the house, my LCD went wacky and I got a bizarre effect. As soon as I panned the camera away from the house, the screen would clear up perfectly. Yet every time I aimed it at the house again, it started giving a static-like, almost negative effect. I called Liz over to verify what was happening, and she couldn't believe it either. She even took a pic of my camera's LCD screen for good measure.

Once we entered the house for our tour of 160 of the mansion's rooms, the camera weirdness continued. We had three fully charged batteries between the two of us, yet we both started losing battery power as soon as we entered the house. I continued to snap pic after pic, but I kept getting completely blacked-out shots, or the strange, colored negative-like effect! I have never before or since seen my camera do anything remotely like this. It almost seemed like a serious camera problem, except for the fact that I was getting some perfectly normal, good shots in between the weird ones.

Liz and I both felt goose-bumpy when our guide explained that when Sarah Winchester dwelled here, she did not allow any photographs to be taken of her. Perhaps she was hanging

around during parts of our tour . . . letting us know that she was still the lady of this house.

It took over an hour to make our way through all of the rooms, and without our guide, I feel sure that we would have gotten hopelessly lost. There are so many twists and turns, false passageways, and hidden doorways . . . it's unbelievable. We moved through the Blue Séance Room, the bedroom where Sarah Winchester died, and the Grand Ballroom where she used to "entertain" her ghostly guests at the stroke of midnight. We saw the bizarre stairway that leads literally into the ceiling, the bathrooms with windows in their doors.

Sarah's Mystery House is filled with cryptic messages and meanings. The number 13 can be found hidden throughout the house: curtain rods have 13 rings, windows and ceiling panels have 13 panes, sink drains have 13 holes, and so on. The symbol of the daisy (which in its perfect form has 13, yep, 13 petals) can also be seen everywhere—in rugs, chandeliers, windows, and walls. There are two very mysterious messages written in the stained glass windows that Sarah herself designed for the Ballroom. The left window reads WIDE UNCLASP THE TABLES OF THEIR THOUGHTS, while the right says THESE SAME THOUGHTS PEOPLE THIS LITTLE WORLD. Although the words are Shakespeare's, no one knows why these particular enigmatic phrases were chosen for the windows.

Time seems to stand still in the Winchester House; an air of secrecy permeates every wall and every floorboard. The confusing, mind-bending twists and turns and perplexing mysteries inside its walls left Liz and I puzzled and intrigued when we stepped back out into the warm California sunshine with three completely dead camera batteries, a handful of bizarre photos, and a whole bunch of questions.—*Shady*

DOOR TO NOWHERE

Spirited Hide and Seek

I just had to write and let you know that my mother and her siblings grew up in the Winchester House—really! My grandfather was manager of the house/property for over thirty years in the '40s through the '60s. They lived in a portion of the original house set aside for the manager and his family. My father was actually a tour guide there while attending the University of Santa Clara, and there he met my mom and married soon after graduation. When I was a kid, our family would always spend holidays visiting grandma and grandpa at the Winchester House. One of my best memories was playing hide-and-seek in the 160 rooms after hours when the tours ended and the lights were off. Very scary! Even scarier was the night I was sleeping on a couch in the main living room and I started screaming loudly, as I had just seen Sarah's body floating around the room. I'll never forget that image of her! It is truly a mysterious, foreboding house, full of life and energy to this day.—*Bill, LostDestinations.com*

R. M. S. QUEEN MARY

137

QUEEN MARY

6A-H1598

13

The Ghost Ship *Queen Mary*

The other world has followed this luxury liner since her maiden voyage in 1934.

Just after the big ship was launched, London astrologist Lady Mabel Fortescue-Harrison told newspapers, "The *Queen Mary*, launched today, will know her greatest fame and popularity when she never sails another mile and never carries another paying passenger."

The psychic noblewoman was right. Now permanently lodged at Pier J in Long Beach, the ship is one of Los Angeles's most famous tourist attractions, a three-hundred-ninety-room floating hotel that also hosts tours, conventions, and maritime exhibits. It's also said to be the most haunted ship in North America.

All sorts of spooky things have happened over the length of the 1,019-foot, 81,237-ton liner. Lights flicker, and on the G deck, thought to be the location of the ship's morgue, doors slam unaided by human hands. Another hot spot is the swimming pool, where the ghost of a middle-aged woman in an archaic swimsuit sometimes dives into the empty basin. She's believed to be the spirit of a woman who drowned there. Some people have seen a young, mini-skirted woman pace around the pool area and disappear behind a pillar. Sounds of shouting and splashing have been heard at the deserted poolside deck as well, and there are also stories of ghostly, watery footprints appearing along the pool's edge.

More unnerving phenomena have been reported in one of the kitchens. During World War II, when the ship was used as a troop transport, a brawl erupted in the galley, and a cook was shoved into an oven and burned to death. Now, near the site of his death, light switches turn themselves on and off, dishes move under their own power, and utensils mysteriously vanish.

Other shipboard phantoms include an elegantly dressed "woman in white" who hangs around the salon's piano, a ghostly officer who walks near the bridge, and a black-bearded man in coveralls who rides the engine-room escalator. The latter is thought to be the spirit of John Pedder, an eighteen-year-old seaman who was crushed to death by a watertight door during a routine drill on July 10, 1966.

For some reason, the engine-room area is the most haunted place on the ship. Staff members and tour guides who go there report clanging and knocking sounds, chains being whipped and dangled by unseen hands, and balls of light moving slowly across the walls. Tom Hennessy, a *Long Beach Press-Telegram* columnist who was initially skeptical about ghosts on the *Queen Mary*, spent a night near the ship's engine room and came out a believer. During his stay, he was menaced by moving oil drums, felt the vibrations of some invisible presence walking toward him on a catwalk, and heard clanging noises that stopped when he approached them.

Hennessy's eeriest experience came at 3:33 a.m., when he heard two or three men talking in the deserted propeller-shaft room. He distinctly made out the words, "turning the lights off," from one of them. A security guard who had monitored the area later told him that no living people had been near the shaft room when he heard the conversation; the guard said that other people had heard ghostly voices there as well.

The *Queen Mary*'s days as a luxury liner may be long gone, but the old lady of the sea has found a new life both as a major tourist destination and a floating home of ghosts.

> **For some reason, the engine-room area is the most haunted place on the ship.**

Whaley House

Officially recognized as the Most Haunted House in California by the U.S. Commerce Department, the Whaley House is a whistle-stop on most major tours of San Diego. This fact should not deter weirdists from making a pilgrimage; its reputation is well deserved. Every volunteer at the house has a story about swinging chandeliers, footfalls on the floor below or above them, smells of lavender perfume and burning tobacco, and seemingly solid, flesh-and-blood figures dressed in nineteenth-century clothes who walk around corners and disappear. The place claims at least seven apparitions, including a small terrier who will lick and hump your leg. The house may have been destined to be haunted, since it was built on the site of a macabre hanging.

Thomas Whaley was a New York businessman when in 1849 he decided to relocate to San Francisco to take advantage of the burgeoning gold rush economy. His retail store there was a hit but burned down in 1851, and Whaley decided to try the milder west, down south in sleepy San Diego. Again he was successful, which allowed him to return to New York to marry his childhood sweetheart, Anna. In 1855, they returned to San Diego and the new home Whaley had built for them on the land where the infamous hanging had occurred. A series of tragedies and triumphs (but mostly tragedies) followed, most notably the death in 1888 of Whaley's eldest and favored daughter, Anna, who shot herself in the chest, despondent over a failed marriage. Her father carried her from the backyard storage building (which is now the facility's outhouse) to the rear bedroom, where she died in his arms. Inconsolable over the loss, he vowed never to live in the home again.

In 1890, after Thomas Whaley's death at age fifty-seven, the family moved back in. The final Whaley descendant passed away there in 1953. Altogether, six family members died in the house, as well as a neighbor child who strangled herself by running into a low-slung clothesline.

The violent death that may have started all this was an example of quick and harsh frontier justice. "Yankee" Jim Robinson, a small-time criminal and would-be pirate, was caught stealing a rowboat in San Diego Bay. While Yankee Jim's henchmen got only a year in the pokey, Robinson was hanged for his crime. At a time when the average man in the county stood about five feet five inches, Yankee Jim Robinson, at six feet four inches, was hanged from a gallows barely taller than he was. Instead of having his neck snapped instantly, the dastardly cur was left to twist and choke, nearly on his tiptoes, for almost forty-five minutes before he was pronounced dead.

Thomas Whaley knew about the hanging but didn't believe in superstitious nonsense, yet over the years he and his family were obliged to change their views. Deborah ("No last names please") has been a volunteer tour guide at the Whaley House for about two years. In that time, she has probably seen the entire panoply of the spectral carnival, which isn't guaranteed to the casual tourist. "I've heard a male voice clearing his throat when I'm in the dressing room changing into my costume," she

ghostly smell. The burly dude never returned.

We asked if anyone saw smoke or if there might be any explanation for the episode. "Well, that was the strange thing," Deborah says. "There was no smoke, just the odor. We all smelled it." Deborah left me alone on the second floor for about twenty minutes, and I did smell the famous lavender-scented perfume that legend dictates was Anna Whaley's choice scent, but

reports. Others who use the second-floor rooms to don their period costumes have experienced similar phenomena.

Thomas Whaley himself often materializes at the head of the stairs to the master bedroom. It is not uncommon for visitors to smell the smoke of his cigar or hear his baritone laughter echoing throughout the house. Thomas's wife, Anna, is also known to make frequent appearances. She is described as a beautiful and graceful woman dressed in a gown of gingham; her flowery perfume and lilting voice envelop the air and are followed by the eerie strains of a distant piano.

The house (or its permanent residents) apparently don't tolerate skeptics well. "There was this man who didn't believe in ghosts and was very vocal about it," Deborah recalls. "He was a police chief and said he was an atheist and the whole thing. He was standing in the hallway talking to one of the volunteers and was suddenly hit square in the face with a puff of cigar smoke. The tour guide smelled it too." Now a sudden convert, the chief made a mad dash for the door and stood panting on the front porch, only to be hit with another shot of the

saw no movement, heard no voices, and felt no ghostly brush across my face, as other visitors have experienced.

One of the most macabre and recurring happenings in the place is connected to the Yankee Jim hanging. "I think he has a sense of humor," Deborah observes. "Sometimes we get visitors coming up or down the stairs [the agreed location of the old gallows] who end up with a red mark across their necks. It doesn't hurt, and most people don't even notice until someone else points it out. One girl ran out of the house in a panic after her boyfriend noticed the thin red line."

Like some sort of biorhythm from beyond, activity in the building appears to come in waves. There is no guaranteed creep show, but the ghosts and noises are reportedly most active in the holiday season, from Thanksgiving to New Year's Day. Phenomena have been reported at all times of the day and night. In addition to regular hours of operation, the Whaley House is open from nine p.m. to midnight for a special showing in the week preceding and up to All Hallows' Eve. It is also open from seven to ten p.m. for nighttime tours in the summer.

Beware the Banditos

If San Diego's Whaley House is too far out of the way, the next best place for ghosts-on-demand in southern California may be Ventura's Olivas Adobe. Local ghost-hunting legend Richard Senate has recently completed a documentary about the site, and the spirits apparently obliged him, making a few fleeting appearances on camera and before witnesses. A midweek afternoon visit, when the place is relatively deserted, is perhaps the best time to look for the disturbed ghost of Senora Teodora Olivas.

Senora Olivas has good reason to keep watch over her home, which was completed in 1851. Her husband, Don Raimundo Olivas, was deeded 2,200 acres of land bordering the Ventura shore in appreciation of his service in the Mexican army under General Santa Barbara. He named his property Rancho San Miguel. By shrewd political maneuvering and hard work, Olivas became one of the wealthiest ranchers in Alta California. Fiestas held at the adobe lasted for days. All of this of course made him a target for bandits, who staged a vicious raid on his home in 1855.

The robbers rounded up the family and servants and then searched the grounds for valuables. Here, the story gets fuzzy. One version maintains that a trusted Indian servant was secretly given Don Raimundo's treasure box, reportedly containing anywhere from $3,000 to $75,000 in gold coins (depending on which story you choose to believe), to bury on the grounds while Raimundo stalled the outlaws. When the servant successfully completed his mission, he returned to the adobe and was shot before the desperadoes realized that he was the only person who knew where the stash was hidden.

The banditos fare slightly better if you go with the second version of events: After one of them struck Senora Olivas to the ground and ripped off her earrings, the group managed to carry off the treasure and make for the hills. They soon realized that a sizable posse had been rounded up to track them down, so the box was buried in the mountains somewhere between Ventura and Santa Barbara. No one has yet found the lost gold. According to Senate, at least one of the criminals got away—but not forever: "A fellow named Encarnacion Berryessa was in a bar in L.A. boasting of his many evil deeds—one of which was the robbery of Olivas's adobe," Senate reports. "The good patrons of the bar took him out and hung him."

Visitors have seen Senora Olivas nervously pacing the high porch along the rear of the house. She is dressed in black and usually disappears in mid-stride. Volunteers at the adobe often hear footsteps going up the creaky stairs or pacing on boards above, but see no one when the area is checked. Rocking chairs in the restored rooms tilt back and forth when no one is near, and objects move from their usual locations overnight in the deserted house. Figures have appeared in the upper windows, looking sternly down on startled witnesses. One night in 2004 Senate managed to capture on a digital camera the image of a bearded male face peering into one of the upstairs windows. The window is eighteen feet above the ground, with no balcony or ledge. A bit of research determined that the face resembles Nicolas Olivas, eldest son of Don Raimundo and his wife. Perhaps he was looking for one of his fingers, which was shot off in the robbery.

The Olivas Adobe is a State and National Historic Monument, and is located at 4200 Olivas Park Drive, south of the town of Ventura, near Highway 101. Although the grounds are open daily, tours are offered only on weekends from ten a.m. to four p.m.

Ghosts Along the Road

Flora Floats Away

If you're walking along California Street in Nob Hill between Powell and Jones and a young, happy girl in an elaborate Victorian-era white gown walks by and smiles at you, smile back. Then watch her very closely. If you see traffic and pedestrians pass through her body, and if she disappears suddenly and completely, you've seen the Nob Hill Ghost.

She's commonly believed to be Flora Sommerton, a young woman who disappeared on the eve of her social debut in 1876. Flora's parents were pressuring her to marry a wealthy young man whom she despised, so rather than bend to their wishes, she took her Paris-made debutante gown and skipped town.

News of her disappearance made headlines across the nation, and a $250,000 reward for her return stood for many years. In 1926, she was finally located—dead, in Butte, Montana, where she had been known as Mrs. Butler and had worked as a housekeeper. According to police reports, her room was filled with newspaper accounts of her disappearance. She died wearing the same white dress that she'd last been seen in as Flora Sommerton fifty years earlier. Ghost hunters say she still walks in that gown, not in the form of an aged, lonely woman, but as a fresh-faced debutante, still trying to find the party that she missed over a century ago.

Hitchhiking Woman

Along one of the many picturesque canals in the little town of Heber, there is a highway. The story is that a married woman was having an affair with another man in Calexico, about 5 miles from Heber, and she wanted to get home before her husband did. The woman was driving home after her afternoon of fun and was speeding. She came to a sharp curve going too fast and crashed through the guardrail and into the canal. She drowned.

I first heard about the "Mujer" from children in the elementary school that I was a student counselor at. I did some investigating and found that almost everyone in the little town knew of the story. On certain nights, the woman will appear and ask for rides into town. If you do not stop, the woman will hitch a ride from you nonetheless, and appear in your backseat. I know of several people that have given rides to the phantom and they report that she is very beautiful and polite. The husband who became a widower left the Imperial Valley and moved to Bakersfield and became a prominent citizen of that city.—*Thief of All*

Don't Look!

If you drive down the 105 freeway down in Filmore, you'll spot the White Lady. After night falls, don't look at her! She'll jump into your car and make you crash down a deep cliff! If you go, check it out. You can see there are over 10 cars down that cliff.—*Carlos*

Ghost Hunting in San Francisco

San Francisco may be a favorite haunt of seafood lovers, sports fans, and bondage queens, but it is also the stomping grounds of a goodly number of poltergeists and banshees caught between the world of the living and the realm of the dead. From Haight Ashbury to Alcatraz Island and all spooky points in between, the city is a hell of a hangout for ghosts.

Jim Fassbinder is not a Ghostbuster, but more of a tour guide to the supernatural. Fassbinder recalls having "shadow friends" from the time he was a child. "When I was about five years old, I was talking to my parents about my invisible friends and mentioned their names," claims the top-hatted escort to all things eerie by the bay. "These were the names of two men who had been killed in a train wreck in Chicago. The supernatural things never stopped happening. I just learned to keep them to myself."

One of San Francisco's most famous phantoms, Fassbinder will tell you, is Mary Ellen Pleasant. Born into slavery, she eventually won her freedom and married a wealthy man who left her a wealthy widow when he died. She was an active part of the Underground Railroad, helping other slaves escape to freedom, and has been called the Mother of Civil Rights in California. Mary Ellen also apparently dabbled in the occult enough to be considered a voodoo priestess. A park and a plaque mark the spot on which her manor once stood at the corner of Bush and Octavia. There, bizarre happenings are said to have been witnessed by believers and nonbelievers alike.

Many people have reported that objects either fall or feel like they are being thrown from the trees. Fassbinder says he was spit on by the surly specter. Other folks assert that the unexpected appearance of a crow is a messenger of Mary Ellen's ethereal presence, and others even maintain that she has taken human form and walked around the park at night.

It is said that if you make a polite appeal on that corner and find Mary *in good spirits,* your request will come true.

Fassbinder will be happy to tell you more about Mary Ellen and a host of other ghosts on his two-hour walking San Francisco Ghost Hunt. For more frightening information visit www.sfghosthunt.com. Be on the alert, however, for loogie-hawking ghouls.

Moonlight Sonatas

This Queen Anne—style wedding cake of a mansion has been at 1925 K Street in San Diego for over a hundred years, surviving a long series of near disasters and neglect. The original resident of Villa Montezuma stayed in the house for only two years, and the place went through a succession of owners before it was declared a historic landmark in 1970. Many occupants suffered financial ruin and other hardships,

giving rise to a legend that the place is not only haunted but cursed. The villa opened to the public in 1972, after the San Diego Historical Society finished extensive restoration work.

With the arrival of the railroad in 1885, San Diego was transformed from a frontier dust trap into a boomtown. Flush with newfound prosperity, civic boosters and the nouveau riche wanted to bring ever dreaded "culture" to the town. To this end, they convinced the staff and a clique of hangers-on of the San Francisco literary magazine *The Golden Era* to relocate down south. One of the group was the flamboyant Jesse Shepard—author, musician, and spiritualist. Shepard was basically a professional hipster, living off the largesse of the rich and influential who doted on his apparent spiritual depth and carefully crafted persona. Although he gave séances, his psychic powers seem to have been limited to channeling great composers. Or at least that's what he told audiences in his dimly lit nighttime concerts, where he performed opera selections and played the piano and harpsichord—quite well from all reports.

Spiritualism was all the rage in the San Diego of the mid-1880s. This belief system was an American invention, begun in the late 1840s by the activities of the Fox sisters of upstate New York. The young Fox girls claimed they could communicate with disembodied spirits, divining deep truths from a series of thwacks and cracking sounds. Somehow the movement morphed into a national craze, even though one of the sisters later admitted that their "abilities" were just a joke to tease their superstitious mother.

Villa Montezuma is a monument to that movement. It was built for Shepard by a pair of wealthy fruit ranchers, William and John High, who had fallen under Spiritualism's spell and longed to be accepted in high society. They sold Shepard a plot of land for $1 and then proceeded to finance the ostentatious home for him on the property.

They intended to make the place a haven for spiritualist philosophy and a meeting place for the cultured crust of San Diego. Shepard moved in a month after the paint dried in the summer of 1887. But the next year he was off to Europe, where the Spiritualism pickings were lush. He returned in 1889 and promptly sold the house, never to return to San Diego. He died at the piano in 1927 during a private recital in Los Angeles, his hands still resting on the keys of the last chord he played. He was seventy-nine years old.

Although the docents who lead tea-drinking dowagers and other assorted tourists through the house nowadays are usually loath to discuss it, the place is reportedly home to at least two ghosts. One has been seen staring at neighborhood kids and passersby from one of the upper-floor windows. She is said to be a resident who lived alone in the house after her husband died, most likely accompanied by the ubiquitous herds of cats favored by old women in that situation. Shepard himself has not been sighted, but footsteps and creaking floorboards, as well as the usual closing doors, are witnessed regularly by volunteers from the San Diego Historical Society. Neighbors report the sounds of piano music coming from somewhere inside late at night. Imprints of a body on Shepard's downstairs bed are smoothed out in the evening, only to reappear in the morning.

Chris Spratley, one of the guides at Villa Montezuma, says he has heard footfalls from the upstairs rooms and other places in the house both when he is alone and with other docents. He revealed that there is a crawl space between the first-floor ceiling and the stained fir wood floor above.

"I think Shepard used the space to spy on people and knock on the walls during séances," he says. "There's a hidden room behind the fireplace too." Pressed further, Spratley admits there have been problems with caretakers who live on the property. "They all seem to go a little weird after a few months in the place. We had this one guy a couple of years back who was okay for awhile, but then he started giving tours in his T-shirt and sweatpants. When he stayed in his room rather than do a tour, we let him go." One volunteer took things further. "He started acting weird too, and after he was fired, he started growing a mustache like Shepard's and dressing in vintage clothes. He insisted that people call him Jesse, which wasn't his name."

Perhaps the ghosts object to other things going on in the house. When I was a lad, in the mid-1970s, my Boy Scout troop (San Diego County Council #937) visited the Villa Montezuma on a field trip. I didn't see any ghosts, but we were blocked from seeing the music room because a photographer was working. "We're going to have to close the door. The light's really messing me up in there," he informed us. Mysteriously, the tour guide didn't protest. I fancied myself a budding photographer, so I managed to sneak away from the rest of the group to take a peek at the test shots left carelessly on a downstairs table. My heart (or maybe some forbidden emotion) jumped into my throat—there were twenty or thirty pictures of a naked blond model lounging over the vintage paisley furniture. The model and crew probably thought it was pretty funny that they had to hide from a bunch of Boy Scouts. No idea whether this sort of thing goes on at the place these days.—*GB*

Ghost Toys with Customers

Toys "R" Us, at 130 East El Camino in Sunnyvale, has been featured on television's *That's Incredible* and other shows. Psychics have said that the store is haunted by the ghost of a man who farmed the land on which the store was built. The man accidentally cut his leg with an axe while chopping wood and bled to death on the spot. The ghost is an apparently playful poltergeist, and employees often have opened the store in the morning to find the aisles strewn with toys or have had balls bounce down the floors or teddy bears float down from the shelves. The ghost also follows people into the restrooms and turns on the faucets. Visit aisle 15C — it always seems to smell of freshly cut flowers. The store managers are happy to live with this mischievous ghost, as their sales climb every time a story is printed about the haunting.

The Haunted Toys "R" Us

On El Camino in Sunnyvale there is a haunted Toys "R" Us store. The story goes that many decades ago when the whole Bay Area was still orchards, there was a worker on a farm who was in love with the orchard owner's daughter. It is not known whether she loved him back or not, but one day he was told that it could never work out between them. He went into the field and started chopping wood to relieve his frustration, but in his fury he wasn't paying attention, and the axe missed the log and went into his leg. He bled to death by the woodpile.

Later, a Toys "R" Us was built in that area. Employees have reported coming to work in the morning and finding toys "played with" when no one was in the store. A few even have stories about being alone in the stock room and seeing boxes move, feeling hands or someone steadying their ladder. It seems that the ghost is lonely and not angry, and no one has reported injuries because of the hauntings. *—Jocelyn Laney*

A Farmer's Daughter Story

I live in the Bay Area, and due to its in-depth history, there are many local legends. One story has to do with a Toys "R" Us in Sunnyvale. Back in the mid 20's when the town was a small farming town, a large farm ran with the help of "field-hands" to take care of the owner's crops. One such man was named Johnny Johnson.

He had fallen in love with the farmer's daughter, and would spend the days working and thinking about being with this lovely lass. One summer day, while chopping firewood with an axe, his attention wandered off when Elizabeth Yuba (his love interest's name) crossed the area he was working in. In a freak accident, the axe missed its mark, and hit his leg instead. Due to his wounds, and being far from help, he died. In that very spot, Toys "R" Us erected their store, and from day one, its employees had the displeasure of experiencing many ghostly incidents—boxes dropping, toys falling off the shelf and many other events on these grounds.

The night crew (needed in order to clean up the flying toys) has witnessed glowing objects and other strange events. This story has been featured on a few paranormal TV shows. *—Matthew Bergendahl*

Ghost in the John

I spent the past few days on vacation with friends in San Francisco. On the drive back to LA, we decided to stop and eat at the Old Yellow House in Sommerland. I have this book of haunted places in the U.S. and it mentioned that this little restaurant has had some ghostly happenings. So without really knowing much else about it, we stopped by.

The whole evening was just eerie. The rain was coming down, and we were the only ones in the entire place! I asked the waiter if he had experienced any ghostly phenomena, but he said he hadn't. He also had been working there for only one week! He did mention that he was forewarned by management not to panic if things in the restaurant happened to "fall."

During the evening I made a trip to the restroom. I have to admit, I was a little freaked out being alone in there. As I was standing up taking care of business, I heard a pretty loud bang right beside my left ear. I quickly looked to my left and saw the stall door swing open! I got the heck out of there without even washing my hands. My friends argued that it was probably just a breeze, but I'm not buying. I know the difference between a breeze and a door opening by itself. It was just like a fist or something hard hit the door from the inside, thus pushing the door out! Freaky.–*Steven*

Haunted at the Hungry Hunter

There is a restaurant in Oceanside called Hungry Hunter. It is located where the 78 West and 5 South freeway meet. It was built on an old Native American burial site. Some nights the waitresses and waiters will be tripped by invisible legs, their hair will get mussed up by invisible hands, trays of food will be thrown from their hands. It doesn't just happen to the employees, it also happens to diners.

I was eating there one night with some friends, celebrating a birthday. I walked to the bathroom and I was pulled away from the door. It was so powerful a pull that I fell onto the floor.
–*Andrea Johnston*

Ventura's Hotel California

Second only to the "Paul is dead" talk that followed the Beatles throughout much of their careers are the rumors and legends about the Eagles' 1976 hit "Hotel California." The lyrics supposedly describe a church that was abandoned and taken over by Satan worshippers. Anton LaVey's Church of Satan did indeed garner a lot of interest and attention in the 1960s, culminating with the admitted membership of celebrities like Jayne Mansfield and Sammy Davis Jr. (before he saw the light and converted to Judaism). Despite the fact that the song is most likely an allegory for the music industry and the hedonism of the 1970s, and that the album cover photos—which purport to show the actual haunted edifice—were really taken at the Beverly Hills Hotel, the legends persist. Many of these stories center on the now abandoned

Camarillo State Hospital near Ventura.

Built in 1936, this facility housed alcoholics, the retarded, drug addicts (jazz great Charlie Parker recorded a seven-month stay in 1947), and more sinister characters such as pedophiles and violently insane criminals. Former patients often referred to the place as Hotel California long before the Eagles had even formed.

The barbaric state of "care" at Camarillo is legendary, and it seemed like something out of the Inquisition rather

than a place where people were meant to be healed. Patients, some of whom were children, were routinely given electroshock treatments, immersed in tubs of hot water and then wrapped in icy towels, beaten, and otherwise abused. Residents were made to wear tan jumpsuits, and any who tried to escape were easily spotted.

"You can check out any time you'd like, but you can never leave."—The Eagles

Parapsychologists suspect that more strange phenomena occur in places where mentally unstable people are grouped, and experiments have borne out this theory. This legendary "snake pit" bears so many psychic scars, it's a prime spot for haunting. Accounts from former employees tell of a man who would routinely enter the women's restroom, only to disappear when someone went inside to look for him. One female janitor saw a man's legs in one of the stalls, but after receiving no reply when she asked him to leave, opened the stall to find it empty.

In 1999, efforts began to turn the site into another kind of institution. It is now the California State University Channel Islands. School officials would rather forget the sinister history of the buildings, but sightings of strange apparitions and moving furniture continue to plague the grounds. Most of the reported happenings seem to occur in the complex located on the far southern end of the campus, which is still used for location filming, since it is the only place that hasn't been touched by the renovation crews as yet.

The look of the place on *Weird California*'s recent visit, just after sunset, with the light of the full moon illuminating the courtyard, was intense enough. But from somewhere inside the building we could hear an intermittent banging on something that sounded like metal pipes. The faraway noise echoed through the dark hallways for many seconds afterward. A crawl space door led to an impenetrable darkness. No apparitions were seen or recorded on film that time, but the place remains a good bet for ghost-hunting thrill seekers, as well as a monument to a time when the mentally disturbed were treated as nonhuman by an ignorant and at times inhuman staff.

Getting Hammered

My brother, Bill, while on a location shoot, was working out of this building at the asylum in May 2004. He's a set builder. While there, little things like the hammers, wrenches, etc. would disappear and then reappear in other rooms. Windows would shut, microwaves thrown on the floor, the walls would knock, and cold spots happened. They would hear children laughing, but no kids were there. A couple of the crew quit—it was too close to the other side for them.

—*Maryanne and Bill Barrett (from ghostvillage.com)*

Hotel Del Coronado

Few who stay in the five-star Hotel Del Coronado know of the eternal guest who lives here—until they run into her late at night. On Thanksgiving Day 1892, a beautiful young woman named Kate Morgan checked in at the ornate hotel. Five days later she checked out with a gunshot wound to the temple. The case was a sensation in local and national newspapers for weeks afterward, and writers have speculated about it for over a century. Contemporary headlines obsessed over the mystery of the "Beautiful Stranger."

Morgan worked the railways, operating as a team with her husband, Tom. Introducing themselves as siblings, Kate would distract the mark by flirting with him, while Tom played sleight of hand with cards. His swindle of choice was Three Card Monte. They made a good living at it, but this charmed existence came to an end on a trip from Los Angeles to San Diego. The couple apparently had a barn burner of an argument, and Tom got off in a huff at the station in Orange. It was the last time they would see each other—perhaps. Kate may have been pregnant, and some historians have speculated that she was ready to file for divorce, a tough road to travel for a woman in nineteenth-century America.

Kate continued on to San Diego and arrived at the "Del" on the afternoon of November 24. She entered through the unaccompanied ladies entrance and had the clerk sign her in as Lottie A. Bernard. She claimed that she was waiting for her brother to arrive. Over the next few days, she complained to the hotel staff of headaches and pains. She asked a bellboy to get her wine and, later, a jigger of whiskey from the bar.

On Monday, November 28, Kate took a train to San Diego and bought a pistol from Chick's Gun Shop, an establishment also frequented by Wyatt Earp while he ran various gambling houses in the Stingaree district downtown after his more famous stint in Tombstone,

Arizona. Morgan returned to the hotel and was found the next morning by David Cone, the hotel electrician. Her body was lying on the stairs leading to the beach, a gun by her side, and a bullet hole in her right temple. The coroner guessed that she had been dead at least six or seven hours.

In his 1990 book *The Legend of Kate Morgan*, trial lawyer and author Alan May theorized that Morgan was murdered by her errant husband, citing evidence such as corrosion on the supposedly new gun found next to her body and the hasty coroner's inquest that failed to ask key questions about the circumstances surrounding Morgan's death.

"Kate is our most famous ghost," says hotel historian Christine Donovan. "We get more interest from the media on that one subject than anything else."

And why wouldn't they? Whether it was murder or suicide, her violent end is custom-tailored for a haunting. On the last five days of her life, Morgan stayed in room 302. After a century of restoration and remodeling, the room has been redesignated number 3327. According to hotel staff, it is usually booked months, even years, in advance, especially around Halloween. Guests have reported swinging fixtures, flickering lights, telephone and TV malfunctions, and dark figures pulling sheets off the bed. One gentleman became so exasperated by phantom phone calls that he finally shouted at Kate

Morgan to leave him in peace. The alarm clock buzzed three times (this was at four a.m.), and the calls stopped. Another guest stopped to unlock her room late at night and saw a pretty woman mirroring her actions a few feet away next door. The figure smiled at her. She wasn't aware that she'd seen a ghost until she realized that the woman was dressed in turn-of-the-century period clothes. Parapsychological snoops have attested to activity in the room as well.

There have been reports and complaints about another room—3519—which has also been extensively studied by psychic investigators. Ashtrays and other objects fall off tables, and footsteps and voices can be heard from the floor above. The problem here is that the next floor is the roof, as an unnamed Secret Service agent discovered in 1983 while staying in the hotel on assignment with then-Vice President George Bush. He immediately demanded to be moved elsewhere.

Manifestations have been recorded in other rooms besides 3327 and 3519, but seem to be confined for the most part to the third floor, Kate's floor. The hallways here are much narrower than the ones below, and the feeling is a little on the claustrophobic side. In 1999, a family staying in room 3343 were driven to hysterics when the mother's reflection in a bathroom mirror laid a singular moment of cognitive dissonance on them: As Christine Donovan reports in her book *Beautiful Stranger: The Ghost of Kate Morgan and the Hotel Del Coronado*, "[H]er eyes were the size of Orphan Annie's (two or three times their normal size) and each appeared to be configured like a bull's eye."

Nonsensitives seem to have an advantage in ghost-watching here. "People who check in looking for the ghost really don't have much luck," Donovan says he has noticed. "Kate seems to like catching people who aren't looking for her. I don't think these spirits want to be conjured."

If you do decide to tempt Kate Morgan, it'll cost you: "Victorian" rooms go for $250 or more, but it's a small price to pay for a good bet to see a ghost—and a babe at that.

A Date with Kate

Kate Morgan checked into room 302 at the Hotel Del Coronado to meet her estranged husband for Thanksgiving. He never arrived to meet her, and a few days later, she was found dead on the hotel steps near the ocean. Since then, guests and staff of the Hotel Del Coronado have noticed strange breezes, ghostly noises and the pale figure of a young lady walking in a black lace dress. Most people also find it exciting and exhilarating to rent the room for the night, just to see if they have a paranormal experience with Kate.—*Ian Bair, San Diego*

Appearing Nightly: Viola!

The Lancaster Performing Arts Centre in the Antelope Valley opened in 1991. From the spring of '92 to the fall of '99, I spent a great deal of time in that theatre as a performer, usher, patron and finally as a backstage crew member.

Being so new, you wouldn't expect this theatre to have a ghost, but that's not the case. While the theatre was under construction, several important people in the community were given a tour. An elderly lady named Viola was in the group. As the theatre was still being built, the orchestra pit (which would house a platform that could be raised to stage level and lowered to orchestra level), was still a huge, gaping hole, waiting for the machinery to be installed. Poor Viola got too close to the edge. She lost her balance and went plummeting to the bottom of the unfinished pit. She was rushed to the hospital and died soon after.

Viola is said to haunt the orchestra pit and the catwalks of the theatre.

Having spent my entire teenage life there and a few years into my twenties, I have had a few personal experiences with Viola. I would come into the theatre during the day to practice using the lightboard, having the entire auditorium to myself. I would hear footsteps, but no one was there. Speakers that were not turned on would snap and crackle. Whenever I had to go to the galleries or the spot booth, which was accessible only by climbing a series of ladders and crawling along the catwalks, I would always have the strangest feeling that I was being watched. Odd noises were everywhere. Whenever I went into the orchestra pit while the platform was at stage level and I could see down into the bottom of the pit, my stomach would always twist into knots of pure terror. I hated it down there!

Viola has never done anything malevolent, as the entire staff can verify. In fact, they are rather proud of their "resident spook," and whenever anything odd happens or something goes missing, people will shake their heads and say, "Well, there's Viola again!" *–Absinthe*

The Entity Haunting

On a sunny afternoon in 1974, parapsychologists Barry Taff and Kerry Gaynor were browsing in Hunter's Bookstore in Westwood when they met a woman whom they assumed was probably crazy. She told them of a particularly violent ghost that was making her life hell. She desperately wanted help. The case would become world famous when it was recounted in *The Entity*, starring Barbara Hershey, released in 1981.

Taff and Gaynor were students at U.C.L.A., working in the psychology department and specializing in, of all things, ghost hunting. Toiling under the famous parapsychologist Dr. Thelma Moss, who had headed many research projects in Kirlian photography, Taff and Gaynor had learned to take most claims about the paranormal with a grain of salt. In spite of the sensationalized-sounding nature of the woman's story, they decided to visit her home, in Culver City, just a few miles south of the campus.

When Dorris Bider (usually referred to as Carla Moran) told them about an evil presence who had sexually assaulted and beat her repeatedly late at night, the investigators politely excused themselves; they had a good laugh in the car on their way back to Westwood. They weren't laughing when she called a few days later and said that others had seen the apparition as well. "This is what we're always looking for—independent verification of the phenomena," said Gaynor during an interview published in *Omni* magazine.

On their next visit, Taff and Gaynor were standing in the kitchen talking to Bider when one of the lower cupboards opened and a heavy skillet flew across the room and hit a wall. They tried to get pictures of small orbs of light that they observed traveling around the house, but when they were developed, the photos showed nothing out of the ordinary. At one point, Bider told Gaynor that the ghost was right in front of her, so he snapped a picture. In it, Bider's face was blurred and appeared to be obscured by something. Another picture taken seconds later did not manifest the same anomaly. When Gaynor pointed the camera in a corner where the witness said the ghost was at the time, there was another blurred area. The investigators decided to return with reinforcements.

The two students loaded up their equipment and called a few photographers they knew who could provide independent observations and possibly capture any manifestations on film. In all, seventeen people crowded into Bider's bedroom as she asked the spirit to show itself. Green balls of light appeared and began to fly around the room. In one famous image, a photographer captured what appeared to be streaks of light arcing around Bider's head. She then asked the figure to show itself, and the speechless group watched as a "greenish white" form began to materialize in a corner. All present agreed that the figure looked male and appeared to be muscular. If any pictures of this manifestation survive, they are out of circulation.

On another occasion, Bider's sixteen-year-old son heard his mother screaming in her bedroom; he burst in, trying to stop another assault. He was struck violently in the head before he could reach her and was thrown back, breaking his arm. Curiously, when the scene was re-created in the movie, the actor playing the son also had an arm broken and a curtain was mysteriously torn from top to bottom.

During a subsequent visit, the investigators covered the walls with black poster board and numbered the panels. Gaynor relates, "The lights appeared. I would call out, 'All right, blink three times on board number two for yes. Blink twice on board number five for no.' It would blink on the exact board that I asked it to. At that point, the level of excitement really increased, because it seemed like we were communicating with something intelligent.

"But I was very concerned that somebody was faking it by projecting light onto the wall. So I said to it, 'If you're really here, come off the wall.' I didn't think anything would happen. But then the light pulled right out of the wall and floated into the middle of the room. It started spinning and twisting and expanding in different directions simultaneously. I had nine professional photographers shooting every angle of that room.

"It was extraordinary because it was floating in the middle of the room and the light was dimensional. It is very difficult to fake something like that. If you project light, you have to project it onto a flat surface. You can't project light into empty space unless you have some kind of very sophisticated laser system."

Bider claimed that there were three entities in the house. Two smaller ones would generally hold her down while the third one assaulted her. After months of abuse, she and her son moved out to try to escape the terror at the house. As is typical in these cases, the haunting followed her. As time went on, however, the activity devolved into simple poltergeist manifestations, and it eventually petered out. Bider moved to Texas and at last report, was in her sixties and suffering from pancreatic cancer. After leaving the Los Angeles area, she shunned all publicity.

Mission San Juan Capistrano

The 1939 hit tune "When the Swallows Come Back to Capistrano" was recorded by Glenn Miller, Gene Autry, and the Ink Spots, but no one has thus far been inspired to sing about the ghosts that haunt this upscale area.

Predictably, the official guide to the Mission San Juan Capistrano given out at the entrance turnstile concentrates on the history of founder Father Junipero Serra and the story of the Spanish colonization of California. The mission was founded by Serra on November 1, 1776, and soon became one of the busiest in the territory. As in almost everywhere the Spanish set down roots, the native population was forced to work as free labor for the greater glory of God and the Royal Crown. The Indians were actually locked up in the buildings at night.

The big deal at Capistrano is, of course, the swallows, whose numbers have dwindled recently due to encroaching development and the loss of habitat for the insects that provide their diet.

When you think about it, it would be peculiar if there weren't any supernatural phenomena in this town, steeped as it is in the history of early California. On the night of December 18, 1812, a catastrophic earthquake effectively leveled the ornate chapel that once stood here, taking the lives of forty worshippers. But enough remnants of the old mission still stand to give the place an authentic, and sometimes ghostly, air. There are no actors to help the atmosphere along, but tourists occasionally report sightings of Franciscan monks walking among the adobe colonnades—and disappearing into thin air. Visitors have also heard bells tolling for mass, even though the mission's four massive bells have not been used in years. In addition, ghost hunter extraordinaire Richard Senate reports that a woman in a white dress, looking like she had just come in from the rain that was falling outside, once entered the gift shop, formerly the priests' quarters. She had jet-black hair and looked "confused and perhaps ill." When a clerk approached to ask if she needed help, the woman walked straight through a wall. The phantom left no wet footprints.

An Indian woman named Magdalena, who is said to have died without confessing her sins, walks one of the upper stories of the ruined walls, carrying a candle that can be seen on dark nights through one of the windows at the back of the church. The mission cemetery, on the east side of the complex, has witnessed strange lights moving about the tombstones at night and even a few instances of spirit voice recordings. The utterings, known as Electronic Voice Phenomena (EVP), can be manifested by anyone with a tape or digital recorder. One said "I'm scared" and "I'm cold," and another whispered more cryptically, "It's happening again."

A few doors south of the mission is the popular El Adobe De Capistrano restaurant, known for its enchiladas, which were often special-ordered by Richard Nixon during his brooding retreats to the Western White House in nearby San Clemente. The building was originally two structures, the oldest built in 1797 as a private home. In 1812, the local courthouse was established next door. After the structures were joined in 1910, the place went through a few different owners, who began to notice strange goings-on in the basement of the courthouse, which served as a jail. Restaurant employees are wary of the area, which now is used as a wine cellar. They report feelings of being watched, cold spots (in an already cold basement), and wine bottles falling off racks.

Historic Ghosts of Los Rios

The Los Rios historical district is a short walk west of the mission, over the railroad tracks. At least three ancient adobes here have recorded even more dramatic activity than the mission itself. Under a huge and ancient pepper tree next to the Rios Adobe, the ubiquitous woman in white scares passersby with her ethereal visits, sometimes accompanied by an evil-looking black dog who apparently spits fire. One legend claims the unnamed woman killed herself with poison on the front porch of a suitor who had spurned her. The Rios family, who still live in the house, have heard footsteps and doors closing late at night. At first, they thought prowlers were responsible, but came to know better after a few tense nights.

The specter of Dona Polonia Montanez sticks close to her old place next door. She was a popular (if unofficial) spiritual leader in San Juan Capistrano during the late nineteenth century and is associated with at least one possible miracle involving a drought-ending deluge. She, or something, manifests as a blue light in her old adobe. Visitors have also heard devout chanting in the two-room home.

In 1778, the mission cemetery was full, so new ground was cleared nearby. The old and hard-to-find cemetery plays host to a classic La Llorona (Crying Woman) spirit, who wanders the area wailing for her lost children. Almost every area in the Southwest originally settled by the Spanish or mestizos has its own version of this classic haunting, usually employed by parents as a cautionary tale to keep kids in line. The cemetery is creepy enough in the daytime and well worth a visit, even though it is gated and locked.

Cemetery directions: From Interstate 5 South, make a left on Ortega Highway and another left directly into a seemingly dead-end road (after the abandoned gas station). The cemetery is on a hill above the 5 Freeway and Ortega Highway.

Cemetery Safari

How people choose to be remembered after their death is often a very personal and revealing look at what sort of people they were while here on earth. This is especially true in California, where so many celebrities lived their lives in the limelight and seem reluctant to let go of the warm glow of fame, even after their final curtain call. But death is the great equalizer, and there are no velvet ropes in the afterlife. In the end, the famous and the anonymous all lie down side by side.

All over the state, there are fascinating cemeteries with graves of people whose names we know well and people who may have been unknowns in life, but who achieved some measure of fame in death. A walk around the crumbling markers or magnificent mausoleums can be a living history lesson, taught by those who preceded us—and who know where we are all headed in the end. Some cemeteries have given rise to legends of hauntings and curses, while others are of interest simply for the offbeat tombstones to be discovered within them.

Every one of those tombstones tells a story. The departed speak to us from beyond the grave, and their words are written in stone. Sometimes they are words of warning or advice to the living. Some tell tales of earthly woe, while others are actually quite lighthearted and inspiring. Whatever the message, each graveyard that we may whistle past offers reminders of life's triumphs and tragedies to anyone who takes the time to read the words inscribed there.

TYRONE POWER

1972   1988
HOUDINI COHEN

MY BELOVED SON
MAMA'S LITTLE BABY

Hollywood Forever Cemetery

Visitors to Los Angeles are disappointed if they go back home without a single celebrity-spotting story to brag about. Imagine the disgrace of traveling all the way from Chippewa Falls, only to remain shamefully silent when your next-door neighbors ask if you rubbed elbows with anyone famous. Now you can travel to the City of Angels in confidence, explorer from the east. There are places in L.A. where you can't swing a dead cat without running across dozens of Tinseltown's famous and infamous. Hollywood Forever Cemetery is one such place.

Hollywood Forever was originally named Hollywood Memorial Park and was opened to the dying public in 1899 by two Isaacs (Lankershim and Van Nuys). It slowly became the place to spend eternity. But by the 1980s and '90s, mismanagement and skulduggery on the part of owner Jules Roth had turned the place into a horror. The property was in a sorry state when it went on the block in 1998. Some families had actually paid to have their loved ones removed from crypts and graves. Tyler Cassity took over the facility and invested "millions" (according to the press release) in improvements and renovations.

Cassity saved the famous old burial ground and renamed it Hollywood Forever Cemetery. Here you can hobnob with such luminaries as Douglas Fairbanks, Peter Lorre, Tyrone Power, Fay Wray, and everyone's favorite Jewish mob boss, Benjamin "Bugsy" Siegel. Siegel's crypt marker sits just above eye level and is shaped like an open book; there is a Star of David above his name and an inscription that reads IN LOVING MEMORY FROM THE FAMILY. One can't help but wonder if

this written send-off was from Bugsy's family or Bugsy's *family.* (Get it?)

Fans of the old *Little Rascals* and *Our Gang* comedies will be happy to know that Darla Hood and Alfalfa are eternally united, at least in burial-plot real estate if not in each other's hearts. Darla is entombed in the Eternal Life mausoleum, while her silver screen sweetheart was laid to rest in the lawn a few hundred feet away.

Alfalfa's headstone bears the name Carl "Alfalfa" Switzer and has an engraved image of a dog that many believe to be Petey, the pooch in the series. Others maintain that it is Switzer's own pet dog and not the motion picture pup. As it turns out, Alfalfa had dabbled in

secretly entombed him here. It only sounds farfetched if you haven't seen it. . . . Believe us, it's freaky. The bust, which was modeled after White at age fifty-three, was actually a prop from a 1969 *Bewitched* episode.

Fan of the punk rock genre? None did it harder or better than the Ramones. Both bassist Dee Dee (Douglas Clovin) and guitarist Johnny (John Cummings) are buried here. Dee Dee is in the more conventional grave of the two. The Ramones' presidential seal logo is emblazoned atop his tombstone along with the tongue-in-cheek phrase, "OK. . . . I gotta go now." The nearby ground is littered with tributes from Ramones fans: candles, Bic lighters, and guitar picks.

But Dee Dee's memorial is positively conventional in comparison to that of Johnny, who planned ahead for his decidedly unpunkish marker. He rises from a granite block in pure bronze, trapped at mid-thigh and clutching a guitar from which he is surely coaxing the first chords of "Now I Wanna Sniff Some Glue." Inscribed around the

professional dog breeding, and the dog on his marker is most likely a reference to that. Carl was shot dead on January 21, 1959, at age thirty-two, in what was deemed a "justified homicide." The shooting was the result of a heated argument between Switzer and a friend over fifty dollars and a lost hunting dog. It seems that dogs played a big part in Alfalfa's life—and death.

Death by misadventure is also represented in the elaborate monument for Jayne Mansfield (who is actually buried in Pennsylvania), star and famous devotee of Anton LaVey and his Church of Satan. Mansfield died in an auto wreck that spared her three children but also killed her dog and driver. Rumors still swirl about a curse put on Mansfield by the goateed LaVey.

David White, who played Larry Tate, Darren's wishy-washy boss on television's *Bewitched*, is buried here too. At least we hope he is dead and not the everlasting victim of Endora's dark witchcraft. Look for yourself. The bronze bust of the actor is so eerily lifelike that one can't help wondering if White stumbled across Samantha's secret—and in order to keep his silence, the comedic coven

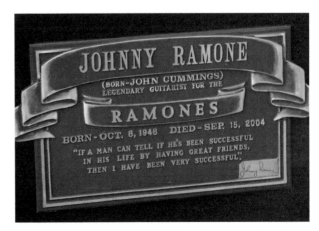

polished stone are tributes from friends such as Vincent Gallo and John Frusciante (the latter, the guitarist for the Red Hot Chili Peppers). Leaning back in the quintessential rock god–axe man pose, the statue of Johnny Ramone is far and away the most visually jarring image in the park. Sitting directly in front of the serene duck pond and framed by the swaying palm trees, the grave is a loud rock shout in this otherwise somber field of memorials, but that was most

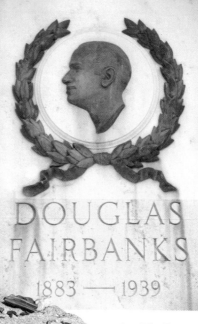

likely by Johnny's design.

Not had your fill of the rich, famous, and dead? How about the man of a thousand voices? Mel Blanc, who breathed life into such classic cartoon characters as Bugs Bunny, Daffy Duck, and Barney Rubble, is buried beneath this hallowed bedrock. His headstone says THAT'S ALL FOLKS.

If this isn't enough reason to visit Forever, and we think it ought to be, there are also the occasional outdoor screenings of well-known movies projected on the walls of the mausoleums. Sometimes the movies fit the spooky graveyard atmosphere, i.e., *The Exorcist*. Other times they're simply Hollywood standards, like *Some Like It Hot*. It makes for a great date. For the past three years, the L.A. film-lovers group Cinespia has been projecting classic films on the wall of the Cathedral Mausoleum in the southeast corner of the park. Up to three thousand viewers arrive early for the shows, carting chairs, blankets, and picnic meals. Often stars represented in the films are actually interred in the cemetery or mausoleum itself. A few families have complained about disrespect for their lost loved ones, but owner Cassity maintains it helps to raise money for upkeep of the cemetery grounds. "Donations" for admission are $10.

Hollywood Forever will sell you a map showing the grave sites of the famous. So the next time you return from a visit to the West Coast, you can hold your head up high. You'll have enough celebrity sightings to become a star in your own right at the next block party or ice-cream social.

Rocket Man

Not everyone interred at Hollywood Forever was famous in life. Some, like Carl Morgan Bigsby, waited until after death to grab the spotlight. Bigsby was a graphic designer, but also a hard-core believer in outer space manifest destiny. To mark his grave, he commissioned an exact scale replica of the Atlas B ballistic missile in gleaming white marble. The real version of this rocket was still undergoing tests in California and Florida when Bigsby died in 1959. He is interred here with his beloved wife, Charlotte.

Where Stars Shun the Spotlight

The award for the most impressive collection of dead celebrities has to go to Forest Lawn Memorial Parks in Glendale and Hollywood Hills. Take a look at this roll call if you will: Spencer Tracy, Humphrey Bogart, Walt Disney, Sammy Davis Jr., Bette Davis, Larry Fine, Clark Gable . . . that's some impressive Hollywood gathering, above or below the earth.

Death must be a good business in Los Angeles. Forest Lawn Corporation has five complexes in different areas of the county, covering over 1,200 acres in total. The cream of the crop is definitely the park in Glendale. The grounds look as if someone took every painting of heaven that has been produced since the Middle Ages and used them as production drawings. Periodic billboard campaigns dot the southland, asking motorists to "celebrate a life" with "pre-planning" courtesy of Forest Lawn.

The 1965 film *The Loved One,* written by Terry Southern, was supposed to have been a parody of the uniquely southern California–Forest Lawn style of overweeningly pastoral resting places for the dead. A walk through the grounds reveals that the film was not far from the truth. The Freedom Mausoleum

is a flag-waver's paradise, with a massive brass statue of George Washington and busts of founding fathers like Benjamin Franklin installed tastefully throughout the buildings. All around the mausoleum complex, 101 Strings–inspired versions of old favorites like "Suwannee River" and "Greensleeves" play on a continuous loop through sometimes static-laced outdoor speakers. Is it comforting or just strange? Does everyone in the graveyard like this music? Can't they at least install an iPod and leave it on shuffle?

The biggest problem when visiting Forest Lawn is that, unlike in Hollywood Forever Cemetery, you are on your own to navigate around it. Forest Lawn silently discourages tourists and fans. Some celebrities had the courtesy to customize their commemorative plaques and markers, so as to stand out from the regular noncelebrity dead, like circus legend Clyde Beatty (cool engraving of a lion) or the original rhinestone cowboy, Nudie (designer of Nudie clothing). Unfortunately, it seems the more famous the person, the more unassuming their sites here tend to be. We did find them, though, along with local celebrities like longtime L.A. newscaster Jerry Dunphy

and right-wing talk show host and father of actress Rebecca DeMornay, Wally George. There's also an A-list of classic television stars: Morey Amsterdam, Freddie Prinze (the talented one), McLean Stevenson, and Isabelle "Weezy Jefferson" Sanford.

We advise a printout from one of the many Web sites that specialize in this sort of thing. The security staff was surprised that locations of celebrity graves were commonly found on the Internet. "Those are supposed to be private" is an oft-repeated phrase when the visitor arrives with pictures and directions fresh off some Web site. So if you go to Forest Lawn, make sure you walk with a dignified grace once you enter, because we're serious about their being sticklers for decorum. Getting eighty-sixed from a swinging Hollywood shindig carries with it a certain cachet; being bounced from a cemetery, no matter how cool the cemetery, is pretty lame.

He'd Rather Be in Forest Lawn

Rumors swirl about what is written on the grave site of W. C. Fields, the famous comedic curmudgeon: He used a fake name, he couldn't afford to pay for it, and others. The most famous story is that Fields's will instructed that his memorial would bear the inscription ALL THINGS CONSIDERED, I'D RATHER BE IN PHILADELPHIA. That rumor stems from a 1925 article in *Vanity Fair* in which Fields proposed the epitaph for himself; it is a play on his oft-uttered quote "I'd rather be dead than in Philadelphia!" which was his birthplace.

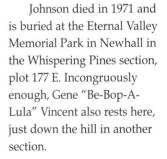

Fields occupies an honored place in the massive and ostentatious Great Mausoleum on the peak of the highest mountain on the Glendale property of Forest Lawn. The location is designed to impress the living with the idea that the dead will appreciate the million-dollar view. Fields's propensity for pseudonyms apparently spilled over into questions about his birth date. He was born on January 29, 1880, then again on April 9, 1889. Most historians (and Fields's own son) have settled on the 1880 date, and this is what appears on the brass plaque on the front of his crypt. No sign of the Philadelphia quote. The Great Mausoleum is open from nine a.m. to four thirty p.m., but only for twenty-minute periods every half hour.

Tor Johnson

Most generation Xers are at least aware of the films of Edward D. Wood Jr., who has been called the worst director of all time. No, the legendary Eddie isn't buried in Los Angeles. He was cremated and scattered at sea after his death, in 1978. But one of Wood's stock players, who usually played a hulking goon or a hulking goonlike zombie, has left us his earthly remains. We speak of the three-hundred-pound former wrestler Tor Johnson.

Swedish-born Johnson made his professional debut under the stage name Super Swedish Angel and became a crowd favorite. Wood introduced him as Lobo in *Bride of the Monster* (1956); he played the mindless assistant to Bela Lugosi's mad scientist character. He went on to appear and sometimes star in at least twenty more films.

The Lobo character was so popular that Johnson reprised it in other features, not all directed by Wood. Lobo became such a legend, in fact, that when Johnson's film career tanked in the late 1960s, he ghouled it up as the character in personal appearances. While he was still among us, a Hollywood makeup-effects artist made a life mask of Johnson, which was used as a mold for an elaborate perennial favorite Halloween mask.

Johnson died in 1971 and is buried at the Eternal Valley Memorial Park in Newhall in the Whispering Pines section, plot 177 E. Incongruously enough, Gene "Be-Bop-A-Lula" Vincent also rests here, just down the hill in another section.

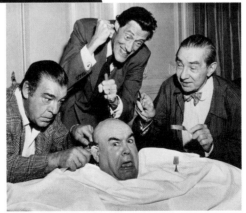

Three horror actors (left to right), Lon Chaney, John Carradine, and Bela Lugosi take time for a snack. The "snack" being served up is Tor Johnson.

Westwood Village Memorial

A scant few miles from the hallowed halls of U.C.L.A. is the Westwood Village Memorial Park. Easily the smallest of the "Famous Dead People Gravesites," it also offers the most bang for your buck. Whereas Forest Lawn in Glendale alone consists of over three hundred acres of peaceful rolling hills, and you could get lost in Hollywood Forever Cemetery if you're not paying attention, Westwood Village is about the size of the clothing section in your average Wal-Mart.

That, however, is where the comparison to the bargain-priced retail outlet ends. This place is the Tiffany's of deceased superstar icons. Jack Lemmon and Walter Matthau are once again teamed up for great dramatic effect here. Tough guys George C. Scott and Burt Lancaster hang out comfortably with a

man's man of a different sort, Truman Capote.

Music legends? Yeah, they got 'em. Carl Wilson of the Beach Boys is here, as well as Roy Orbison. Frank Zappa is said to occupy the unmarked grave just eight feet west of Orbison's (grave #100).

Television stars Carroll O'Connor (Archie Bunker), Jim Backus (Thurston Howell the Third), Jonathan Harris (Dr. Smith), and Sebastian Cabot (Mr. French) all now make Westwood Memorial their eternal TV land.

Looking for hotties? It's going to be hard to beat this collection of exquisite leading ladies: Natalie Wood, Dorothy Stratten, Donna Reed, and the one and only candle in the wind, Norma Jeane Mortensen, a.k.a. Marilyn Monroe.

Westwood is even the final resting place of two young stars of the movie *Poltergeist* who were taken way before their time: the adorable Heather O'Rourke, who died on the operating table at the tender age of thirteen, and the beautiful Dominique Dunne, who played O'Rourke's older sister. (Dunne was tragically strangled by an estranged boyfriend.)

If death seems to be an unfair yet certain eventuality for everyone, consider the situation of the very much alive and breathing (at least as of this writing) comedian Jerry Lewis. Jerry's longtime partner, crooner, and former Rat Pack member Dean Martin is entombed in a crypt here at Westwood Memorial. Most days Martin's marble stone is covered in lip prints of every size, shape, and color, proving that even in death, Dino gets more action than his wacky and annoying former sidekick.

Hey, Laaaaaady!!!!

Ah, the Futility of It All

A fitting epitaph for a defeatist Beat poet can be found at Green Hills Memorial Park in Rancho Palos Verdes. It reads simply DON'T TRY, and is inscribed on the grave marker of Henry Charles "Hank" Bukowski, whose drunken exploits in life were immortalized in the film *Barfly*. The movie starred Mickey Rourke in the role of the brawling and slovenly, yet somehow endearing, Bukowski. Despite the portrayal in the film, Bukowski was actually an extremely prolific and well-respected author of both poetry and prose, having more than forty-five books published before his death in 1994 at the age of seventy-three. The grave of the antisocial antihero writer sits on a hillside by itself, set apart from the other dead in the cemetery, just the way Buk would have wanted it.

"Gorgeous" George

Another resident of Valhalla Memorial Park is "Gorgeous" George Wagner, the famous and flamboyant entertainer who reigned as the King of Pro Wrestling from the late 1940s until his retirement in 1960. Wagner was an unsuccessful wrestler until he came up with the idea for his famous persona. He grew his hair long, bleached it blond, and had it permed into flowing curls. For every match, he entered to the strains of "Pomp and Circumstance," with the train of his satin cape carried by a male assistant, who would disinfect and perfume his master's corner of the ring before George would even think of entering it. He would also do the same for (or to) the opponent's corner.

Wagner used every opportunity to cheat—gouging eyes, punching, and pulling noses—supposedly out of view of the clueless referee, which delighted or infuriated fans and sometimes caused riots to break out. In many ways, Wagner is the father of modern pro wrestling. He apparently had his name legally changed to Gorgeous George sometime in the 1950s.

Location: Block J, Section 9370, Lot 4—northeast of main fountain.

Lived Fast, Died Young

You don't have to be driving a fancy foreign sports car to get a case of leadfoot on Highway 46 in Cholame. You can bury the needle on a rented Toyota Camry and still feel like a causeless rebel when the road is that flat and open. No matter if your waist is a little larger than it was when you were 24 years old, or that your hair doesn't have enough body to do a proper DA. When you've got the pedal to the metal, the sun to your back, and the right tunes blasting out of your stereo (or the rental car's stereo), you are James Dean—heartthrob, idol, movie star, immortal.

The sign that commemorates James Dean—with his name still intact.

So it is with these romantic and admittedly immature notions that I race toward the intersection of Highways 46 and 41, anxious to see it, the site of the crash that thrust Dean into the big matinee in the sky. I don't know what to expect, but it seems natural to anticipate the twisted horrible remains of the famed Porsche Spyder. Maybe they kept the blood on the dashboard. That would be so cool.

I arrive at the crossroads, but I don't expect the memorial to be there. In fact the actual site of the crash is not even a paved road anymore, and it's about a half a mile east of the junction that now stands there.

The actual memorial is in the parking lot of the Jack Ranch Café. I am anxious to behold the spectacle that it is sure to be. If there is a tribute to a man who lived his life by the credo, "Live fast, die young, leave a beautiful corpse," it has to be nothing short of breathtaking.

Pulling into the restaurant's parking lot I see it, but I don't want to believe it. It's a sign. A stainless steel sign, ok, but it's still

just a sign. Not only that, but all the letters of his name have been yanked off the stupid sign. Stupid, stupid sign.

It's a sign, in front of a tree, surrounded by a rock garden. Whoopee!!!

No Spyder, no shattered windshield, no blood. I mean I know this happened in 1955, September 30, at 5:59 p.m. to be exact, but I was expecting something more . . . theatrical. This guy was James Freakin' Dean, a Hollywood legend. Give me some blood.

I walk into the restaurant, hoping to use the restroom, and maybe get some information from a waitress. The walls are lined with newspaper clippings, and photos of the young actor, but the girl behind the counter doesn't know much about the memorial. "Some rich Japanese guy put it up there, like a long time ago," she offers in an annoyed monotone, as if she's been asked a thousand times before.

A different sign behind the counter informs me the restroom is only for customers, so I order a bag of butterscotch cookies, and ask politely for the key to the boys' room. I wash my hands and pay for the goodies, and consume them all in the Toyota before I am a half mile away, doing a law abiding 55. I probably shouldn't have wolfed them down in one sitting. I've been trying to lose some weight . . . you know, the waistline and all, but dammit, I'm a rebel.—*Joe O.*

N'yuking It Up with Curly

The greatest stooge of all, Jerome "Curly" Howard, n'yuks it up at the Home of Peace Memorial Park in Los Angeles in an area called the Western Jewish Institute.

Curly, one of the famed Three Stooges comedy team, suffered a stroke during the making of his ninety-seventh *Three Stooges* film in 1946, and eventually wound up in a North Hollywood sanitarium. After years of spending all his money on drinking, eating, and women, Curly was in a mental state that made him a problem for the nursing staff, and it was suggested that he be placed in an institution. But his brother Moe, always looking out for his younger brother (whom he referred to as Babe) would not hear of it. Curly died at the age of forty-eight. Years later Moe would recall that every time he slapped his brother Shemp (Curly's replacement in the act), he would think of Babe.

Gram Parsons's Death Pact at Cap Rock

Mystery hangs over the Joshua Tree National Park, a vast expanse of rock piles, stark mountain ranges, and the twisted, treelike yucca cacti that give the park its name. Perhaps because of its desolately beautiful, otherworldly landscape, the Joshua Tree region has long attracted eccentrics living on the farthest fringes of southern California exurbia. UFO devotees insist that there is a secret spaceship base hidden somewhere in the brush-dotted hills. UFO contactee and cult leader George Adamski claimed that he got a saucer ride from "long-haired Venusians" aboard one of the ships cruising above Highway 177, just east of the park.

Other desert residents tell of bizarre happenings in and around the park. They've seen camper trucks dematerialize on the Morongo Valley highway, furtive three-fingered aliens buy supplies in Joshua Tree drugstores, and glowing, robotlike humanoids wander across the national park outback.

One of the oddest places in Joshua Tree is the Gram Parsons "memorial" on the north side of Cap Rock, in the center of the park. Parsons, a talented, troubled musician who almost single-handedly invented the country-rock genre, was a regular visitor to the park until his death at the Joshua Tree Inn on September 19, 1973. The cause of death was a massive drug overdose.

When Parsons's body was taken to Los Angeles International Airport, en route to the family burial plot back in Georgia, his friend Phil Kaufman snatched the coffin off the freight ramp. Kaufman, a former drug smuggler and rock manager who had once produced Charles Manson's solo music album, had made a death pact with Parsons obligating him to cremate the latter's corpse at Joshua Tree's Cap Rock, a "power spot" that was one of the musician's favorite hangouts. Sure enough, Kaufman and an accomplice brought the body out to Cap Rock, laid it on the desert floor, and set it aflame in a macabre little ceremony. The two men were arrested soon afterward but were released when it was found that no California laws prohibited body-snatching or impromptu cremations.

In the thirty years since his death, Parsons has become a cult figure among rock and country musicians and fans. The little grotto where the strange ceremony took place is covered with eulogies, quotes from Parsons's songs, and fanciful drawings left by admirers. It's a modest monument, but a fitting one left to this strange land's most famous devotee and victim.

The Curse of the Green Man

Artist Peter Ledger, the man behind the face of this unique tombstone found in Oakhill Cemetery in Oakhurst, was born in Australia in 1945 and grew to fame as a graphic artist, creating imaginative hand-painted and airbrushed illustrations. In the late 1970s, he won awards for his advertising posters and album cover art, and during his stint at Marvel Comics, he created the series "Warriors of the Shadow Realm." He later worked in Hollywood on storyboards and designs that have become coveted collectors' items. In 1983, he moved to California with his American wife, Christy Marx, also an artist, and they eventually made their home in Oakhurst. On November 18, 1994, while driving home from Monterey, Ledger was hit by a tractor-trailer and died on impact.

His son, Julian, who works in the film industry doing special effects, created Peter Ledger's one-of-a-kind bronze headstone; to cast the form of his head, Julian used a life mask his father had made in the 1980s. Julian also meticulously sculpted a poem Ledger himself wrote in 1991 with the intent of it being used as his epitaph, along with various symbols that were meaningful to him: clouds (he was an amateur pilot with a love of flying), an eagle logo (Ledger designed it), Greek and Spartan helmets (which often featured in his artwork), grape vines (he had a passion for food and wine), and Celtic knot work (among other mediums, Ledger also worked with leather).

According to a Web site posted by Ledger's widow, Christy Marx

PETER LEDGER EPITAPH

25 OCT. 45 – 18 NOV. 94

DEAD, ROTTEN, IN THE GROUND,
TO SEE NO MORE, TO HEAR NO SOUND,
TO TASTE NOT OF THE TANG OF WINE,
NOR FEEL THE CURVE OF LOVE ENTWINED,
TO RIDE NOT ON THE WAVES OF AIR,
NOR PENETRATE DEEP NEPTUNE'S LAIR,
THE POWDERED SLOPES NO MORE TO RUN,
NO FLASHING SHAFT NOR BUCKING GUN,
TO DINE NOT FROM THE LADEN TABLE,
UNMOVED BY WORDS OR SONG OR FABLE,
TO BUT LIE ENTOMBED ANON,
'TIL BODY, MIND AND EARTH ARE ONE.

(www.christymarx.com /ledger/memorial.htm), an interesting story—"The Curse of the Green Man"—goes along with this exceptional headstone, which took two years to create. While the tombstone was still a work in progress, Marx placed a sculpture of a mythic Celtic character called the Green Man, which Ledger had purchased, on his grave site to mark it. This

Green Man was subsequently stolen, angering Marx, who took out the following ad in the Personals section of the local newspaper:

> To the person or persons who stole the head of the Green Man from my husband's grave. My husband was an artist. He painted this Green Man with his own hands to look like aged bronze. I placed it on his grave as a temporary marker and you took it.
>
> Only the lowest form of scum would desecrate a grave. If you have any shred of decency, you will return the Green Man to Oakhill Cemetery where he belongs. If you do not, you are thrice-cursed. Cursed once for defiling the dead, cursed again as a thief, and finally the Curse of the Green Man is upon you which will bring you misfortune, bad luck and misery for the rest of your days.
>
> Return what you have stolen or never know peace again.

Marx notes that a Fresno TV station saw the ad and featured her story on the local news—and the very next day, the Green Man had been returned to its rightful place.

Ironically, the bronze face of Peter has now turned an eerie shade of patina green, due to the oxidation—we assume.

Brownie the Railroad Dog

Poor old Brownie, he just couldn't keep away from speeding trains. Brownie was a stray mutt who wandered the tracks near the Union Pacific Railroad stop in Victorville in the late 1930s. He got a home when the stationmaster rescued him after he was injured in a traffic accident and nursed him back to health. For years afterward, Brownie faithfully (and probably annoyingly, after a while) announced the arrival of every train coming up the track from the treacherous Cajon Pass. Legend has it that crews often threw cooked meat out the door of the moving train when Brownie appeared, nipping at the heels of the caboose. Brownie would chase passengers' dogs away when they tried to exit the cars for a simple poop stop.

When he was finally hit and killed chasing the steel wheels of his beloved 5:15 in 1945, the boys at the station gave him a decent burial and a headstone, which now sits in a park next to the tracks. The headstone, which originally read BROWNIE / A RAILROAD DOG / A FRIEND AND A PAL was apparently replaced recently, the original most likely a victim of vandalism. It sits at the base of a tree among scores of cranky homeless people. "Dammit! Don't put me in your picture!" one of them boomed out while we zoomed in on poor Brownie's simple monument. The park is apparently the local one-stop crack shop too. Newer model cars automatically arouse suspicion. Visit in the day, and don't forget to look in on the burned out and abandoned Spook House next door. Brownie's eternal resting place is in Forrest Park—16906 South D Street (at Sixth Street).

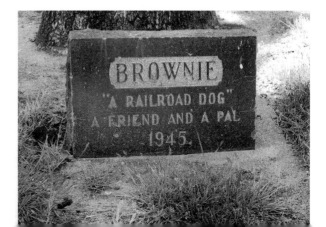

Where Little Pets Rest in Peace

Alas, the happy hunting ground for pets of the rich and famous is way out in Calabasas, but it is worth the drive, even if you don't plan to provide Fido with a deluxe resting place. Visible from the freeway is a sign high on a hill overlooking the cemetery that reads L.A. PET PARK. This is probably one of the few graveyards around where pets are actually encouraged to come, so long as they are on a leash.

The L.A. pet cemetery was founded in 1928, early enough to receive the worldly remains of Rudolph Valentino's beloved Doberman, Kabar. Kabar must have been a highly spirited animal, because visitors have reported doglike panting and a wet tongue on their hands near his grave. Other, unidentified pets have also been seen cavorting about the grounds, evidently blissfully unaware that they are dead. Celebrity burials here include Hopalong Cassidy's horse Topper, Mary Pickford's pup, and at least one of the Petey dogs from the *Little Rascals* series. Here, dogs and cats lie together in peace.

Cemetery regulations specifically state that "No upright monuments are permitted," but an exception was apparently made for one of the most locally famous and beloved of pets: a cat called Room 8. From 1952 until her death in 1968, the precocious feline lived her weekdays in room 8 of the Elysian Heights elementary school near downtown L.A., and was featured in international news reports. When Room 8 died, donations poured into the school from all over the world for a large gravestone, which features a portrait and her name in gleaming white, highlighting the carved letters.

Although the maintenance nightmare that surrounds, say, Jim Morrison's grave in Paris is unlikely to plague the eternal residents of the Los Angeles pet cemetery, the caretakers here do seem overly cautious. Staffer Sandy Dunaway looks like a gentle soul whom anyone would be happy to call Nana, but when asked about the interment locations of the more notable four-legged friends, she quietly but firmly says, "You must understand that the owners want their privacy," and hands out a helpful promotional folder. Among donation forms and ads for flower companies are photocopies listing three separate psychologists who specialize in coping with the death of a pet. One features a session of therapy called Pet Loss Bereavement Coaching. Grieving owners may also avail themselves of numerous pet death support groups.

Even without directions to the celebrity sites, an hour spent wandering the ten-acre grounds is rewarding.

1949 1963
PUSSY CAT
BELOVED DOG
OF
MOM AND
THE MOREY AMSTERDAM'S

1941
SATAN 1958
FOREVER IN OUR HEARTS
LEO M. SMITH

Visits with L.A.'s Underground Residents

In L.A., everybody's always coming or going—except the dead. They're the only permanent residents here. I frequent the cemeteries of the Los Angeles area to find the most interesting of our dearly departed and document them on my website, "Beneath Los Angeles." Here is a sampling of some of the hundreds of examples of cemetery weirdness I've captured over the years.—*Steve Goldstein*

A Weeping Lady
Angelus Rosedale Cemetery

Flying Codonas
A family circus act ended in tragedy, but resulted in this striking monument, complete with a broken trapeze ring at the bottom. Inglewood Park Cemetery

"This ATM Is Closed"
Don't come looking for cash at the grave of Daniel Steven Burley. Forest Lawn Cemetery, Glendale

"I'm Fine, Thank You"
Stage and screen actor Sgt. Vince E. Bushey is fine, thank you! Forest Lawn—Hollywood Hills Cemetery

"Died Against His Better Judgement"

Charles Henry Rolker had a hunch that death wasn't a good idea! Woodlawn Cemetery, Santa Monica

"Hurry! The Party Has Started!"

Don't be late for the great beyond!

Ralph "Poopsy Doll" Butcher

Forest Lawn–Hollywood Hills Cemetery

Weeping Lady

A woman weeps over F. W. Blanchard, designer of the Hollywood Bowl and creator of L.A.'s first art gallery, Blanchard Hall. Hollywood Forever Cemetery, Los Angeles

"On Vacation"
Laura Frances Gill is vacationing in an
unknown land . . . called Santa Barbara.

'64 Corvette
What we can't have in life,
perhaps we can have in death.
It's yours, Boo Boo!

The Living-Room Grave
This grave gives new meaning to
"warming your bones by the fire."
Pull up a chair and make yourself
at home in the Home of
Peace Cemetery.

DROOPY
TO A WONDERFUL LITTLE PUP
WHOM WE'LL REMEMBER ALWAYS
NATALIE & BETTY BACALL

KABAR
MY FAITHFUL DOG
RUDOLPH VALENTINO
OWNER

abin Grave

restless life of toil and
over mountains, this
wanderer can call
s Rosedale Cemetery
Angeles home.

Droopy, Kabar, Meatball, and Pukie

At play forevermore in
Los Angeles pet cemete
Calabasas are Droopy (
hood dog of Lauren Ba
Kabar (Rudolph Valenti
Doberman), Meatball (A
Sandler's bulldog), and
cat of the Barrymore fa

"PUKIE BARRYMORE"
MY DEAR LITTLE CAT
LIONEL BARRYMORE

TAUBER
FAMILY

MAX
LANDR

MEATBALL
MY FIRST SON

Welcome to Necropolis!

Incorporated in 1924, the city of Colma actually has a lot more dead residents, an estimated two million, than it does living, around 1,200. There are seventeen cemeteries within the city's two square miles, accounting for approximately 73 percent of the total acreage of the town. Some of the boneyards contain some fairly noteworthy former folks, such as denim pioneer Levi Strauss, publishing potentate William Randolph Hearst, and Tombstone gunslinger Wyatt Earp.

So just how did this city end up with so many dead occupants? The Colma official Web site, www.colma.ca.gov/briefhis.html, tells the story colorfully, if not always with the best grammar.

A California State Law was passed in the late 1800's, State Penal Code 297 stated - prohibited any burials anywhere except an established cemetery such as one by a city or county, church, ethnic group or military. You could no longer bury a body on the homestead or along the wagon trail.

San Francisco had many cemeteries established by the time gold was discovered. Hundreds of thousands arrived bringing diseases, followed by deaths and filled their cemeteries to capacity.

Cemetery owners started looking for new locations to expand or relocate their burial grounds. They were frustrated in their attempt to buy San Francisco property. Land was too valuable for cemetery use said real estate promoters.

The San Francisco City Fathers passed Bill #54 & Ordinance #25 on 3-26-1900 stating that no further burials will be allowed in the City & County of San Francisco. With no further burials, they became a place of neglect and vandalism. They then became a health hazard.

Colma became the chosen area for cemeteries. . . .

In August of 1912 the San Francisco's Board of Supervisors declared intent to evict all cemeteries in their jurisdiction.

On Jan. 14, 1914 Removal notices were sent to all cemeteries, branding them as "A public nuisance and a menace and detriment to the health and welfare of city dwellers." Ordinance 2597

There were many delays to this order as the cemeteries and some citizens fought to have it revoked. By Nov. of 1937 the legal battles were over and bodies not removed were now ordered to be removed.

Colma Cemeteries now inherited hundreds of thousands of additional bodies.

This all led to the incorporation of the cemetery area that became known as Lawndale on August 5, 1924. . . . We kept Lawndale until the United States Postal Service informed us there was a Lawndale in Southern Calif. We went back to the name of Colma. This was on Nov. 17, 1941.

City of the Dead

I live here in San Francisco and wanted to write to you about the city of Colma. It is often called the City of the Dead due to the fact that it has many cemeteries, which include a Jewish cemetery, Chinese cemetery, pet cemetery, and so forth. It is known that this town has more dead people than living. The reason there are so many cemeteries is because in San Francisco it is "not allowed" to bury people. Some kind of ordinance that passed in the early 1900's I think. You should check it out.—*Leticia*

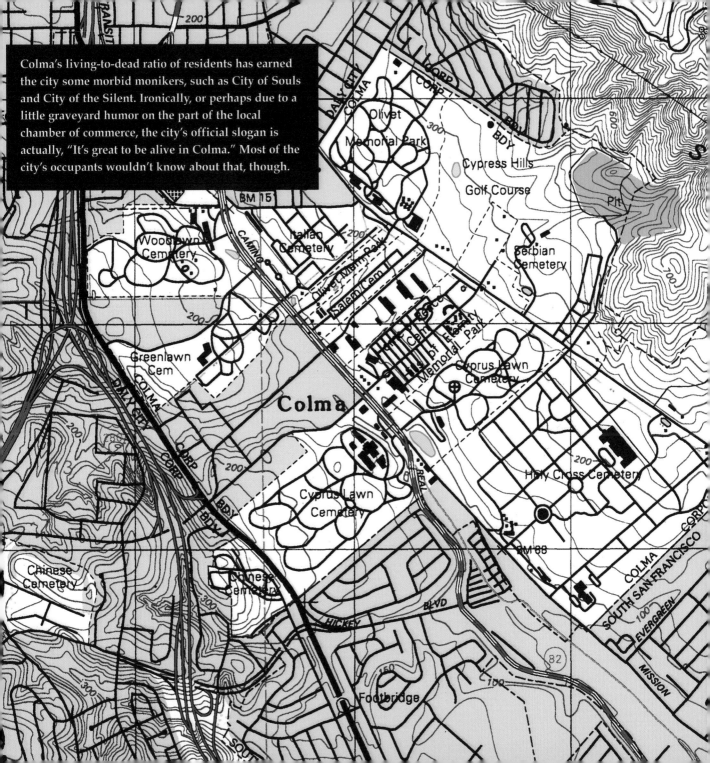

Colma's living-to-dead ratio of residents has earned the city some morbid monikers, such as City of Souls and City of the Silent. Ironically, or perhaps due to a little graveyard humor on the part of the local chamber of commerce, the city's official slogan is actually, "It's great to be alive in Colma." Most of the city's occupants wouldn't know about that, though.

Abandoned
in California

Stepping into a strange world that others once inhabited and then left forever can be a very unnerving sensation. Who were the people who once lived here? What were their lives like? Why did they leave, and where did they go? These are the questions that race through your mind while you wander inside these forsaken monuments of rotting wood, broken glass, and peeling paint.

Without a doubt, some of the weirdest places in California are the ones it has abandoned. Whether they be hollow-eyed homes with forgotten tales to tell, ghost towns whose fortunes turned from boom to bust, or decommissioned institutions that have outlived their usefulness, these vacant and crumbling places possess an aura that is foreboding and captivating at the same time. Some of them speak of the optimistic dreams of those who created them. California is, after all, a land of promise and opportunity. Abandoned places are poignant reminders that these promises may not pan out, that even our best laid plans and intentions might crumble to ruin in the end. Other abandoned places are, and may always have been, just plain creepy. They might have been home to people who lived in the shadows of sunny California—the mentally disabled, the terminally ill. Perhaps it's a by-product of the suffering that transpired within their walls, but wandering the empty hallways of these places can make even the staunchest skeptic believe that tortured spirits from the past may linger on, haunting us until this day.

There is no denying that people will conjure up all manner of fantastic stories about places that have been left to wither in the winds. Do the tales spring forth from overactive imaginations, or is there really something weird going on behind some of California's most forlorn façades? This is the question that we ask ourselves each time we cross a darkened threshold to explore another abandoned California ruin.

"Goodbye God, I'm Going to Bodie"

In 1859, gold was discovered in the hills north of Mono Lake and the town of Bodie was born. Because of its isolation on the eastern side of the Sierras, far from any mountain passes, Bodie grew slowly. Then came the big silver and gold strikes of 1877, and the rush was on. Soon the bitter adage, "Goodbye God, I'm going to Bodie," coined by a young girl confiding to her diary as her family prepared to move, was heard all over the country.

Bodie's population had exploded to 10,000 people by 1879, making it one of the largest cities in California. At its peak, this bustling Wild West metropolis boasted over 2,000 buildings, including seven breweries, more than sixty saloons, a red-light district, and even a Chinatown complete with opium dens. Bodie was wild. The hard climate (temperatures in the 100s during the summer and twenty feet of snow in the winter) brought in hard people. The volatile atmosphere of money, gold, and liquor meant that murders were a daily occurrence. Bodie had the dubious reputation of being one of the roughest towns in the Old West, and that's saying something.

Like a thousand other boomtowns, Bodie's glory days were short-lived. By 1881, the mines began to play out, and Bodie slipped into a long decline. In 1892, a massive fire destroyed half of the tinderbox town in a single day, and in 1932, a toddler playing with matches started a second big fire, which claimed many of the remaining structures. The entire town was eventually bought by local merchant and banker J. S. Cain, but by World War II, Bodie was essentially dead. Empty and untouched for decades, its abandoned buildings were protected by Cain's full-time, live-in caretakers until 1962, when Bodie became a State Historic Park.

At one time, hundreds of late-nineteenth-century mining boomtowns were scattered all over the West. Most are gone: burned down by vandals, ravaged by antiques collectors, and dismantled by salvage operations. However, thanks to Cain's caretakers, Bodie is the best-preserved, most authentic mining ghost town in the American West. Nearly two hundred buildings, "held in a

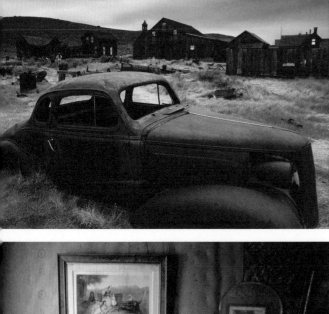

state of arrested decay," are filled with dust-covered merchandise and forgotten possessions, untouched since the 1940s.

On my first trip to Bodie, during a family vacation in 1973, the place was still more or less deserted. We could drive right into the center of town and park. It was mind-boggling to stand quietly among the elegantly weathered buildings. You could feel time grind to a halt as the wind blew tumbleweeds down Main Street. It was untouched and perfect, a ghost-town hunter's dream. Unfortunately, that's no longer true. Today Bodie swarms with tourists

all summer long, and rental RVs pack the parking lot, a quarter mile from town.

Still, that first trip sealed my fate. I became completely fascinated with the realization that places like this occurred all over the West. Since then, I've visited Bodie many times, and its surreal charms continue to draw me back. Closed and difficult to gain access to at night, Bodie had remained one of the top locations on my "Someday I have to do night photography in there" list. When the opportunity finally presented itself through a photo workshop, I leaped at the chance.—*Troy Paiva*

Lost Resorts of the Salton Sea

"The assembled forces of the river reached the intake, and the trembling wooden structures that stood between the pioneers and ruin, besieged by the rising flood, battered by the swirling currents, bombarded by drift, gave way under the strain and the charging waters plunged through the breach. . . .

"Then a new and alarming phase of the river's destructive work developed . . . a great gorge through which a new-made river flowed quietly to a new-born and ever-growing sea. The roar of the plunging waters, the crashing and booming of the falling masses of earth that were undermined by the roaring torrent were heard miles away."
—Harold Bell Wright, *The Winning of Barbara Worth*, 1911

The Salton Sea is one of California's true oddities, a great salt lake in the middle of a desert. (*See* Fabled People and Places, page 61.) Over the centuries, it has flooded and dried up many times. Ancient watermarks on the surrounding mountains suggest that it was over twenty times its present size as recently as the year 1500. The deepest part of its mucky bottom lies over three hundred feet below sea level.

In 1905, heavy rainfall caused the Colorado River to inundate a dike that was built to provide water for the Imperial Valley's farms. The Salton Sink, dry at that point, took the brunt of the flooding waters for almost two years. When the berms were finally fixed, a fifteen by thirty-five-mile artificial lake remained. The town of Salton and a Southern Pacific railroad siding (and some say an entire railroad engine) were completely submerged. In 1944 and '45, the crew of the *Enola Gay* made secret flights to the sea, sharpening their aim for the Hiroshima run and adding a few dummy atomic bombs to the treasures that await explorers when the water inevitably dries up again.

The main water supply for the sea is the New River, which was formed relatively recently in geological terms and has basically evolved into a slough for phosphate and nutrient-rich agricultural runoff, giving it the distinction of being the most polluted river in America. The river is given life (if that is what it

Skeletal mobile homes now stand waist-deep in stagnant water and salt-caked mud . . . and rusted signs advertise long-closed bait shops and liquor stores.

may be called) from various mysterious sources south of the border in Mexicali. Almost immediately it is inundated with what locals refer to as *agua negra,* the outflow of hundreds of illegal sewage operations. This may actually be the only source for the river. There are laws in Mexico against this sort of thing, but there are, of course, ways to keep such nuisances in check. With no border patrol agents to stop it, the river crosses into the United States and makes its way through the Imperial Valley, picking up more foul molecules on its way.

When it finally reaches the Salton, this chemical smoothie feeds massive algae blooms, which periodically choke most of the oxygen out of the water, leading to mass die-offs of aquatic life. Much of the shoreline appears to be ringed by pleasant stretches of white sand, until a closer look smashes that illusion. The beach is really littered with dead and dying fish and birds, lying on the billions of bleached bones of those that preceded them. Thousands of pounds of sun-dried fish jerky await the seagulls. The smell is unpleasant and gives little hint of the recreational bonanza that was once the Salton Sea.

Sometime in the 1930s, eager developers realized that the populations of Los Angeles and nearby Palm Springs could provide a steady stream of weekend fun seekers to the sea, which was then in relatively good shape. For a while, they were right. Towns sprang up around the shore to cater to fishermen, campers, and boaters. Resorts appeared and did a brisk business, entertaining everyone from Joe Six Pack to the Rat Pack.

In the 1960s, as overeager agribusinesses boomed in Imperial County, the runoff reached biblical proportions and the water level began to fluctuate wildly. Whole towns and sections of towns were suddenly swamped by ever more saline flooding. In the late '70s, two major storm seasons ripped through the region, inundating many of the resort towns. Things got so bad that the entire shoreline area of Bombay Beach had to be abandoned, leaving just a trashy-looking trailer park burial ground. Skeletal mobile homes now stand waist-deep in stagnant water and salt-caked mud. A gutted old easy chair sits sentinel on the scene, and rusted signs advertise long-closed bait shops and liquor stores.

People do still live in Bombay Beach, though—a population of about three hundred and fifty steadfast souls, protected by a twenty-foot-high berm surrounding the remaining streets and homes of the dilapidated community. There seem to be far more homes than people. A few children scrape out whatever games and mischief their imaginations can dream up. Adults have long ago forsaken the outdoors and stay inside with satellite TV and Internet connections, if they have them. The median annual household income as of the 2000 census was about $17,000.

Some sixteen miles north of Bombay Beach on Highway 111 are the remains of the North Shore Beach and Yacht Club. Abandoned in the late 1970s, the facility became a rehab center and then an old folks home before it was finally left to the elements. It's now used sporadically for location shoots when a rock video calls for the ubiquitous run-down building to be transformed into a rockin' roadhouse. The windows are boarded up, and the soot-encrusted shadow of an elegant stairway crawls up the wall in the lobby. The beachfront swimming pool is fenced off and filled with trash, and a playground sits half-buried in fish and bird bones. Watch out for the bored (and overzealous) caretaker. He'll leave his TV dinner long enough to drive the two hundred feet or so to holler at trespassers.

The Department of the Interior and the agriculture industry are in a race against time to save the sea before it becomes incapable of supporting any sort of wildlife. We wish them luck.

Salton Sea Test Base

I've spent a lot of time exploring the abandoned places along the sea's edge, but one of my favorite, seldom-talked-about spots is the Salton Sea Test Base. Opened by the navy in 1942, the eight-thousand-acre southwest shore facility served as a training base for PBY Catalina seaplane operations. Abandoned in the mid-'70s, the SSTB was used for live-fire military training exercises through the '80s, completely destroying all of the structures at the facility.

Today only the marines and Navy Seals use the Test Base for training. Surrounded by signs warning of unexploded bombs and almost inaccessible due to encroaching sand dunes burying sections of the access road, the base has always held a fascinating attraction for me. One night I finally slipped over the dunes and into the base just to see what was out there. As I expected, all the base buildings were gone and the long seaplane pier had been bombed down to its pilings. The only structures still evident were the concrete ordnance-storage bunkers. As I rode my mountain bike out of the SSTB late that night, tripod slung over my shoulder, several Apache attack helicopters on maneuver buzzed me repeatedly. No doubt I was leaving an infra-red trail visible in their night scopes. Plainly trespassing on restricted government land, I high-tailed it out of there.
–Troy Paiva

Salton Sea Is a Creepy, Creepy Place

This place is nuts. Murky and really, really, really creepy. In the '40s, '50s, or maybe '60s the Salton Sea was rendered "the largest fishing population in a man-made lake in the world" and it was a hot spot for communities and an aspiring yacht club. But the salinity levels became so high that fish by the millions, as well as birds drinking the water, died. The communities that grew around the lake vanished or simply moved to Niland. They were left in abandonment utterly and completely.

Further north of the communities is the yacht club, lavishly designed with a Frank Sinatra kind of rat-pack-casino-Mafia look. The road to the yacht club off the highway is laced evenly on both sides with palm trees. The club had all the amenities, an open walk-around roof as well as a lakeside pool and spa. Half under water, there is a small convenience store, not to mention the Texaco gas dock, and its ancient sign. The dock was crushed and lies on the side of what seems to be a breakwater. This is a must for anyone that likes creepy things. The motel is adjacent to the yacht club. It's two stories high and fully boarded up with yet another empty swimming pool with u-shaped boundaries. The motel is a Hitchcock movie just begging for attention. I shot two rolls of film here, and none of the pictures came out.

Legend says that there is an island that people refused to leave when services were no longer available to get them to and from the shore. The island in the Salton Sea was used for drinking, swindling, and getting away from any rules. Local legend says that from the shore late at night you can hear a band playing from the island. This information was given to me via locals. This is a place where you absolutely do not want to be caught at night.—*Paintchips*

For Hunters Point, the Ship Has Sailed

In the first half of the twentieth century, San Francisco was the busiest port on the West Coast, and the Hunters Point Shipyard was its busiest repair facility. The yard opened commercially in 1867 with the construction of the West Coast's first permanent dry dock. At the time, it was one of the world's largest.

Within weeks of the 1941 attack on Pearl Harbor, the entire shipyard was seized by the navy, and during World War II the War Department transformed Hunters Point into a vital repair base. At its peak in 1945, it employed over 18,000 workers. During the postwar years, the Naval Radiological Defense Laboratory operated there, its major responsibility being the study and decontamination of ships used in the nuclear weapons tests at the Bikini atoll. The NRDL also built a cyclotron "atom smasher" at Hunters Point and conducted top secret research on the effects of radioactive fallout on humans and animals.

Between the slipshod documentation of the NRDL's dirty playthings and other unknown contaminants from the day-to-day operation of a major shipyard,

no one really knows the extent of the toxic mess left behind on the isolated south side of the base. The NRDL was shut down in 1969, and in 1974 the navy decommissioned the entire base. Most of the area has remained uninhabited and inhospitable ever since.

Stories of widespread radioactive and chemical contamination as well as its location beside one of the toughest, most crime-ridden neighborhoods in San Francisco have kept the once bustling five-hundred-acre shipyard out of the public eye for decades. The entire facility has been locked and off-limits to the public for over thirty years. After a series of phone calls to various local and federal agencies, *Weird California* was granted night photography access to the long-deserted yard.

Dozens of abandoned corrugated-metal warehouses and decrepit office buildings stand scattered around name-less potholed streets. Red brick dry dock pump houses, dating back to 1867, slowly decay in the fog-shrouded air. These are some of the oldest buildings in San Francisco, utterly forgotten. Giant gantry cranes loom over broken and flooded dry docks as an endless stream of airliners streak across the sky from the nearby San Francisco and Oakland airports.

Security is tight. The SFPD and Department of Defense police maintain a strong presence at the shipyard. Inside the fence, it's quite safe, while just outside, gang warfare runs rampant.

On the hill above the dockyards is a now empty residential neighborhood. Built in the early twentieth century, all eighty-six homes were seized by the navy for officers' housing in 1942. When the base was decommissioned, the homes were abandoned. They have stood untouched for thirty years, slowly weathering, taking on the look of a postapocalyptic movie set. It's spooky to wander down the middle of these desolate, debris-covered streets and hear car chases and gunfire just a few blocks away. The entire relic-strewn base is just minutes from the downtown of one of the West Coast's largest cities. Most of San Francisco's citizens have no idea of this place's checkered past and toxic legacy. Many don't know it even exists.

PUMPRoom1

Abandoned TB Ward, Keene

One of the first places we visited while researching this book was also one of the creepiest—an abandoned ward for tuberculosis patients in Keene. The land on which it rests has been owned by the United Farm Workers (UFW) Union since the 1960s and is home to the Chavez Center. At the entrance to the property is UFW founder Cesar Chavez's grave and monument, complete with an appropriate quote from his friend Robert F. Kennedy chiseled into the stone. Be sure to stop in at the main building before you enter the grounds so that the staff knows you're there, or you could be arrested for trespassing. You can also look at Chavez's office, left in a state of suspended animation since 1993, when the storied labor leader died.

The abandoned TB ward is about a quarter of a mile

back on the main road. Teresa Delgado, the Chavez Center receptionist, recalls hearing strange stories from old-timers who used to stay there during classes and teach-ins in the 1960s and '70s. UFW staff and guests would often hear ghostly footsteps, lights would turn on by themselves, and a few noncorporeal residents were even sighted making appearances around the grounds late at night.

The main building is in surprisingly good repair for all the neglect it has suffered. High school kids and Halloween thrill seekers have entered the halls and rooms from time to time and thrown files and furniture around, but most of the rooms are almost barren. On the south side of the front entrance, a white-tiled room is spattered with red paint and handprints, some at impossibly high places on the wall. It's either someone's idea of a macabre joke or perhaps the remnants of some guerrilla film production. A door at the rear of the building was open, and we ventured in only a few feet before the fear of pigeon-incubated encephalitis or perhaps something else we couldn't see drove us back into the overcast daylight. Numerous NO TRESPASSING signs also helped as an excuse. Through one scum-encrusted window we could see a bulletin board that still bore an ancient handwritten list of daily drudgery for long-forgotten patients.

There are three other buildings on the property, splayed in varying directions, all connected by concrete walkways covered by decrepit wooden roofs. An old light fixture hangs from one of the open hallways like the skeleton of some executed convict, swaying in the breeze of the mountain pass where these buildings lie. A porch in the rear of the complex has lost over half of its protective railing, leaving an unwary visitor with a ten-foot drop to the dirt and rubbish heaps below.

As if this weren't enough, termite-infested storage sheds line the rear of the complex, where there also is the detritus of some sort of motor pool facility. We also found a huge old safe with foot-thick walls sitting exposed in the yard—its gaping innards now a spawning tank for mosquito larvae.

Beyond a battered school bus (with the slogan Smells Like Children spray-painted in red letters) lies a small rocky hill which inexplicably bears three large rusting symbols mounted on poles: a six-pointed star, a cross, and what appears to have been a crescent and star. Omni-denominational cult activity, or some sort of paean to the former residents? Apparently, the theory must have been that Buddhists weren't subject to tuberculosis.

Where Old Planes Go to Die

At the junction of State Highways 58 and 14 sits the old road town of Mojave. Located on the western fringe of the upper Mojave Desert, the town is famous for its large airport, where Burt Rutan designed and built his around-the-world-without-landing *Global Flyer* and his more recent *Space Ship One* which won the X Prize.

Since the 1970s, the airport has also seen the storage and ultimate demise of countless more mundane aircraft. The lined-up tails can be seen for miles in every direction. Most of the planes are put into mothballs by struggling airlines during economic downturns. Many more are the entire fleets of now defunct carriers. Inventory peaked in 2002 after the 9/11 attacks when 360 planes in suspended animation lined the taxiways and runways, their windows and engines covered with plastic to seal out the blowing desert grit. Maybe someday these planes will fly again.

Behind the stored aircraft on the far side of the runway is the boneyard—the place where old planes go to die. An airliner's life span is not measured in years, but in pressurization/depressurization cycles. After thousands of takeoffs and landings, airplanes can no longer

withstand the pressure of high-altitude flight without major parts replacement. Most jet airliners reach the end of their operational lifetime in about twenty-five years. These worn-out planes are parked on the desert flats and cannibalized to keep newer versions of the same model flying. Eventually, when the series is retired, the entire manufacturing run of planes makes its way to the boneyard, where the airliners are recycled. When the last parts of remaining value are removed, the skeletal fuselage is dragged to the recycling area, systematically dismantled, shredded, and melted into raw aluminum ingots.

At any given time, a half-dozen planes are in various states of disassembly. Some airframes are nearly complete, with only a few high-value parts removed. Others are just broken chunks of random fuselage, stacked on piles of railroad ties or flopped on their bellies in the dirt.

Because of the Mojave's relative proximity to Hollywood, a few planes are held in reserve for use in film work. Dozens of action movies and videos have been shot here, including *Speed, Die Hard 2,* and *Swat.* If the movie has a scene with blowing up airliners, it was probably filmed at Mojave.

You need permission to get in. (Sneaking in will guarantee instant arrest and potentially being eaten by guard dogs.) But poking around in these junkyards at night is an unforgettable experience. The planes are chopped and gutted like fish—their huge tails lie in the sand, weeping fluids and moaning in the bitter wind. Virtually untouched airframes stand in line on flat tires, waiting for death, monuments to obsolete technology. The boneyard is an unforgettably evocative and romantic place.–*Troy Paiva*

Most jet airliners
reach the end of
their operational
lifetime in about
twenty-five years.
These worn-out
planes are parked
on the desert flats
and cannibalized
to keep newer
versions of the
same model flying.

Secret Nazi Camp

Nazis in Los Angeles? Why would such evil choose to make its home in the land of dreams and make-believe? The truth is not simple, and it is surprising. There is much more to this brush-choked canyon than a sun-baked offshoot of National Socialism.

Rustic Canyon, a gouge in the Los Angeles coastline, has a history of nonconformity. Bohemians flocked there after World War II. Will Rogers bought into the area, and by 1928 his property extended all the way to the beach. The folksy Rogers famously said he never met a man he didn't like. But if he had survived past 1935, he might have run into a few people who would've tested that friendly thought.

In 1933, a widow named Jessie Murphy made plans to build a formidable home in the canyon. The widow Murphy, for some reason, seemed intent on ensuring her self-sufficiency. Her home would include a 295,000-gallon spring-fed water tank and a 20,000-gallon tank for diesel fuel, as well as electric generators and a twenty-two-bedroom mansion. Just when the basic amenities were finished, there was a disastrous fire, and in 1938 Murphy abandoned her project, depressed and disgusted. The property passed to Norman and Winnona Stephens, who located Murphy's original blueprints and, by 1942, had finished the work.

Attic at Rustic Canyon

the heart of darkness begins. The massive concrete water tank appears on the right, littered with charcoal that used to be a gargantuan wooden cover.

Farther down, the overgrown asphalt road divides several times. More narrow stairways lead up and down, seemingly going nowhere. Ruins of the old Stephens complex are not hard to find, although all are overgrown with trees, brush, and ivy. The entire length is lined with cypress and eucalyptus trees, and it's not difficult to imagine shiny black Model T's and Pierce-Arrows making their way through the compound, dropping off more recruits for Herr Schmidt. Keep an eye out for square concrete holes along the way. They're entrances to underground passageways full of debris, seemingly leading nowhere.

Everything is covered in graffiti. (One that's particularly strange: "Bart Simpson is an agent of the international Zionist conspiracy.") Orange and avocado groves planted in the early twentieth century still bear fruit in the spring and summer months. What looks to be an old hotel blocks the path farther on. Stop and add a piece from the rusting metal building to an impromptu sculpture in the driveway.

Hikers in Rustic Canyon have all commented on the brooding and sinister nature of the place. Almost all have said not to try it alone, if only to have a partner along when bitten by one of the many rattlesnakes living in the valley. Happy exploring!

At this point, the story begins to play out like some spy thriller from the 1940s. One of the workmen at the property saw "troops dressed in paramilitary outfits" and someone running the show, whom he referred to as "an overbearing German named Herr Schmidt." Seems Herr Schmidt had either convinced Mrs. Stephens that the Third Reich would win the war, or that the United States would be turned into a postapocalyptic nightmare. Whichever, with her acquiescence he began teaching survivalist classes. Unfortunately, Schmidt was also caught sending secret messages to his Nazi contacts and was arrested by the government. The Stephenses were later cleared of any charges.

If you venture to the now derelict Stephens House, it's best to allow a full day for exploration. The hike begins from the end of Queensferry Road in Pacific Palisades, among multimillion-dollar homes that hug the hillside, many with elaborate security systems and high walls to keep out the hoi polloi. Head up the fire road to a fence bordering the street, which hides a staircase that disappears down the steep slopes of the canyon. An ornate wrought-iron gate is easily bypassed, and the descent into

Canadian night photographer Larrie Thomson and I circled the back roads in the Barstow-Mojave-Ridgecrest triangle. We jabbered and joked over walkie-talkies as we crisscrossed the high desert, driving nose to tail, searching out locations for that night's photo shoot. It was getting near dark, and we had yet to find the right creepy spot to set up the cameras and make our full-moon time exposures. We rolled north on 395. As we cruised into Red Mountain, the eastern shoulder of the highway sloped away to a series of ramshackle building barely visible from the road. An abandoned mine complex. We'd hit a photographic motherlode!

Spinning a quick U, we hid our vehicles across the highway behind tall creosote piles. As the sun went down, we gathered our gear and pretended not to see th NO TRESPASSING signs while squeezing through the rusty barbed wire fence.

The Atolia Tungsten Mine, we would learn, was

established in 1905. By 1916, it was a full-fledged town with a modern school, four restaurants, and even a newspaper. Between 1916 and 1918, it produced $10 million in ore. By World War II, the mines had played out and the town folded up and blew away in the Mojave wind. Today the site contains about a dozen buildings, all in various states of disrepair. Some are largely intact, others tattered and partially collapsed. Anything of value is long gone.

opposite sides of the twenty-five-acre site well into the evening, each absorbed in the lonely isolation of the desert night. Every few hours we'd cross paths. "Did you see that giant owl on the transformer?" "No, but check out the Acid House."

The Acid House reeked of toxic chemicals spilled everywhere. Sinks and spray booths were scorched with chemical burns. My sinuses instantly burned, and I felt my DNA begin to unscrew. Nice place to hide a body. O

Around midnight, a bitterly cold late-winter storm blew through. The moon ducked behind the clouds, pushing exposure times to the twenty-minute mark. Used to desert shooting at night in shorts and T-shirt and typically unprepared, I had to borrow an embarrassingly dorky stocking cap from the Arctic explorer Larrie.

Later that night we could hear loud and raucous voices on the westerly wind. It was a group of kids across the highway partying, spinning donuts in their hand-me-down pickup trucks, and drinking beer. We saw them, but they never saw us. We ignored them until we started to hear the echo of gunshots off the hills followed by the unmistakable plink of corrugated metal buildings being hit with bullets. They were hitting all around us! We surprised them into silence with our hollering to "Stop shooting!" but soon the firing began again. We decided it was probably best to move along to our campsite behind some even more remote abandoned buildings twenty miles down the road. *—Troy Paiva*

Today the site contains about a dozen buildings, all in various states of disrepair. Some are largely intact, others tattered and partially collapsed.

Exploring the Ruins of the Sutro Baths

You can hardly wait your turn. It is 1896, and you are about to enter the spectacle that everyone in San Francisco is talking about. Inside, you will rent one of the 20,000 swimsuits and grab one of 40,000 towels. Up to 10,000 people may share your experience tonight, half of whom are in line with you trying to peer into the great unknown beyond the ticket vendor. It is a bit chilly this evening (as San Fran nights can be), but you do not hesitate in your shuffle forward. Anyway, you've heard that one of the seven giant bathing pools inside (each almost 500 feet long) gets up to 80 degrees in temperature.

In 1881, Adolph Sutro, the colorful and somewhat eccentric mayor of this great city, bought a large portion of the western headlands where this palace of public decadence now stands. Rumors have circulated about the wonders found inside, and you are sure, at the estimated price tag of $1,000,000, that some must be true. You cannot wait to feast your eyes on the rare artifacts from Egypt, the fine art from around the world, or maybe even a stuffed gorilla or some other mysterious beast.

At last you're in. You change into your suit in one of the 517 private dressing rooms and walk out onto the promenade through a classic Greek portal into a massive enclosure. The laughter and shouts of thousands of people mingle into a rollicking display of frolicking folks. Like mad lemmings they leap and plunge into the pools. They jump from the springboards, glide from the swinging rings, and race down the seven toboggan slides. You take a breath of the salt air and curl your knees into your chest for a cannonball. It is pure bliss, and you are sure that this place, the legacy of Adolph Sutro, will last forever. But it won't.

I can hardly wait my turn. It is 1999 and my first night in San Francisco. It is very late at night and a damp fog makes the atmosphere

8127. SUTRO BATHS, SAN FRANCISCO, CAL.   COPYRIGHT, 1900, BY DETROIT PHOTOGRAPHIC CO.

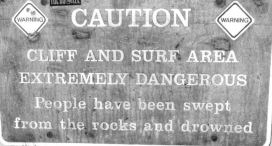

THE BRONZE

WARNING

CAUTION

WARNING

CLIFF AND SURF AREA
EXTREMELY DANGEROUS
People have been swept
from the rocks and drowned

thick. My path to the sea seems all too ominous as wind-sculpted cypress trees stretch in unison around me, pointing me toward the wonderful and strange place known as the ruins of the Sutro Baths.

Hundreds of feet below me stands a moving postcard of haunting beauty. In the valley below is America's Parthenon, a series of ruins spanning three acres. Concrete walls and clubhouses sit in overgrown plants and wild lilies. Still standing are the 700-foot-long battered break-waters constructed with some 750,000 cubic feet of concrete. Gone is the amphitheater that could seat 3,700 people. Gone are the boxing dwarfs and other famous performers who once enter-tained here. Most of the structure was lost in a fire in 1966, but what was left was purchased by the Golden Gate National Recreation Area in 1980 for $5,500,000.

Looking out on the remains, it is as if some force above poured concrete from the sky, creating staircases and tunnels in the nooks and crannies of the cliffs. Some of these stairways lead to nowhere and some end abruptly at the edge of the grinding surf. Once that same tidal water was used to fill the six saltwater pools (there was one fresh water) bringing in a combined total of 1.7 million gallons in a matter of an hour. Rusty pipes still exist, possibly the means by which the used water would be carried up the coast away from the bathing patrons.

While the collective joy that once existed here may never be rekindled, the site still has a lot to offer the inquisitive explorer. The ruins are completely accessible and quite extensive. A giant

cave dares you to enter—but you are sure to retreat, spooked by the sound of the powerful surf. If this place, once a palace of recreation and social graces, could fall into such decay, one may wonder what the ruins of Disney World will look like in some inevitable future. Should you decide to visit the Sutro Baths, be attentive to the warnings posted. Though I saw but one sign, its message was clear. One false step and your plunge into the water could very possibly be your last.—*Ryan Doan*

INDEX

Page numbers in **bold** refer to photos and illustrations.

WEIRD CALIFORNIA

By
Greg Bishop, Joe Oesterle, and Mike Marinacci
Executive Editors
Mark Sceurman and Mark Moran

ACKNOWLEDGMENTS

GREG BISHOP

In no particular order, I would like to thank my parents, Sigrid Hudson, Robert Larson, Paul Young, Walter Bosley, Nick Redfern, Adam Gorightly, Richard Senate, Scott Lindgren, Bill Moore, Tim Cridland, Lisa Davis, Jeremy Bate, and Skylaire Alfvegren. Inspiration and early guidance were provided by Robert Anton Wilson, John Keel, Robert Sterling, Kenn Thomas, and though I never knew or talked to him, Edward Abbey. I would also like to express my appreciation to all the people I interviewed who were helpful and welcomed me with openness, eagerness, and a sense of wonder that was infectious.

The music of the Tuscan-based band Calexico was on my car stereo constantly as I traveled to many locations for research and interviews.

Contributing Photographer Troy Paiva
captures the disappearing man-made world with his evocative and exotic night-photography technique. Troy uses old and obsolete low-tech equipment to create brilliantly lit tableaux of the abandoned debris of a modern, dispos-able culture—taking pictures of junk with junk. In 2003, Troy published *Lost America*. He also contributed material to *Weird U.S.* and *Weird Texas*. Troy's Web

JOE OESTERLE

I would like to thank the numerous bartenders, waitresses, and gas station attendants I met along the way. Waitresses tend to know a little about everything in their town, gas station guys can be relied on to point you in the right direction whether you're looking for the world's largest rubber band ball or a building in the shape of a giant hot dog, and bartenders always have beer.

MIKE MARINACCI

I would like to thank my mother and father, who passed on to me both a love of California history and culture, and the desire and ability to write about it; my *Weird U.S.* editors, who gave me the opportunity to tell these stories; and most of all, God, for the chance to enjoy the mysteries and wonders of His creation.

Publisher: Barbara J. Morgan
Assoc. Managing Editor: Emily Seese
Editor: Marjorie Palmer
Production: Della R. Mancuso
Mancuso Associates, Inc.
North Salem, NY

PICTURE CREDITS

All photos by the authors or public domain except as listed below:

SHOW US YOUR WEIRD!

Do you know of a weird site found somewhere in the United States, or can you tell us about a strange experience you've had? If so, we'd like to hear about it! We believe that every town has at least one great tale to tell, and we're listening. It could be a cursed road, haunted abandoned site, odd local character, or bizarre historic event. In most cases these tales are told only in the towns in which they originated. But why keep them to yourself when you could share them with all of America? So come on and fill us in on all the weirdness that's lurking in your backyard!

You can e-mail us at: Editor@WeirdUS.com,
or write to us at:
Weird U.S., P.O. Box 1346, Bloomfield, NJ 07003.

www.weirdus.com